KU-548-703

The Representation of the Past

Museums and heritage in the post-modern world

Kevin Walsh

ROUTLEDGE

London and New York

First published in 1992
by Routledge
11 New Fetter Lane, London EC4P 4EE

Simultaneously published in the USA and Canada
by Routledge
a division of Routledge, Chapman and Hall Inc.
29 West 35th Street, New York, NY 10001

© 1992 Kevin Walsh

Set in 10/12 pt Sabon, Monophoto
by Selwood Systems, Midsomer Norton.
Printed in Great Britain
by Butler & Tanner Ltd, Frome and London.

Printed on paper manufactured in accordance with the proposed ANSI/NISO Z 39.48–
199X and ANSI Z 39.48–1984

All rights reserved. No part of this book may be reprinted or reproduced or utilized in any
form or by any electronic, mechanical, or other means, now known or hereafter invented,
including photocopying and recording, or in any information storage or retrieval system,
without permission in writing from the publishers.

British Library Cataloguing in Publication Data
Walsh, Kevin
    The representation of the past: museums and
    heritage in the post-modern world. – (Heritage:
    care, preservation, management)
    I. Title   II. Series
069

Library of Congress Cataloging in Publication Data
Walsh, Kevin
    The representation of the past: museums and heritage in the post-modern world/Kevin
    Walsh.
    p. cm. – (Heritage: care, preservation, management)
    Includes bibliographical references and index.
    1. Museum techniques. 2. Museums – Educational aspects.
    3. Popular culture. 4. Mass society. I. Title. II. Series:
    Heritage.
    AM7.W35 1992
    069′.5–dc20   91–30400

ISBN 0–415–05026–X
ISBN 0–415–07944–6 pbk

069

PETERLEE
COLLEGE LIBRARY

7944-1

Editor in chief   Andrew Wheatcroft

The Heritage: Care–Preservation–Management programme has been designed to serve the needs of the museum and heritage community worldwide. It publishes books and information services for professional museum and heritage workers, and for all the organizations that service the museum community.

The programme has been devised with the advice and assistance of the leading institutions in the museum and heritage community, at an international level, with ICOM and ICOMOS, with the national and local museum organizations and with individual specialists drawn from every continent.

Forward Planning: *A handbook of business, corporate and development planning for museums and galleries*
Edited by Timothy Ambrose and Sue Runyard

The Industrial Heritage: *Managing resources and uses*
Judith Alfrey and Tim Putnam

Museums 2000: *Politics, people, professionals and profit*
Edited by Patrick Boylan

Museums and the Shaping of Knowledge
Eilean Hooper-Greenhill

Museums Without Barriers: *A new deal for disabled people*
Fondation de France and ICOM

The Past in Contemporary Society: Then, Now
Peter J. Fowler

The Representation of the Past

97102939

PETERLEE
COLLEGE LIBRARY

069

AA44-1

The 1980s and early 1990s have witnessed a marked boom in the ... um
... is
the
nes

This book is due for return on or before the last date shown below.

illy
of
m-
om
ige
at
the
eir
s a

ni-
in

ed

of

Don Gresswell Ltd., London, N.21   Cat. No. 1207   DG 02242/71

Contents

99102939

y No.

Acknowledgements

First I should like to thank my colleagues in the Department of Archaeology at the University of Leicester for both their support and help. Special thanks must go to the following: Frances Condron, Shaun Hides, Alan McWhirr, Deirdre O'Sullivan and Rob Young.

I should also especially like to thank the following for their comments and help: Robert Hewison, Neil Lang, Nick Merriman and Susan Pearce.

I am indebted to the following people and organizations for material and help with my research: Martin Bell, The British Tourist Authority, CADW, John Corner, David Harvey, English Heritage, Mark Fisher MP, Pete Garside, Tom Greeves, The Heritage Co-ordination Group, Pete Liddle, Heather Lomas, Jane Malcolm-Davies, Geoff Marsh, Graham Murdock, The National Trust, RESCUE, Tim Schadla-Hall, Prof. C. G. Screven, Andrew Selkirk, The Society for the Interpretation of Britain's Heritage, Hilary Spencer, Carol Stapp, Dominic Tweddle.

Introduction

At the time of writing, winter 1991, a number of nations are at war; the stock market and the value of gold and oil fluctuate in an almost unprecedented manner. Warfare seems to boost stock market values the world over. The wealth of nations oscillates by the second, responding to events that are taking place many thousands of miles away. A possible war in the Gulf immediately results in price increases at petrol pumps all over the world, the war begins and stock markets rally and the price of oil tumbles. Economic processes are today more removed from the daily experiences of more people than ever before.

This remoteness from economic processes is reflected in the remoteness, for most people in the First World, from the harsher aspects of life. The tabloid press hankers for the blood of innocent Iraqis, and patriotically wishes 'our lads' good luck. Politicians welcome the absence of casualties, as if the Iraqi civilians do not exist. It is this distancing from many of the processes which affect our daily lives that is modernity, or more recently, post-modernity. Many acts of endeavour, bravery, stupidity and barbarism have taken place in the name of modernization. Most of us exist in a society where any real hardship is nonexistent, although our prosperity is another society's poverty.

Museums and heritage have contributed to this distancing from the processes which affect our daily lives, and have promoted an uncritical patriotism which numbs our ability to understand and communicate with other nations. War seems acceptable to many of those who will only have to suffer the vetted images transmitted, via global telecommunications networks, into their living rooms. The histories of warfare, poverty, oppression and disease have been transformed into media of shallow titillation – from 1066, to World War I and the Blitz. During the summer of 1991, a series of mock battles is planned by the conservation organization English Heritage. The diary of these events mentions a 'Civil War Battle Spectacular', an event which the reader is told is 'Subject to developments in the Gulf' (Historic Buildings and Monuments Commission 1991: 17). Surely a mock battle is just as tasteless when a country is not at war. If warfare is to be represented and discussed, the most obvious time for this is when a country is at war.

Organizations with an imperative for capital accumulation trivialize and package experiences which are, essentially, neutered reproductions of possibly the most horrible and tragic ordeals any person might experience. Success for the promoters of such experiences is measured on the computer spreadsheet package, and promotion within an organization is guaranteed if the profit column on the printout is more impressive than the year before. This is the world of the 'post': post-modern, post-ethical, post-moral.

The disadvantaged are remembered once a year in charity telethons, where surrogates for the Welfare State salve the consciences of those people who shudder at the thought of paying too much income tax. A new prime minister in Britain has spoken of a classless society, while cardboard cities continue to grow, and unemployment rises once again. Mostly working-class young men, disproportionately Black, Asian and Hispanic in the case of the US army, go to war to fight for a nation that shunned democracy.

Written partly out of anger and despair during the early part of 1991, this writer feels that museums, and the heritage industry especially, have to shoulder at least some of the shame for society's unquestioning acceptance of the need to go to war, the horrors of which most of us have thankfully never had to experience. This uncritical stance, combined with a debilitating jingoism, is partly a product of the emergence of nations and nationalism, along with the concomitant articulation of related positions of patriotism promoted by some museums and the heritage industry.

Since the nineteenth century representations of the past have, perhaps unwittingly in most cases, contributed to a form of institutionalized rationalization of the past. As people have been distanced from the processes which affect their daily lives, the past has been promoted as something which is completed, and no longer contingent upon our experiences in the world.

The processes of modernization uprooted many millions of people from familiar localities and re-placed them within towns and cities which in themselves represented and promoted the intensification of production, consumption, travel, communication and all of the other experiences which are common to many societies today. The modern world opened up new horizons of expectation, legitimated through an omnipresent idea of progress.

This new fleeting experience of life in the modern urban world demanded that the past be held onto, but as with all processes of modernization, the past became something which emerged as yet another form of institutionalized discourse, often articulated through the museum and the academy. The past was gradually isolated and obscured, and was promoted as that which was no longer important to and contingent upon people's daily experiences. Rationalized in the removed and rarified discourse of the professions, the past was sequestered from those to whom it belonged. This process has been one which has steadily intensified to the point where, during the later twentieth century, the past has emerged as a reservoir of shallow surfaces which can be exploited in the heritage centre or on the biscuit tin.

Fundamental to this book is a belief that the experiences of (post-) modernity – both the modern and so-called post-modern periods, which may in fact be one and the same – are experiences which have gradually distanced people from many of the processes which affect their lives. This has been not just a distancing from their pasts, or their roots, but a distancing from the economic, political and cultural systems that influence, or even control their lives. This distancing is partly reflected in the development of the professions, which provide services based on an implicit notion of trust – trust that the consumer has in the professional (see Giddens 1990). This trust to a certain extent has been abused, and has enhanced the ability of certain groups to provide services, including representations of the past, which have been beyond question. Accepting that life in the (post-)modern world demands the existence of reliable professions, what is needed is the development of intersubjective discourse between the providers and the consumers of such services. But what we have seen in the context of heritage is an increased distancing of the providers from the consumers. Required responses to problems are assumed to occur naturally within a benign market, which by its very nature seems to deny the possibility of communication. What is necessary is a rearticulation of discourses based on the locality, a manageable context which permits the development of democratic discourse.

The first chapter of this book outlines briefly some of the main characteristics of modernism and modernity concentrating on the idea of progress and the distancing of people from the processes which affect their daily experiences. The emergence of the museum is considered as a part of these developments, especially within the context of society's need to articulate both a certain appreciation of progress, and an appreciation of a certain conception of time in an industrial, urban society.

Chapters three and four go on to consider the political developments of the post World War II period, specifically concentrating on the impact of the New Right. The New Right's emphasis on the radical individual, freely operating in the market-place, is considered as part of a post-modern condition. An important element of this condition has been the emergence of the heritage industry, an industry, or rather, a leisure service, which has been concerned to market ephemeral images of the past. To put it at its most bland, the commercialization of pasts, where the emphasis has been on a consideration of superficialities rather than a concern with the discussion and consideration of the past and its contingency upon the present, has been an attack on both democracy, and people's understanding of their places. One of the most important effects of heritage has been its intensification of the modern emphasis on promoting the past as that which is entirely complete and removed from the present. This has served to neuter the past and permit its manipulation and trivialization in the present.

Chapters five and six go on to consider in turn the development of the conservation and preservation movements, which more often than not have been concerned to preserve a very limited heritage which has concentrated on the preservation of that which represents the highest achievement of the nation. In the case of Britain, this achievement is seen by many as the castle and the country house. This discussion also considers the emergence of industrial conservation, and the impact of the combination of selective conservation and post-modern architecture on our sense of place.

The second of these two chapters considers more specifically what some have labelled the 'heritage industry'. Again, a brief consideration of the origins of this leisure service are considered. This discussion too, goes on to argue that the selection of a few unrepresentative images of the past, neutered by dazzling media, exacerbates the feeling of placelessness which is common in the (post-)modern world.

Chapter seven ties together the discussions of the previous chapters, and argues that the emergence of heritage should not just be considered as a characteristic of a climate of decline (Hewison 1987), but that it should also be seen as part of a wider service-class culture which expanded during the 1980s. The ideological nature of heritage is considered with reference to the survey work carried out by Nick Merriman (1991). Finally, this chapter considers the heritagization of space: the reduction of real places to tourist space, constructed by the selective quotation of images of many different pasts which more often than not contribute to the destruction of actual places.

Chapters eight and nine offer a framework for re-emphasizing the importance of places or localities. Partly derived from Fredric Jameson's idea of cognitive mapping (1988b), this framework offers just one way in which people might wish to appreciate the past of their own or any locality. Chapter nine considers the potential role for museums, especially those which adhere to the beliefs of the new museology as it is understood outside Britain. An emphasis is placed on the role of ecomuseums – museums which take a more 'holistic' approach to the understanding of places and the ways in which people interact with their environments.

The concluding chapter brings some of the main points of the book together, arguing that the key to the future of the past is an emphasis on providing public facilities which enable people to come to terms with their own places. The free public provision of such services is undoubtedly an important part of any struggle to enfranchise people *vis-à-vis* their pasts. But as the book argues, one of the most worrying aspects of the post-modern condition has been the increasing emphasis on the role of the radical individual in the market-place and a denial of the importance of societies and even communities. The hope is that the final chapters of this book will offer just one way of enhancing the importance of people and places in a world where the anonymous marketing director and the mercenary multinational increasingly dominate our daily lives.

The idea of modernity

1

Modernity: a brief definition

Jurgen Habermas has defined modernity as, 'The epochal new beginning that marked the modern world's break with the world of the Christian Middle Ages and antiquity [that] is repeated, as it were, in every present moment that brings forth something new. The present perpetuates the break with the past in the form of a continual renewal' (Habermas 1989: 48).

Modernity has its origins in the Renaissance, and the emergence of modern science – the discovery of 'truths' and 'facts', or rather claims for the possibility of objective truths about the world and 'Man's' place within it. The 'meta narratives' which emerged during the modern epoch were essentially discourses which implied a rigid objectivism, and through this, the potential of a thorough analysis of the world. Such meta narratives might include Darwin's Theory of Evolution and Marx's analysis of capital. Modernism can thus be considered as a set of discourses concerned with the possibilities of representing reality and defining eternal truths.

The idea of progress

An essential proposition of modern thought is an idea of progress, a belief which developed as a constituent part of Enlightenment thinking, and provided modern thinkers with a faith in the ability of humankind to manipulate and exploit their environments for the benefit of society. Such a society could escape from the debilitating elements of the past, and could move ever forward to new horizons. If modernity has a particular essence, it is a belief in rational advancement through increments of perpetual improvement.

Enlightenment thinking provided the foundations of modernity, and must be seen within the contexts of European voyages of discovery and the Renaissance, and the establishment of world-wide trading, and Imperial, networks. These developments along with the foundation of new nation-states within Europe, notably Italy and Germany, can be seen as important elements in the foundation of modernity.

A fundamental of Enlightenment thinking was a conception of a society which was advancing, a society that potentially knew no bounds, a society that could overcome any of the problems that it was either forced to confront, or confronted out of choice. Progression through the exploitation of the environment, combined with a faith in humankind's dominant position in the scheme of things, must be central to any appreciation of modernity. 'Since the beginning of the modern era the prospect of a limitless advance of science and technology, accompanied at each step by moral and political improvement, has exercised considerable hold over Western thought' (McCarthy 1984: v).

The belief in progress was in part based on Newtonian physics, as was the Enlightenment's concept of time. A belief in growth provided a secure model for progress in all aspects of knowledge. To a certain extent it was this shift from the mythical/superstitious frameworks of the pre-Enlightenment period, to the rationalized lifeworld of modernity, which was to be symbolized by the museum displays of the nineteenth century. Such displays doubtless contributed to the idea of progress which helped develop an 'horizon of expectation':

> The horizon open to the future, which is determined by expectations in the present, guides our access to the past. Inasmuch as we appropriate past experiences with an orientation to the future, the authentic present is preserved as the locus of continuing tradition and of innovation at once; the one is not possible without the other, and both merge into the objectivity proper to a context of effective history.
> (Habermas 1987b: 13)

The idea of progress influenced many areas of thought, including the understanding of language. 'Speech and writing were considered to have improved during the past, and conscious attempts were made to foster further linguistic advance in the future. The progress of language seemed to have special significance because of its intimate relation to positive intellectual and social change' (Spadafora 1990: 12–13).

Pessimistic views of history began to disappear during the 1730s, and hardly existed come the latter half of the eighteenth century. Certainly in Britain, the idea of progress in history was fundamental to the way people thought about the past and was undeniably more important than the previously pessimistic outlooks.

By the turn of the century it would seem that the idea of progress was widely accepted amongst the educated classes of the First World. Whether progress was apparent to other societies, whose suffering seemed to be an essential element of industrialization, is doubtful.

During the eighteenth century, the Christian vision of history developed, with an emphasis on the correlation of past events with scriptural predictions: 'the eschatologists of high eighteenth century Britain gave the Biblical prophetic programme a concrete chronological order and made it amenable to their historical understanding' (ibid.: 131). In contemporary Christian thought the idea of progress was inextricably part of a wider optimism in the divine program for spiritual advancement.

The wider conceptions of history tended to articulate frameworks which were essentially concerned to promote the idea of progress, or during the later nineteenth century, a form of progressive evolutionism. James Mill's *History of British India* (1817) saw societal development as moving through stages 'from primitiveness toward a high level of civilisation (as determined by contemporary Europe)'. India was deemed to be near the lowest stage of development (Spadafora 1990: 397). Such an understanding of the world gave justification to the idea of the 'white man's burden': the duty of the European to colonize and educate those who were perceived as being less fortunate. It was such a belief in progress, and the rationality of the European economic and political system, which gave rise to the myth of the struggling savages' [sic] subsistence economy (Sahlins 1974: 1–39).

The height of the popularity of the idea of progress was probably during the mid-Georgian period, rather than the mid-Victorian period (Spadafora 1990: 387). But despite this, there is no doubt that for many Victorians, the nineteenth century was a period of great advances in both the arts and sciences, although many began to realize that progress in industrialization and urbanization was not progress for all. Despite this, it is undoubtedly true that, 'Rarely has a single idea played so central a part in an intellectual world. To begin to understand that world requires that we recognize the significance of the idea of progress within it' (ibid.: 415).

The idea of progress is an idea which has underpinned the teleological nature of many representations of the past, an ordering of the past which came about through a new conception of time and history, both of which can now be considered.

Time in modernity

Time is a culturally specific construction, although years and months are based on natural cyclic periods. The week is in fact a purely cultural unit of time, as are hours, minutes and seconds. Despite this, humans often seem to consider time as a universal or absolute phenomenon. Time, as it is widely understood in the First World today, has its roots in the Enlightenment. This idea of time is undeniably linked with the idea of progress and is crucial to any understanding of the modern world and any disciplines which adopt an historical perspective.

It is probably the Judaeo-Christian concept of time which has had the greatest influence on the modern understanding of time. This Jewish concept of time was based on the 'linear concept of time, founded, in their case, on a teleological idea of history as the gradual revelation of God's purpose' (Whitrow 1988: 51). Christians saw the crucifixion as a unique event, and it is this emphasis on the non-repeatability of events which is crucial to explaining the western idea of linear and non-cyclical history (ibid.: 57).

Roman culture also emphasized an idea of linear history, attributing the success of the Roman Empire not to one person in the present, but to many ancestors during Rome's past. As Whitrow illustrates, Tacitus often cited documents and authors and developed a critical form of history. He recognized the historian's role as a judge of previous human actions. But as Marwick comments, 'For the Greek and Roman writers history was unabashedly "exemplar history", a preparation for life, especially political and military life' (Marwick 1989: 29).

During the Middle Ages there seems to have been little concern with a fastidious observation of time. According to Whitrow, people rarely even bothered to date their letters (Whitrow 1988: 84). It was with the advent of accurate timekeeping during the latter half of the seventeenth century that the modern experience of time developed. The idea of time as an entity in itself emerged, a belief that there was in fact a definable context of time. Newton's concept of mathematical time, as outlined in his *Principia*, understood it as a straight geometrical line. Newton went on to develop a concern with chronology, which, during the late seventeenth and early eighteenth centuries, was symptomatic of a wider concern with the authenticity of the Bible and its chronology (ibid.: 131).

For much of the later Medieval period, time was considered to be a destructive force. 'The typical Renaissance image of time was as the destroyer equipped with hour-glass, scythe or sickle' (ibid.: 132). However, during the Renaissance an awareness of change through time developed, and a more optimistic perception of time and its effects emerged.

By the eighteenth century, for many people an appreciation or new awareness of time had developed. This was a period of 'discovery' of historical perspective. In 1795 Condorcet's *Sketch for a Historical Picture of the Progress of the Human Mind* was published. In this 'Condorcet expressed his belief in the inevitability of human progress and in the power of science and technology to transform man's knowledge and control over himself and society' (ibid.: 147).

During the nineteenth century a more scientifically coherent justification of linear time emerged. The unidirectional nature of time was legitimated by Becquerel's discovery of radioactivity in 1896. Subsequently explained by Rutherford and Soddy in 1902, the decay of radioactive elements was shown to be uniform and linear.

The idea of progress and history

As discussed above, central to modernity was a belief in progress, but often this was a progress achieved through destruction, often a destruction of lifestyles that had not really altered since the early Middle Ages, or even the late third and second millennia BC. The Industrial Revolution was responsible for the uprooting and disturbance of large sectors of the population. It was partly as a result of this newly imposed rootlessness that an enchantment with the past emerged during the nineteenth century. Despite the fact that the Victorian period was dominated by industrial and scientific progress, it 'was also an age dominated by a fascination with the past' (Bowler 1989: 1). Of course, it is understood that societies prior to those of the nineteenth century had an interest in the past, but these interests were quite different from the histories and archaeologies which had their roots in the Enlightenment, and developed into the foundations of the modern disciplines of the twentieth century.

It can be argued that pre-industrial society's awareness of the past was an experience which was entirely more organic than that understanding of the past which was to develop in the modern urban world. In the rural, or pre-industrial context, there seems to have been an appreciation of the processes which had, and still did, affected daily life. The past was something which was present in the construction of the sense of place. This may be considered as a more organic form of history, one which recognizes the crucial contingency of past processes on present places. Places, natural and human-made features, acted as 'time-marks', physical phenomena which exist in the present but possess, for those who know them, a temporal depth which gives them a special meaning. An important form of such a time-mark is the boundary, the perceived periphery of a community's locality. These may range from boundaries made of stone in prehistory, to parish boundaries, and enclosed fields.

In this book, it is considered that a sense of place is an attachment to, or knowledge of, one's locality, an understanding or appreciation of the processes which have affected a place, both through time and space. Such a sense of place is not based on a narrow parochialism or chauvinism, but rather an understanding of how other places and people have affected one's place throughout history. This idea of a sense of place will be considered at length in chapter seven.

The experiences of industrialization and urbanization destroyed for many people this organic, or contingent, past. The sense of the past developed by the new urban mass was one that had to be created, in the same way as their places had to be created. The experiences of modernization wrenched a vast proportion of the population from settled, well-established lifestyles, where the past had been a part of their daily experience. 'The Victorians' fascination with the past was the product of an age obsessed with change, desperately hoping that history itself might supply the reassurance that could no longer be derived from ancient beliefs' (ibid.: 3). The move from the rooted place, to an ephemeral, transitory urban experience, resulted in a conception of the past which was dominated by change – progress towards the ever more modern world. Towards the end of the nineteenth century, there does seem to have been a developing awareness of the importance of the past, but this importance was increasingly neutered by the developing perception of the past as something which was separate and had a limited contingency for modern societies. This point will be expanded later in the book.

Also, the idea that such a past was essentially a tale of progress towards the modern was rarely ever questioned by the majority of people. As Dellheim argues in his discussion of the Victorian appropriation of images of the Middle Ages,

> Liberal England's middle-class politicians and businessmen appropriated medieval forms to create pedigrees for their values and to legitimize their quest for hegemony. Although their concern with historic paraphernalia superficially reinforced the authority of traditional symbols, actually it diminished the prescriptive force of the past by reinterpreting its meanings in the light of progressive aspirations.
>
> (Dellheim 1982: 179)

The Victorians tended to believe that social development was a movement in a purposeful, positive direction – a progression towards a meaningfully constituted society. It was this understanding of the nature of progress which saw its clearest articulation in Whig history: the belief in inevitable trends, based on freedom of thought and commercial enterprise. 'Evolution was the sum total of a vast multitude of individual progressive acts, allowing middle-class values to be seen as the driving force of an essentially purposeful system of nature' (Bowler 1989: 8).

This idea of progress was reflected in the work of Adam Smith, whose *Wealth of Nations* (1776) articulated the belief that, despite the fact that people are inherently selfish, their efforts for self-improvement would benefit society as a whole. If uninhibited by 'unnatural' controls, then the economy and society will develop naturally, and in a trend that will be in the interest of everybody. Contrary to Darwin's emphasis on the uniqueness and haphazard nature of all evolutionary developments, it would appear that there was a profound belief in the inevitability of progress as the basis to Victorian evolutionism.

It is this model of progress that contributed to early ideas on societal development in prehistory. This kind of linear interpretation clearly lent itself to static display in museums, although it was probably not until just after World War I that such ideas were represented explicitly in museum displays. It is in part for this reason that today many archaeological and historical displays still follow this basic formula. It is of course very difficult to avoid, and it is the aim of this book to approach some ideas on how this might be achieved.

To an extent, the modern idea of history and its concomitant conception of time implied that the future had already begun. There was a belief in an acceleration and advancing of historical events. Habermas considers that,

> At this time the image of history as a uniform process that generates
> problems is formed, and time becomes experienced as a scarce
> resource for the mastery of problems that arise – that is, as the pressure
> of time. The 'Zeitgeist', or spirit of age, one of the new words that
> inspired Hegel, characterizes the present as a transition that is
> consumed in the consciousness of a speeding up and the expectation
> of the differentness of the future.
>
> (Habermas 1987b: 6)

For Stephen Kern, author of *The Culture of Time and Space*, 'Thinking about the past centred on four major issues: the age of the earth, the impact of the past on the present, the value of that impact, and the most effective way to recapture a past that has been forgotten' (Kern 1983: 37).

There was also a concern with the problem of fixity for the past. In 1654, Bishop Usher informed the world that creation took place in 4004 BC. In the 1770s Comte de Buffon considered that the earth was at least 168,000 years old. By the early nineteenth century the age of the earth was reckoned by some to be infinite. During the first half of the nineteenth century the aging of the earth was the province of geologists until 1862 when the physicist Lord Kelvin argued that the earth was probably between 100 million and 20 million years old. This reduced time scale forced biologists and geologists to develop theories of catastrophe which allowed them to hypothesize great surges in development. For the majority of people, however, these debates over the geological age of the earth probably had little impact on their perceptions of history, once it was recognized that the biblical chronology, epitomized by Usher, had been revealed as false. For most people there was probably little difference, conceptually, between a 100-million- and a 20-million-year-old earth.

Despite the realization that humans have had a relatively short past on the earth compared with the planet's age, there was a growing concern with discovering humankind's past. Kern argues that especially during the late nineteenth century, as a consequence of new recording technologies, people became more and more aware of the fact that the present was the result of the past. 'The phonographic cylinders, the motion pictures, and the preservation societies constituted silent arguments for the persistence of the past and its impact on the present' (ibid.: 40). During the late nineteenth century a new appreciation of the contingency of the past on groups of people developed. A belief that people were constituted by the traces of their pasts emerged. This was ghoulishly elaborated by Bram Stoker's *Dracula* (1897): 'The blood of several centuries of victims flowed in the veins of the four-hundred-year-old hero along with blood of his ancestors – more ancient, the Count boasted, than the Hapsburgs or the Romanovs' (Kern 1983: 41). This differed from the pre-modern 'organic' sense of the past, where the locality or the place was filled with historical meaning because it had been occupied by a definable community for a long period of time. The later Victorian awareness of the past tended to consider the histories of groups of people who were often separated across space. The impact of modernization had further ruptured many links that had existed between many groups; such disturbances necessitated the articulation of new historical traditions. The definition of historical associations between peoples who were now, more so than ever before, removed from their own places seemed necessary for many groups of people who wished to maintain an identity.

Life in time may have become more important for some people, especially if they had lost their spatial roots. Kern believes that this may have been true of Jews, for whom spatial roots were usually only a dream. However Judaism, as with most religions, shows a reverence for the past. It is this rootedness in time which perhaps gives Jews such a great strength and faith. Kern also argues that with the decline of a religious conception of humankind during the late nineteenth century, there may have been the development of a belief that if humankind no longer had a place in God's eternity, then perhaps they had a place in history (ibid.: 50–1).

The first 'modern' histories were produced in the early nineteenth century. It was Condorcet who had hoped that the history of humankind would be modelled on the history of modern science and rationalization. But for most historians, the first 'true' history was written by Leopold von Ranke, whose *History of the Latin and Teutonic Nations* was published in 1824. Ranke's aim 'was the misleadingly modest-seeming one of pre-senting the past as it really was, discovering what actually happened on the basis of a systematic and comprehensive survey of existing evidence and of new evidence that could be collected' (Atkinson 1978: 16).

During the Victorian period the modern discipline of history expanded. Macaulay wrote multi-volumed histories of England, while the historical novel flourished. Interest in the excavations of Assyrian cities by Henry Layard, and the work of Heinrich Schliemann at Troy, was extensive. Schliemann's activities often reached the front pages of newspapers, and Gladstone himself wrote the preface to Schliemann's *Mycenae* of 1875 (Bowler 1989: 48). The teaching of non-ancient history in universities also developed during the nineteenth century. In 1866 William Stubbs was appointed to the chair of Modern History at Oxford, and in 1868 the new Ecole Pratique des Hautes Etudes opened at the Sorbonne.

Early archaeological thought

Contemporary with the emergence of history as a discipline was the development of modern archaeology, which was different from anti-quarianism in its emphasis on the use of artefacts in a consideration of human development, and of course, progress, through time. An early example of the influence of the modern episteme of progress was the work of Christian Jürgensen Thomsen, who in 1816 became the first curator of the Danish National Museum in Copenhagen. He was the first to arrange the collections systematically on the basis of the Three-Age System in a linear developmental scheme of technological change, moving from the use of stone artefacts, to bronze and ultimately to iron. This followed on from the earlier eighteenth-century work of Nicolas Mahudel among others.

The Danish National Museum was opened to the public in 1819. After a few years, the museum was rehoused in part of the Christianborg royal palace, where one room was assigned to each of the Three Ages. Thomsen made a concerted effort to educate 'peasants' who visited the museum, working on the assumption that these were the people most likely to discover prehistoric artefacts. Trigger believes that the motivation behind Thomsen's work was patriotism, but 'The antiquarian research of the eighteenth century and the evolutionary concepts of the Enlightenment were indispensable preconditions for his success' (Trigger 1989: 73). It was his development of relative dating techniques that made his contribution to the understanding and presentation of prehistory of crucial importance.

As mentioned above, modern university history began its development during the early to mid-nineteenth century. This development was mirrored in archaeology, with J. A. Worsaae's (1821–85) appointment as Denmark's Inspector for the Conservation of Antiquarian Monuments in 1847, and then in 1855 his appointment as the first Professor of Archaeology at the University of Copenhagen.

In Britain, Enlightenment archaeology took hold in some areas. Notably the Scottish antiquarian Daniel Wilson (1816–92), influenced by Worsaae, used the Three-Age System to organize the artefacts which belonged to the Society of Antiquaries of Scotland in Edinburgh. Wilson recommended that the British Museum reorganize their artefacts on the basis of the Three-Age System, but this plea was ignored for many years. By and large the prehistoric archaeology that had been pioneered by the Scandinavians was disregarded by antiquarians in England, and the more scientific approach to the study of artefacts did not really develop in this country before the late 1850s.

Archaeology was seriously hampered in its development as a serious academic discipline by the problem of a limiting biblical chronology. The acceptance of human antiquity was largely brought about as a result of the work of two geologists, William Pengelly and Hugh Falconer. Their excavations at Brixham Cave near Torquay yielded stone tools and bones of extinct animals in close proximity. Other geologists visited the site, including Charles Lyell, and supported the assumptions of Pengelly and Falconer regarding the antiquity of humankind. During 1859 and 1860, a number of papers were published supporting the belief that humanity was far more ancient than had been previously accepted.

John Lubbock, with the publication of his *Pre-historic Times* in 1865, promoted the idea that humankind had developed from the primitive savage, and had arrived at its current position through a steady linear progression and advancement: 'Lubbock ended his book with a hymn of praise to progress' (Bowler 1989: 81), and his hypothesis challenged the theological doctrine of the era, which accepted the idea of degeneration from a state of grace. Some, including the Duke of Argyll in his *Primeval Man* of 1869, argued that the evidence only proved that humans had developed technologically. Nothing could prove that they had not possessed an equivalent moral or spiritual capacity and as Bowler says, 'His argument illustrated the extent to which evolutionary anthropology rested upon an assumption about the integral nature of economic and moral development' (ibid.: 81).

The archaeological counterpart to the linear progressionism of anthropology was developed by the French archaeologist Gabriel de Mortillet, assistant curator at the Museum of National Antiquities at Saint-Germain-en-Laye. His analysis of flint tools was based on a firm belief that any subdivision of such material should be based not on palaeontological, but on cultural, criteria. This progressive sequence comprised the Chellean Epoch (which included the large stone handaxes discovered by Boucher des Perthes whose work on the Somme gravels led to an acceptance of the antiquity of humankind), the Mousterian which was followed by the Solutrean, and finally the Magdalenian. Mortillet was convinced that this was the result of a natural progression in human development. This sequence is still central to the teaching of early prehistory in the Western world.

Another form of progressionism which developed during the nineteenth century was the belief that the cultures of living peoples could be compared, if they were considered as unilinear developments at different stages of progress, ranging from simple to complex. Such studies were based on ethnographic data gathered from around the world by missionaries and explorers (Trigger 1989: 59). A form of institutionalized racism was established. Since the Victorian period, archaeology and history have continuously been used as supportive evidence for the superiority of white European peoples, the most disastrous form manifesting itself in the incorporation of Kossina's archaeological research on Germanic origins into Nazi racist ideology (ibid.: 163–7).

The development of museums

An important element of Enlightenment and modern thought was a concern with the nature of 'man's' [sic] position in the order of things. Early museums were influenced, to a large extent, by the classical ordering of the universe:

The Representation of the Past

> ... the Classical *episteme* can be defined in its most general arrangement in terms of the articulated system of a *mathesis*, a *taxinomia*, and a *genetic analysis*. The sciences always carry within themselves the project, however remote it may be, of an exhaustive ordering of the world ...
>
> (Foucault 1970: 74)

Whereas proto-museums were concerned with the naming and ordering of the universe, as will be illustrated below, the museums which developed during the nineteenth and twentieth centuries were clearly more influenced by the modern idea of progress and the modern preoccupation with representing humankind's place in a world which was recognized as being constituted by fleeting and opaque experiences, a world where humankind was just one element amongst all other phenomena. Thus the modern museum has attempted to represent processes and experiences which are recognized as transient through static and objectifying displays, a form of display which will be considered later in this chapter.

The 'proto-museum'

In the fifteenth and sixteenth centuries it is possible to discern the emergence of proto-museums. These largely took the form of private collections, or cabinets of curiosities. Francis Bacon, in 1594, was quite explicit in his belief that no learned gentleman should be without a 'cabinet'. Bacon identified the 'specific role it had to play in contemporary endeavours to comprehend and to encapsulate "the universal nature"'. Such cabinets would to modern eyes seem full of random miscellaneous objects, but 'those very traits of diversity and miscellaneity which serve in our eyes to impair the serious intent of these collections were essential elements in a programme whose aim was nothing less than universality'. In terms of historical or archaeological material it would appear that greatest importance was attached to classical objects, or antiquities from Egypt. An interest in objects from closer to home certainly developed, possibly as a consequence of the already developed interest in more exotic objects (Impey and MacGregor 1985: 1–2).

Eileen Hooper-Greenhill (1988 and 1991) has traced the development of early museums employing Foucault's concept of 'effective history'. This requires the researcher to identify and articulate the important nodal points in the history of the phenomena under study, and she identifies the Medici Palace as the first 'nodal-point' in the development of museums (Hooper-Greenhill 1988: 70).

Clearly a product of the Renaissance, the Medici Palace was a private collection, and essentially an articulation of conspicuous consumption. The display was not a display as such, but rather a collection of exotic *objets*, designed to signify the importance of the owner, for 'Along with economic independence, and greater wealth, came an emphasis on the importance of a life in the present rather than the contemplative ideal of earlier times' (ibid.: 80).

Objects were ordered in the display through correspondences, through analogies, and the emphasis on the ability of *man* [sic] to know or to discover through the power of the gaze. Humankind was perceived as being able to take a position within the order of the universe, and from this position develop a rational understanding of that universe, and thus appreciate the superiority of humankind's position therein. Part of this emerging experience was the recognition of historically sited cultures that were in some ways superior, and that through the appreciation of this history, Renaissance society could mirror that superiority. During the Renaissance, the Classical period gradually came to be perceived in a new light. No longer was the past feared. Instead 'A gaze informed by the idea that classical artefacts were the product of a superior epoch' emerged (ibid.: 124).

What was equally important about this proto-museum in the Medici Palace was the fact that it was primarily a private institution, a privileged gaze, available only to those who had mastered the world through trade and the amassing of wealth. 'The "first museum of Europe" was constituted for the sole benefit of the family who owned it' (ibid.: 150). The collection was perceived as giving the collector a certain kudos: 'not only did the creation and enrichment of a museum constitute an occupation worthy of a nobleman; they were also means of acquiring renown and prestige and of turning the owner's home into an almost obligatory sight for everyone' (Olmi 1985: 13).

'The cabinets of the world' are identified by Hooper-Greenhill as being a development of the late sixteenth and early seventeenth centuries, and they were quite common across Europe, taking varied forms. The cabinets of the world should be differentiated from the cabinets of curiosity, represented by the German *Wunderkammer*.

Such a collection was meant to be no less than a representation of the 'universe', although as Hooper-Greenhill comments, 'The absolutely crucial question of what this "universality" might be now or might have been during the late Renaissance is never raised' (Hooper-Greenhill 1988: 159). Such cabinets, and the ways in which they were organized, were attempts to represent the world, and its order, as it was perceived by their owners. The aim was to constitute 'the world as a view' (ibid.: 161).

The Representation of the Past

The world was divided into macrocosm and microcosm. Macrocosm represented God and that which he created (nature), and microcosm represented 'Man' who was responsible for 'Art'. Nature and art were presumed to be fundamentally intermeshed and a network of complex correspondences linked the two categories.

The *Kunstkammer* of Rudolph II at Prague Castle can be considered as 'Encyclopedic' in its design, and represents a perceived position of man as master of his universe (ibid.: 211). It should be made clear that whereas the museum displays which emerged during the nineteenth century and are still common today attempted a form of didactic linear narrative, a representation of progress through the ordered display of artefacts, the *Wunderkammer* attempted an articulation of universal knowledge through the possession and identification of objects. To name an object is to know it and understand its position within the order of things. The aim of most displays of the late Renaissance period was to represent a sense of unity between the various material phenomena extant in the two spheres of creation, art and nature, highlighted above.

The elevated conviction of the museum as a public service did not really develop until the late seventeenth and early eighteenth centuries. And not until the nineteenth century could museums be considered as being truly public, and thus providing some sort of public service.

It is the institutional collections of the seventeenth century that represent the intermediate position between private 'cabinet' and public museum. Hunter believes that the basic difference between the 'private' cabinet and the institutional collection lay in the fact that the institutional collection 'had a potential for continuity which their private counterparts ordinarily lacked' (Hunter 1985: 159). This potential was due to the fact that institutions had a corporate life that was external to those of their members. A good example of such a collection was that of the Royal Society, which opened its museum in 1666.

England's first public museum was the Ashmolean which opened in 1683. The form of the Ashmolean, after its new building was completed in 1683, made it 'the first modern museum, specifically designed to display its collections, organized so that the University could use it for teaching purposes, and regularly open to the public' (Hudson 1987: 21).

The modern museum movement in Britain had its foundations in the philosophical societies that emerged during the late eighteenth and nineteenth centuries. The Sheffield Society for the Promotion of Useful Knowledge, established in 1804, and the Bradford Philosophical Society, established in 1808, are two examples of such. Brears and Davies point out that many of these societies were actually quite short-lived and had collapsed due to problems caused by the Napoleonic Wars (Brears and Davies 1989: 16). After the Napoleonic Wars many new societies were formed. In the north of England, the Leeds Philosophical and Literary Society was formed in 1818. This was followed by the establishment of similar societies in 'Sheffield and Hull in 1822, Bradford, Whitby and York in 1823, Wakefield and Scarborough in 1827, Halifax in 1830, and Doncaster in 1834' (ibid.: 17). Many constructed purpose-designed museums, and, as a result, were important pioneers of the museum movement. Others shared facilities with other organizations, including libraries and theatres.

These philosophical societies' collections usually consisted of objects collected by people with interests in geology, natural history, antiquities and ethnography. Objects were usually donated. Local people and those who had travelled abroad would make donations. The Empire and 'informal Empire' (i.e. those countries that were not officially a part of the British Empire but were under British influence at the time, e.g. Argentina) would have been an almost limitless resource as far as museums were concerned.

The proto-museums developing in America during the eighteenth century were also of the cabinet of curiosities type. An example of such a proto-museum was the Charleston Museum in South Carolina established during the 1770s. The pattern of real museum growth in the US was the opposite of that in Europe. In the US public museums existed years before the great private collections which, in Europe, were the primogenitors of museums. Early American museums, such as the Charleston Museum and Peale's Museum in Philadelphia, both of which opened during the late eighteenth century, were committed to displaying their collections to the wider public. However, these early museums were clearly more akin to the cabinets of curiosity as far as the mode of presentation was concerned: 'the collections piled up in a completely disorderly, unplanned fashion yet, ... this old-fashioned chaos had a strong appeal for children and other unsophisticated people [sic], for whom a museum was, more than anything else, a chamber of wonders, a romantic place which scientific arrangement could and did only spoil' (Hudson 1975: 37).

Proto-museums can be considered as the early articulations of 'objective' understandings of the known world. Such representations were usually only available to the ruling and mercantile classes who had been involved in the 'discovery' and 'mapping' of the known world. However, the processes of modernization, industrialization, urbanization and empire-building brought a vast new populace into increased contact with the developing political, economic and cultural networks which were a part of modernity. Such dramatic developments required the expansion of public institutions which could impart a feeling of belonging to, and knowledge of, the modern world. Therefore, the emergence of the modern museum can not be considered without a discussion of the economic contexts within which it developed.

Industrialization

The development of the public museum should be seen as the consequence of a number of interrelated factors, including the modern idea of progress and the emerging historical disciplines. But just as important was the impact of industrialization, urbanization and the consequent development of local government and social education programmes.

While the ideas of progress, linear time and history developed, so did the fabric of the societies in which these ideas emerged. It is difficult to say which came first, the idea of progress and scientific rationality, or the processes of industrialization which fundamentally transformed the way most people lived and thought. There is no doubt though, that in order for the processes of industrialization to be successful, a foundation of rational and scientific thought was necessary.

Before the Industrial Revolution, many communities were probably more firmly rooted in their own localities. These communities, whether they were in mercantile centres, villages, or market towns, would probably have possessed a sense of place, or rootedness, to a much greater extent than many people have had since the middle of the nineteenth century; many generations had lived in the same place.

The developments in Enlightenment thinking went hand in hand with the processes of the Industrial Revolution; the latter itself emerged partly as a result of the scientific advances made by Enlightenment thinkers, which in turn influenced modern thought itself. The confidence that emerged out of Enlightenment thought, and the perceived success of industrial capital, combined to create a conception of a society that potentially knew no bounds.

The Industrial Revolution intensified people's experiences of life in many ways. Factory work imposed a rigid awareness of and adherence to time. An increase in population, combined with the experience of urbanization, led to the destruction of insular rural communities with an appreciably slower way of life, even if it was harder. All of these experiences combined to impose a different spatial–temporal awareness, an awareness which contributed to the loss of a sense of place, a loss which we shall be concerned with more extensively in subsequent chapters.

The Industrial Revolution, with its roots in the seventeenth and eighteenth centuries, had its most profound effects on nineteenth-century Britain. Brief comparisons of industrial production between 1815 and 1885 illustrate this point. In 1815 Britain was producing 0.243 tons of pig iron; in 1885 7.4 million tons were being produced. Coal output in 1815 was *c.* 13 million tons; in 1885 it was 159.4. Between these two dates the population of England and Wales increased from 10.16 million (1811) to 25.97 million (1881), and by 1885 16,594 miles of railway had been laid (after Checkland 1971: 6).

Urbanization was of course the most important consequence of industrialization and population increase. The greatest movement to the urban centres took place during the 1840s. By the 1850s the size of the urban population was greater than that of the rural, and by the 1860s the ratio of urban to rural dwellers was 5:4 (ibid.: 33). By 1881 twice as many people lived in urban areas than rural.

The processes of modernization were mirrored in most Western nations, most importantly in the United States of America. What makes the US important is that, rightly or wrongly, it is often perceived as the nation which sets the 'standards' for consumer culture; what is commoditized in the US today, will be on sale in the rest of the world tomorrow. It is in part for this reason that a brief description of North American modernization is necessary.

The US experienced industrialization, and its consequences, some years after Britain. The 1860 census revealed the fact that five out of every six Americans still lived in rural areas, although it was apparent by this date that a shift away from agriculture was emerging (Degler 1984: 132).

During the fifty years leading up to World War I the population of the United States tripled, and the number employed in industry increased by about 550 per cent (ibid.: 259).

During the middle of the nineteenth century, despite being a predominantly rural nation, the US was greatly influenced by industrialization and experienced modernization to the same extent as European nations. In 1846 the first transatlantic steamship line was established. By 1844 the first electric telegraph had been set up between Baltimore and Washington, and by 1861 31,256 miles of railway had been laid. By 1890 this figure had increased to 166,703 (Brogan 1985: 387–9).

After the Civil War, the light bulb, the telephone and the phonograph were available thanks to the technical ingenuity of Americans. It should thus be clear that despite the US's relatively small industrial and urban development, it was still an important force in areas of scientific and technical progress. There is no doubt that the industry had a much greater influence on life in the east than in the west of the US. It is for this reason that we should not be surprised to find that early developments in American museums occurred in the east.

As with other industrializing nations, the population of the US expanded greatly during the nineteenth century: between the years 1860 and 1890 the population increased from 31 million to 63 million. Simple arithmetic reveals that the increase was in the order of a million per annum. This increase in population was matched by the increase in the size of the markets and the increases in consumer spending. It was during this period that the highly successful mail-order firms emerged such as Montgomery-Ward and Sears Roebuck (ibid.: 395).

The other factor that contributed to the transformation of the United States was immigration. At the height of nineteenth-century immigration in 1882, 788,992 arrivals were recorded. However, this was not the overall peak: during the 1900s roughly a million immigrants per year were entering the US. In fact, during the period between 1820 and 1920 the total figure for immigration to the US stood at 38 million (Degler 1984: 298). This immigration was not without its problems, and Brogan describes the reaction of some old Americans as 'nativism' (Brogan 1985: 414). Some may prefer to call it racism or xenophobia. The perceived threat posed by immigrants, and negroes brought to the US as slave labour, led to the formation of groups that ranged from the proto-fascist Ku Klux Klan, to the more 'patriotic' Sons, and Daughters, of America.

As in all industrializing nations the phenomenon that affected people's everyday lives more than any other was probably the experience of urbanization. In 1850 less than 13 per cent of Americans lived in urban areas. By 1920 over half of the US population was living in cities, by 1950 this figure was 60 per cent and by 1980 it was closer to 75 per cent (Degler 1984: 332). The period of greatest urban expansion was between 1860 and 1890; for example during the decade between 1860 and 1870 the increase in urban population was 59.3 per cent. The impact of urbanization on the experience of modern people is crucial and it is to this, the changing experience of daily life, that we should look for an explanation of why the past has become an important resource or requirement for modern society. Many of the reasons for such a need have been articulated elsewhere, most notably by David Lowenthal in *The Past is a Foreign Country* (Lowenthal 1985: esp. 396–7).

Local self-government

The processes of industrialization along with concomitant experiences of urbanization led to the need for a new form of local government: a tier of government which could take on the responsibility for the provision of a wide range of services that were essential to the successful running of an urban place.

In Britain during the 1840s, there was a developing awareness of the need to deal with the problems of urbanization. During the 1850s and 1860s the newly developing towns and cities of Britain began to involve themselves in efforts to improve conditions in their localities, and thus, possibly the proudest period of British local government emerged. The mid- to late Victorian period saw local government probably at its most influential, certainly more so than during the 1980s.

Victorian civic pride manifested itself in various ways, the most obvious being the construction of splendid town-halls, such as in Birmingham and Manchester, both begun in 1832.

Local government became responsible for almost all of the amenities necessary for the managing of urban areas, from sanitation to leisure. The effect of local authorities on the everyday lives of the Victorians should not be understated.

Despite the often disorganized nature of early Victorian local government, with each area of responsibility devolved to separate local institutions, museums and libraries did begin to appear in many larger towns. This was partly due to the efforts of William Ewart, a Liberal MP who urged the development of public libraries and museums. Thanks to Ewart the Museums Act became law in 1845 and permitted the various philosophical societies to transfer their collections to public bodies.

> Mid-Victorian cities began to take new pride in themselves, not as 'county' capital, local second-bests to London for an old-fashioned social round, not just as places where a lot of money was made, but as growing points of a new world order, where the expansive power of trade could be allied to traditional cultural standards of amenity and style.
>
> (Best 1971: 81–2)

The squalor and appalling lifestyles of the industrial working class continued throughout the century, but to a certain extent the quality of life was improved due to the efforts made by the many people who believed in local government. Attempts were made not only to improve the material living conditions of people, but also to develop and enhance recreational and educational facilities.

In the United States, as well as in all industrializing nations, there was an obvious need for local government, but it does not appear to have developed to the same extent as it did in Britain: 'Americans have never distinguished themselves, except perhaps for the TVA [Tennessee Valley Authority], by their social planning; for the most part, social institutions have been left to develop freely and under the stimulus of individual interest' (Degler 1984: 339). There does not seem to have been the same emphasis on the provision of cultural or recreation services, such as parks, libraries and museums. One notable exception was New York, where nearly 20 per cent of the land was parkland. Recreation as with many aspects of American life was in the main provided by the private sector.

The experience of urbanization

Crucial to this perception of modernity is the idea of 'distancing', or Giddens' 'disembedding' (Giddens 1990). The experiences of modernity, especially for the urban dweller, are experiences influenced by processes which have been increasingly removed from the local. These range from economic processes, to the provision of services. Distancing has been a fundamental experience of modernity. Whereas the resources of the locality would have satisfied much of a pre-modern community's requirements, modernization removed those processes from the direct experience of the community.

Part of this distancing has been the institutionalization of many of the services that modern societies rely upon. Life for the urban dweller has had to develop on an implicit notion of 'trust', a faith in the ability of people whom one does not know to provide an efficient and reliable service. This is as true of the car mechanic as it is of the museum curator.

Weber considered that the processes of modernization continuously subsumed all forms of institution: technical, economic, scientific, governmental, artistic and cultural. Instrumental/purposive rationalization led to a society that articulated rationalization in terms of means/ends decisions. Actions were justified rationally only within the accepted framework of modernity's progression, through the scientific, technical, and thus, rational control, of nature for humankind's desired ends.

However, an all-consuming rationalization does not necessarily imply a de-differentiation, or an homogenization of modern societies, where all services – cultural, education, and professional services such as legal and financial advice – are concentrated in the hands of one faceless organization. In fact modernity has witnessed the opposite process. Since the Enlightenment there has been an increasing emergence of 'expert cultures', of which the museum is one. Habermas feels that the 'differentiation of science, morality, and art, which is characteristic of occidental rationalism, results not only in a growing autonomy for sectors dealt with by specialists, but also the splitting off of these sectors from a stream of tradition continuing on in everyday practice in a quasi-natural fashion' (Habermas 1987a: 355). He has argued that the existence of separate specialist communities denies access to any form of 'universal' knowledge. Rather than one homogenizing faceless organization controlling modern societies, all forms of service have been monopolized by many different expert groups, who in their own way deny the wider public access to much information and knowledge. This practice effectively works as an ideological tool. The acceptance of separate institutional disciplines serves to negate any demand for any form of totalizable knowledge. These structures of knowledge have their consequence in 'the cultural impoverishment and fragmentation of everyday consciousness' (ibid.: 355). Capitalist, and non-capitalist states alike, have always encouraged a diversity of their own forms; that is to say, cultural heterogeneity has only been welcomed as long as it remained 'in line' with the wider hegemony.

This institutionalization of knowledge and services is a part of Giddens' 'disembedding mechanisms', processes which have removed social relations from local contexts and from the daily experiences of people's lives. Expert systems, such as museums, are disembedding mechanisms. The expertise of the professional, from the accountant to the curator, or even the heritage manager, is knowledge based on trust, a guarantee 'of expectation across distanciated time–space', where the expert is removed from public access, and therefore the quality of any service is only guaranteed by a sometimes unjustified trust in the professional (Giddens 1990: 28). It is the processes of studying, interpreting and representing the past, that have been increasingly removed from the day-to-day experiences of the public. The institutions invite, or rather, impose, a need for 'trust' on the part of the public. Expertise has had to be taken for granted, otherwise the public would not use the services provided by the professional. Part of that relationship is an implicit contract between public and expert which ensures that the expert is beyond criticism, and can therefore demand trust and respect from the public: '*Trust in systems* takes the *form of faceless commitments*, in which faith is sustained in the workings of knowledge of which the lay person is largely ignorant' (ibid.: 88).

The idea of disembedding, or the continual distancing from the local, of the processes which affect people's lives is an important element in the experiences of living in the (post)-modern world, and will be considered at greater length elsewhere.

One of the most important elements in this distancing is money. Money throughout the (post)-modern period has increasingly worked outside the material environment within which people work. Since the Industrial Revolution, the money markets have increasingly improved the potential of money to work externally to people and places; basically, money is not restrained by space.

> Money is simultaneously everything and nothing, everywhere but nowhere in particular, a means that poses as an end, the profoundest and most complete of all centralizing forces in a society where it facilitates the greatest dispersion, a representation that appears quite divorced from whatever it is supposed to represent. It is a *real* or *concrete abstraction* that exists external to us and exercises real power over us.
>
> (Harvey 1985: 3)

The processes of modernization have been largely concerned with the domination of space, the development of processes which enhance the ability of capital to overcome the constraints of space. Throughout the nineteenth century and into the twentieth, this constraint was increasingly mastered. The advent of telecommunication systems and international banking enhanced the ability of money to work 24 hours a day to make a profit while its owners slept.

The triumph of time over space is one which is crucial to the idea of distancing the remoteness of processes which affect our daily lives from the actual experiences which affect those lives. As Harvey argues, the victory of time over space has had its consequence in increasing efforts to overcome the constraints of space, and economic processes since the nineteenth century have been ever increasingly removed from the direct experiences of ordinary people (ibid.: 15).

Modernization, therefore, has contributed to the production of new forms of 'dis-located' space. The urban environment was created out of the imperative to modernize; this resulted in the creation of a new form of intensified experience, intensified because of modernity's need to produce and reproduce itself with ever increasing regularity. The urban city or town developed as a new form of concentrated space, catalysts for the inputs and outputs of capital, new places of enhanced consumption and production.

The destruction of a sense of place and the experiences of time–space compression can not be overemphasized. The re-placing of the majority of the population in modern urban environments, combined with the concomitant imposition of rigid timetables and enhanced communications led to a modern society which was no longer restrained by time–space boundaries. For many it would have seemed that during the nineteenth century the world shrunk. An ability to make 'connections' with the processes which affected daily experiences began to disappear. A security of place, which was partly a consequence of a knowledge of, and trust in, local relationships and experiences for many people was lost for ever.

The modern place

The places which the processes of modernization produced symbolized the idea of modernity. The enhancement of the economic system, which did for many people bring wealth, as well as hardship and squalor, was the epitome of the idea of progress. The technology/science meta narrative provided the foundations for the 'profitable' exploitation of the environment for humankind's benefit, to an extent which was undreamt of a century earlier. The rationalization and institutionalization of life was enhanced through the urban form. The city represented the state's ability to organize and control the populace with hitherto unprecedented efficiency. Unrest in the city was avoided through the development of a sophisticated and reliable form of local self-government. Municipal authorities provided the amenities which ensured a basic quality of life for the majority of the city's inhabitants, from hygiene to the arts. The urban environment provided the contexts for controlled economic and social production and reproduction.

Modernity witnessed the emergence of unfettered consumption, what Xenos has termed the invention of 'scarcity'. 'The discourse of scarcity and abundance that marks the nineteenth century accompanied the creation of an environment carefully crafted to elicit sensations of opulence and desire' (Xenos 1989: 85). The urban environment was one where a large body of people began to appropriate 'style'. There was an emergent consumption of superfluous goods, which hitherto had been confined to a very select group. The city involved 'cohabiting' with others to a degree which had rarely been experienced prior to industrialization. The consumption of superfluous commodities was part of a trend towards the construction of an image of self in the light of one's relationship to others, a construction of identity through the consumption of goods and services which has intensified throughout (post-)modernity.

For many, the perceived success of modernization, combined with the powerful meta narratives which constituted modern thought, resulted in a view of modern society as one which was, or already had, overcome the past. Modernity opened up routes to every potential horizon of achievement. It was as if the past had been overwhelmed by the success of modernity, and the progressive road to the future had been freed of many, if not all, obstructions.

The development of the museum has to be considered as an integral part of the modern condition and the concomitant processes of modernization which have been considered in this chapter.

Integral to modern thought was an idea that the 'realities' of the world were potentially knowable, and 'From this it follow[ed] that the world could be controlled and rationally ordered if we could only picture and represent it rightly'

(Harvey 1989: 27)

The representation of the past had to be ordered if it was to make any sense. People's developed awareness of time and progress, coupled with the modern understanding of history, was reflected and reiterated in the museum displays of the nineteenth, and more frequently, twentieth centuries.

The first museums boom

... if antiquarianism was a natural and appropriate expression of the spirit of the eighteenth century, then archaeology, with its much greater emphasis on order, method and conformity, is a true child of the nineteenth.

(Hudson 1987: 22)

The early decades of Britain's modern museum service may be considered as commencing with the establishment of the British Museum, which was created by an Act of Parliament in 1753. The museum opened at Montagu House in Bloomsbury in 1759. During its formative years it was little more accessible than the Renaissance cabinets of curiosity, as entry was restricted to 60 visitors a day. However, this was increased to 120 by 1808, and daily opening was introduced in 1879.

It was the acquisition of the Elgin marbles in 1814–15 that gave the museum its international reputation in the field of classical antiquities. Its perceived aims would appear to have been the ordering and under-standing of the world. This was obviously an aim closely tied to Britain's perceived role as imperial master of the universe.

From such elitist beginnings a number of factors came together which resulted in the first 'museums boom' during the second half of the nineteenth century. In 1860 there were about 90 museums; by 1880 the number was closer to 180. The reasons for this boom were a combination of the factors discussed earlier in this chapter. These various processes conspired to create a new experience, or consciousness, of time and space. The pressures of urban life, the ordering of time through adherence to rigid timetables in the factory, the ordering of space through the control of domestic property by landlords, as well as the intensified experience of urban life, and the impossibility of avoiding interaction with other people, all contributed to this emerging consciousness. Museums were, and still are, part of this modern experience. However, this was clearly a class-based experience, and museums, although partly an educational provision, were never really successfully 'sold' to the working classes. However, they allowed an educated middle class to develop an awareness of the wider spatial and historical contexts within which they lived.

Many of the museums that were built during the 'boom' were built in the industrial cities of the north of England, where the emphasis on civic pride and the provision of public facilities seems to have been stronger. The Education Act of 1870 was also an important factor, as was Queen Victoria's Jubilee of 1887. This year saw museums opening in Bootle, Halifax, Sheffield, Plymouth and Leeds; several of the larger ones were of the 'Greek Temple' type (ibid.: 26).

The foundation of modern museums is essentially a part of the emergence of modern ideas regarding order and progress, and the related experiences of time and space, with their roots firmly placed in industrialization and urbanization. These ideas and experiences are fundamental to the forms of historical and archaeological study that have been undertaken throughout the twentieth century as well as the nineteenth. The basic form of representing the past through the static museum presentation has not really altered in spite of many changes in fashion and style.

The *modern* museum: a critique

The modern period saw endless voyages of discovery, which for many revealed the world as finite and knowable. One consequence of this was the development of maps, and a kudos attached to objective spatial representation. The museum display articulated a similar sort of perspective. The developing ability to place objects in ordered contexts often implied a unilinear development of progress. Such representations implied a control over the past through an emphasis on the linear, didactic narrative, supported by the use of the object, which had been appropriated and placed in an artificial context of the curator's choosing. This type of display is closed, and cannot be questioned. The display case is a removed and *distanced* context, a context that can not be criticized. At the same time it is an artificial context, perhaps even a non-context. In a way, museums attempt to 'freeze' time, and almost permit the visitor to stand back and consider 'the past before them'. This is the power of the gaze, an ability to observe, name and order, and thus control.

The emphasis on objectifying the perceived processes of human development is a form of rationalization of modern societies, and as mentioned earlier, Weber and more recently, Habermas, have considered that the rationalization of society has to an extent penetrated every institution, including museums (Habermas 1984: 157).

Weber argued that modernization could be considered as the rationalization of society; the capitalist project had, as its aim, rational economic action, and the state had as its goal, the rationalization of administration. Specifically modern societies are considered as being subjected to forms of 'purposive-rationalization', where all action is directed to the attainment of some goal, usually economic, at the expense of open democratic discourse where all members of a society can develop an awareness of the processes which affect their lives. It is the all-pervasive nature of rationalization which is important to note, and museums as a part of the structure of an emerging system of local government in Britain made a tacit contribution to this process in the field of administration through a rationalization of learning and leisure. That is not to say that independent museums did not follow a certain purposive rationality, as nearly every museum employed a similar didactic style, based on accepted rational forms of knowledge developed out of the Enlightenment.

Museums: time and progress in modernity

Time was a frontier that remained for the most part unconquered until the modern epoch, in the same way that street lighting allowed the frontier of night to be conquered, and the telegraph allowed speed of light communication; the museum display allowed control over history. The museum display is a representation of past progress, authoritatively produced and often beyond question. It is itself a created past, implying by its authority a command over time and space.

It was imperative that the increased population of the nineteenth century, concentrated in urban areas, was exposed to certain conceptions of time. Such a vast increase in numbers, coupled with such a profound change in the geographical location of the population, would have demanded a subtle but rigid code of practice. The imposition of a well-defined system of time would have been, and still is, crucial. Museums should be considered as part of the project necessary for the imposition of capitalist time – a precise time, a time that flowed in linear progression.

Factories obviously required workers to observe strict timetables, working-hours, clocking on and clocking off; rates of pay were by the hour and pay was docked for lateness. It was not until the advent of the railways in Britain, and in fact, in many countries, that a national time was required. Time varied from city to city, from town to town; railway timetables required the imposition of a standardized time and rigid timekeeping across the country. Time is a frontier and context that we all share. The development of time as linear progression is a phenomenon that large groups of people who are actually dispersed in terms of space (and therefore time) can share, or rather, it is a restraining influence to which are all subject. The advancement of this common restraint by museums has doubtless helped develop a certain sense of time, and then, over the decades, maintain a certain *status quo*.

> The buying and selling of time, as labour time, is surely one of the most distinctive features of modern capitalism. The origins of the precise temporal regulation of the day may perhaps be found in the chime of the monastery bell, but it is in the sphere of labour that its influence became embedded in such a way as to spread throughout society as a whole. The commodification of time, geared to the mechanisms of industrial production, breaks down the differentiation of city and countryside characteristic of class-divided societies. ... Together with the transformation of time, the commodification of space establishes a 'created environment' of a very distinctive character, expressing new forms of institutional articulation. Such new forms of institutional order alter the conditions of social and system integration and thereby change the nature of the connections between the proximate and remote in time and space.
>
> (Giddens 1984: 144)

Undoubtedly there was a gradual imposition of a public universal time: 'as the railroads destroyed some of the quaintness and isolation of rural areas, so did the imposition of universal public time intrude upon the uniqueness of private experience in private time' (Kern 1983: 34). As discussed earlier, the experiences of modernity were primarily linked to various forms of dislocation, in a way, the destruction of difference between places. That is not to say that the urban form is an homogeneous one, but rather, to argue that the wrenching of people from 'secure' places with a strong sense of community rooted in time and space must have resulted in a feeling of loss, or rather an experience of disorientation.

The Representation of the Past

It can be argued that time, as represented in museum displays, is a product of what is essentially a Western conception that developed during the Industrial Revolution. 'Most social analysts treat time and space as mere environments of action and accept unthinkingly the conception of time, as measurable clock time, characteristic of modern Western culture' (Giddens 1984: 110). The argument is that museums, which have their roots in the late eighteenth and nineteenth centuries, not only reflected what was becoming the accepted conception of time, but were also reinforcing this conception. This is an example of what Giddens refers to as structuration: 'One of the main propositions of structuration theory is that the rules and resources drawn upon in the production and repro-duction of social action are at the same time the means of system repro-duction (the duality of structure)' (ibid.: 19).

Museums have also contributed to a certain conception of time, a time that is concerned with *progress*. The majority of museum displays follow an accepted didactic, linear narrative that either consciously or uncon-sciously imposes a rigid framework, where time and space are sequestered by the curator. The development of evolutionary and progressionist models, such as the Three-Age System in archaeology, is an excellent example of such a preoccupation with progress.

During the nineteenth century, a change occurred in the understanding of how societies developed. Clearly influenced by Darwin's writings, 'The paradigm for the interpretation of cumulative changes was no longer the theoretical progress of science but the natural evolution of the species. With this, the thematic of rationalization was transformed into that of social evolution' (Habermas 1984: 151). This revised model for under-standing society made sense in the light of the historical developments of the nineteenth century. There seemed to be a belief that techniques of production, which had not developed as a result of work carried out in the natural sciences in any case, could be better understood empirically through an evolutionary model. Also, the development of civil liberties seemed to conform to a more progressionist/evolutionary model. And the development of functionalist economic models seemed to possess the characteristics of organic self-maintaining systems (ibid.: 152).

This change in the conception and understanding of Victorian society was reflected in the modes through which museums displayed their material. Consider the differences between the early cabinets and proto-museums, with their displays linking natural and artefactual objects in the same displays, and the nineteenth-century museums with their differentiation between the new emerging disciplines. Displays of archaeological material followed the evolutionary approach based on the Three-Age System developed in Denmark. This understanding of evolution was represented in the displays of Pitt-Rivers. When in 1883, the 14,000 items in his collection were moved to the Pitt-Rivers Museum in Oxford, the artefacts were arranged according to these evolutionary ideas. The ethos underlying this museum was, according to Hudson, that people 'must be shown that all man-made objects follow in an ascertainable sequence, and that improvements are being made all the time' (Hudson 1987: 34). This mode of display was not one that was peculiar to Britain. In the United States, George Brown Goode, who took over the US National Museum in 1879, developed a sophisticated and extensive system of taxonomy for this museum. Goode believed that history was progressive and followed a linear path, which moved in increments of advancement and was also largely about 'great men and patriotic acts' (Kulik 1989: 9).

Today, there are still many museum displays which owe their form to this model of representation. The argument is not necessarily that this model, in all its forms, has outlived its usefulness but rather that the shortcomings of the progressionist, linear narrative, need to be considered more carefully.

This form of display is still popular with many major museums, including the British Museum. For example, the prehistoric displays are still essentially Three-Age oriented. One such display, entitled 'Industrial Progress', is a representation of the evolution of Bronze Age metalwork. The display case is filled with sequences of axeheads and spearheads. Each artefact is named and positioned within the modern unifying framework, and each series of artefacts is divided into a phase. The phasing of evidence reveals the emphasis on technology of many museum displays, with the implicit categorization of peoples through the curator's perception of their technical achievements. The success of such displays relies on the aura of the object. The emphasis is on the object for itself, artefact for artefact's sake. Hoards are neatly arranged on a velvet background. For example, the Anglo-Saxon Burials case in the Medieval gallery at the British Museum, contains six cast gilt-bronze saucer brooches, four cruciform brooches, six disc and composite brooches, four small-long brooches, and four square-headed brooches. One of the Celtic cases contains *ten* penannular brooches. The auratic display, where the 'beauty' or aesthetic quality of the object is intentionally the predominant characteristic of the display, is oppressive in its impressiveness; the medium consumes the message and the auratic display is itself a form of spectacle, suppressing the ability to interpret. The display is a sensual experience, usually for those with the expertise to name and therefore know the object. There is little emphasis on the interpretation and understanding of the contexts of production, use and deposition of the object, there is little archaeology or history. Commenting on the nature of such displays, Shanks and Tilley have observed:

> Display of the artefact conveys the timeless ability of Man[*sic*] as
> toolmaker-artist. As such the visitor need only approach the artefact
> with finely tuned sensibilities; the artifact's universal truth is
> communicated via direct intuition. But whose sensibilities, whose
> intuition, whose 'humanity'? As the aesthetic qualities of the artifact
> are supposedly immediately perceptible, context and critical analysis
> become relegated to optional supplements.
>
> (Shanks and Tilley 1987: 73)

In the museum, the viewer's perception of the object is often constructed
through her/his acceptance of the naming/identification of the object by
an 'authority'. The display often promotes a process of de-differentiation
as each object is placed within the legitimating context of the modern,
linear narrative, which tacitly promotes the modern idea of progress. The
homogeneous form of the museum display represents the past as an
undifferentiated path of progress towards the modern, where our discovery and acquisition of past material culture legitimates the modern
Western position as the inheritor of civilization. This is nowhere more
obvious than in the acquisition, some may say looting, of classical material
culture, and its subsequent display in museums.

The museum display not only reinforces the idea of progress, through its
emphasis on technological advances, but also, through the emphasis on
the auratic object. This is especially so in the national museums which
often have access to the 'richest' objects. The gravity attached to aesthetics
denies a consideration of the wider, more common processes that would
have dominated the everyday lives of ordinary people.

A slightly different articulation of the idea of progress is apparent in the
Museum of London, which is undoubtedly one of the best museums in
Britain. Despite this, the all-pervasive modern rationality of progress is
still manifest.

The underlying theme in the story of London's development as represented in the Museum of London's displays is that of steady advancement. This advancement has been achieved through the continuing
expansion of London's trading links, until 'By the middle of the nineteenth
century when Britain was "the Workshop of the World", London was
its largest port and industrial centre' (Museum of London 1985: 41).
Despite acknowledging the poverty and problems caused by this expanding urban mass, the underlying theme is that of a progress that is 'bright'
and welcoming, whilst that temporary set-back, which was the Dark
Ages, is displayed in a darkened room. The Dark Ages are represented
as a period of history which was an embarrassing hiccup on the road of
progress, a road which the visitor knows will come out at the other end,

as progress demands that there will always be a light at the end of the evolutionary tunnel. The implied failure of the Dark Ages in producing anything worthwhile is remedied by the Medieval London display, which illustrates 'London's chequered rise to pre-eminence not only as the seat of the nation's Government but as the magnet of society and fashion and as the primary centre of industry and international trade' (ibid.: 21).

The criticism here is not aimed at displays concerned with trade as such, but rather, the implicit notion that humankind is always progressing, and that expansion and progression are inherently good – good to the point that even the problems of urbanization can be defeated by the ever successful forward march of humankind.

> The coming of the industrial revolution and the rapid population expansion brought to London hitherto unprecedented problems of poverty, overcrowding and disease. To deal with these, services such as main drainage and new systems of administration had to be evolved.
>
> (ibid.: 41)

As E. H. Carr comments in *What is History?*, 'Progress does not and cannot mean equal and simultaneous progress for all' (Carr 1987: 116). Progress in the realms of economy is often seen from the point of view of those who benefited from its development and not of those who suffered. Such displays are however potentially emancipatory, or could hint at such a potential, as the idea of progress is important at the cultural and moral level, though such progress is rarely represented explicitly.

In a museum display, the object itself is without meaning. Its meaning is conferred by the 'writer', that is, the curator, the archaeologist, the historian, or the visitor who possesses the 'cultural competence' to recognize the conferred meaning given by the 'expert'. The object in the museum display is given meaning through various media – the written text and association with other objects, often articulated within the tacit assumption of technological progress from which human progress is concomitantly assumed. A group of samian bowls placed in a salad bar in a Pizza Hut would probably not take on the same meaning as a similar assemblage situated in a display case at the British Museum.

Conclusion

The emergence of the museum was a part of the experience of modernity – the developments in science and technology, the Industrial Revolution and urbanization, as well as the consequent changes in the experience of time and space. All of these constituted the Victorian society which produced the ideas of civic pride and a recognition (in some classes) of the need for education. The museum can be considered either as an ideological tool which reinforced the held conceptions of order, time and progress or as tools of emancipation, representations of other places and other times which opened people's eyes to a world other than their own, and thus helped them maintain a sense of place, and make connections with those processes which had influenced their current position in the order of things. It is in fact most likely that the museum did, and still does, have both of these effects, effects which are largely dependent on the context of reception. However, there can be no doubt that the emancipatory potential of the museum has never been entirely realized, and that now, more than ever, this potential needs to be articulated. This need is partly a function of the increasing intensity of the modern and post-modern experience.

Post-modern societies I

2

This chapter considers the network of economic, political, social, and cultural contexts within which heritage and the post-modern representations of the past have developed in Britain, and to a much lesser extent, the US.

The basic structures of modern societies in Europe and the US were laid down during the nineteenth century. Throughout the twentieth century, we have witnessed changes in technology and science that have influenced our daily lives more intensely than ever before. One immediately thinks of the radio, the television, the aeroplane, the car, and most importantly, the emergence of information technologies.

Whilst accepting that these developments have changed the everyday lives of the majority of people in the First World, the modern consciousness has its roots firmly in the nineteenth-century experiences of industrialization and urbanization. These changes in experience have been changes by degrees, an intensification of experience, and most importantly as Harvey claims, an intensification of the experience of time–space compression (Harvey 1989: chapters 15–16). This experience is, in turn, a product of developments in the nineteenth century.

The media used in museums through which people have learned about their pasts have altered very little since the nineteenth century. There have been a few notable developments, including the emergence of 'folk-life' museums. However, the static, modern display, which contributes to the maintenance and promotion of an idea of linear progress, even if the display only depicts one theme or period in isolation, is still predominant in the late twentieth century.

There have of course been developments in the various forms of mass communications, such as cinema, television and radio. All of these have greatly influenced people's perceptions of the past, from the great classical epic movie, to the documentaries on archaeological and historical themes. The impact of these media should not be wholly ignored, but it lies beyond the scope of this book.

Post-war Britain

Britain by the early 1950s was one of the most densely inhabited countries in the world. Four-fifths of the British people lived in urban areas, and half of these lived in the London area, or in the major six provincial areas. Another important structural development is the increase in car ownership. Before the war, there were just under 2 million private cars; by 1955 this figure had risen to over 3.6 million. Even then, people still tended to travel within their local areas rather than nationally (Marwick 1990: 32–3).

Immediately after 1945, Britain was still divided upon class lines, despite two world wars, which many had hoped would see the end of this social structure. The upper classes, during the nineteenth century and into the twentieth, had been supremely successful at integrating the emerging industrial gentry, and conceding to the more successful middle classes access to some of the trappings of ruling-class lifestyle, such as education in the public school system. 'In the nineteenth century, the upper class elaborated on older traditions in evolving a distinctive ethos inculcated through the major public schools and, in lesser degree, Oxford and Cambridge universities. There was created an upper-class "box" of attitudes and life-styles into which newcomers could be socialized' (ibid.: 36).

Meanwhile, the war had strengthened working-class identity. The Labour Party, which had largely been responsible for domestic policy during the war, and had developed the policies for the 'New Jerusalem' of the post-war period, had helped develop a new working-class consciousness and confidence, a strength which the New Right attempted to destroy during the 1980s.

One of the most important developments in post-war Britain was the creation of the welfare state – the public provision of education, health care, housing, social security, and to an extent, cultural facilities, to everybody either free, or at a cost which was affordable. The welfare state is an important phenomenon, not just because of what it achieved in terms of promoting a civilized society, but because of the fact that it represents a form of political economy which became the principal target of New Right critique during the mid- to late seventies, and finally of attack during the 1980s, once they had achieved power.

The 1950s saw the emergence of relatively large sectors of society which had the means for new forms of commodity consumption. The emphasis on the nuclear family as a 'centre of consumption' developed throughout the 1950s and into the 1960s (ibid.: 63). After the war, there was a re-emergence of leisure activity. Visits to holiday-camps and day-trips to the seaside were popular recreational activities for many families. The development of the tourist industry and the articulation of the 'tourist gaze' have been scrutinized by a number of writers, most recently by John Urry (Urry 1990).

During the 1950s and 1960s the average earnings of working-class and middle-class households increased substantially. Between 1955 and 1969 average weekly earnings rose by about 130 per cent. Of course, there was inflation (between 1955 and 1969 retail prices increased by 63 per cent) but although the costs of food and other necessities increased in relative terms over this period, the *relative* prices of cars, washing machines and televisions actually fell. 'Television sets had been a rarity in the early 1950s; but by 1961 75 per cent of families had one, and by 1971 91 per cent' (Marwick 1990: 114–17). This statistic alone should illustrate the point, that for the majority of the British public the later post-war years brought unprecedented relative wealth. These consumer goods, along with a developing leisure industry, were still the mechanisms necessary to ensure a pliant and productive work-force, which more often than not was still required to work within a monotonous Fordist mode of production. Britain, along with the majority of the Western world, emerged as a nation of consumers with an ever increasing appetite for new commodities.

The story of this growth is one of an appetite which has accelerated to the point where the commodities themselves have hardly altered in terms of their function, but the surface style of those commodities has changed and continues to change rapidly. During the late 1970s and throughout the 1980s 'surface' marketing emerged; an emphasis on style and the immediate experience became increasingly important.

The New Right

The Welfare State of the post-war decades, which was legitimated and reinforced by a period of consensus politics during the late 1950s and 1960s, came under the close scrutiny of the emerging New Right during the 1970s. Right wingers on both sides of the Atlantic considered that the post-war political economies of the West required profoundly different strategies. Despite the fact that the economic policies identified with the New Right were most conspicuous in the UK and the US, the style of economic planning adhered to by the architects of the New Right took on currency in many other Western, and First World nations, including those with socialist governments.

At its most basic, the New Right can be considered as a reaction against the Welfare State, and in the US, as a reaction to the 'New Deal'-based political economy. The New Right achieved its greatest 'successes' in Britain and the United States, where this political philosophy was articulated and practised under the labels of Thatcherism and Reaganism. Any consideration of the roots of the post-modern condition, and of heritage, demands a recognition of the influence of this strand of political culture and its economic practice.

A reaction to welfarism

The New Right believed that the social democratic states could not protect society from the threats posed to the patriarchal family and the 'white nation'. 'For the Conservative New Right the greatest threat to the survival of the free world lay in the erosion of national will and political authority which was the legacy of postwar social democracy' (Gamble 1988: 57).

Thus the New Right has aimed to discredit the social democratic concept of universal citizenship rights supported by the mechanisms of the state. This should be replaced with a concept of citizenship rights which would be achieved through property ownership and the right to participate in the market.

By the 1970s it was apparent to those on the Right that the Keynesian-based economic policies of the post-war period were failing. This failure was perceived as being intensified by the oil price rises of the early 1970s.

Fundamental to the thought of the New Right has been a rejection of 'the idea that welfare or social and economic rights are to be regarded as basic rights of citizenship alongside rights to civil and political liberties' (Hoover and Plant 1989: 52). Mrs Thatcher objected to the idea of an 'entitlement society' which accepts that people have the right to a set of services or goods independent of their own economic performance. Essentially, for her, the individual should have only their political and civil rights defined, not their socio-economic rights. Here the individual can only claim the right to participate in the deregulated, unfettered market.

Elementary to the economic practice of New Right Governments, as well as those influenced by their philosophies, has been an emphasis on supply-side economics. Supply-siders consider that it is repressive fiscal policy which denies individuals increased access to the market-place. Therefore, cuts in taxation act as an incentive to work, and thus, increase the supply of goods. These goods, it is assumed, will then eventually 'trickle' their way down to all levels of society. Hoover and Plant point out that supply-side theories are in effect a complement to monetarism, and 'certainly share many of the monetarist assumptions about the nature of the capitalist economy and the nature of human motivation in the economic sphere' (ibid.: 28). The emphasis of this type of economic policy is on the individual acting as a 'free agent' within a benevolent and neutral market system, which in turn ensures naturally a just allocation of economic rewards to those who deserve them.

The foundation for much New Right thinking comes from the Austrian school of economics, which lays emphasis on the 'conception of economic dynamics, in particular the role of the entrepreneur in changing and modernizing the economic structure' (Green 1989: 7). Hayek, the most influential member of the Austrian school, emphasized the 'special' knowledge of the individual who can react within a particular place to the demands of the market. It is in this context of unfettered, free marketeering that the service sector, and more specifically as far as this book is concerned, the leisure-service sector, has been allowed to flourish. The atomistic market economy provides little in the way of controlling mechanisms, and therefore 'quality control' is left to the vagary of the market. 'In all of these approaches the revitalizing spirit of unfettered profit-making is lauded. Thus, for example, even if privatization of an industry does not change market structure it is claimed to raise efficiency' (ibid.: 8).

The suite of policies which aimed to remove restraints from the market included the policies of deregulation which were common to both Reaganism and Thatcherism. The architects of this policy argued, once again, that businesses and the individual can operate more freely in a market that is freed of what the New Right perceived as restrictive practices. In the United States Reagan deregulated those organizations which were responsible for environment and worker protection. Such agencies included the Environmental Protection Agency, the Product Safety Council and the Occupational Safety and Health Administration. This move was justified with the argument that deregulation would free businesses from unnecessary costs and would therefore allow them to invest in new products and thus initiate new growth (Hoover and Plant 1989: 32). In Britain similar policies were followed, most infamously the deregulation of the stock market, widely referred to as the 'Big Bang'. Also, the policy of Enterprise Zones was developed – areas which were to be immune from the usual controls, especially those imposed by local authorities.

The reduction of local-authority power over Enterprise Zones was only the tip of the iceberg. The sustained attack on the powers of local government in Britain has been one of the most disturbing aspects of Government policy. During the 1980s there were at least fourteen pieces of central-government legislation dealing with local government. Despite the New Right's emphasis on the role of the individual and the implicit notion of reducing central government's role in society, the opposite in fact occurred.

The underlying reason for the attacks on local government was central to the British Government's unending desire to reduce the Public Sector Borrowing Requirement. The PSBR is the amount of money that the Government spends on all public services, and local-government expenditure is obviously an important part of this total. At the same time, central government attempted to reduce the role of local government from the opposite end, through policies which were aimed at giving the individual consumer a greater influence over the services which she received from the local authority. Such policies have included the right to buy council houses, the removal of financial control of schools to each individual school, and the poll tax. These strategies reject the idea of a wider community, the need to provide policies for all people who require housing now and in the future, and the need for a locally based education policy.

An emphasis on the enhanced role of the individual in the market-place has also led to attacks on the professions, especially those in the public sector. The New Right perceives the professional ethic as being a constituent part of the set of Welfare State restrictive practices which detract from the operation of a truly free market. Those on the Right tend to consider that 'this is because the professional ethic is a self-serving myth, which has enabled the professions to bamboozle the rest of society into paying them monopoly rent. Professionals are sellers of services who have managed to control the supply of the service they sell. Because they control the supply, they can control its market value' (Marquand 1990: 19). As with all marketable commodities the New Right believes that all professional services should also be subjected to the mechanisms of the market.

Mrs Thatcher particularly disliked civil servants and academics (though she made good use of some of them), whom she bracketed with the clergy as representing the 'anti-industrial spirit' which she deplored: 'nowhere is this attitude [suspicion of making money] more marked than in the cloister and the common room. What these critics apparently can't stomach is that wealth creators have a tendency to acquire wealth in the process of creating for others.'

(Perkin 1989: 486–7)

There is no doubt that some professions do operate restrictive practices and should be forced to compete; however, there does appear to have been an emphasis on attacking certain specific groups of professionals.

The removal of restrictions and the opening up of the market to the inexperienced and the unqualified is dangerous in the extreme, and can actually lead, in some cases, to fatalities. A critique of the professions must be based on a healthy awareness of their fallibility, rather than a blinkered unleashing of potentially nihilistic market forces.

In many areas, including museums, there has been an attack on pro-fessionalism. This is not because of a desire to see the quality of the service improve, but rather due to a craving for economic 'efficiency', the imperative to survive in the market-place. The need to survive in the market has had its consequence in a new emphasis on those who can produce something of financial worth. There has been a new and danger-ous emphasis on the need for 'doers' rather than 'thinkers'. This emphasis was manifested, for example, at the Victoria and Albert Museum in 1988, when a number of academics were forced out as part of the wider mission of profitability. Such policies can only lead to the damaging of the reputations of such an institution's expertise and professionalism. The consequence of such policies 'has been not only a gap in the academic generations which may never be repaired but a brain drain of some of the best scholars and scientists, principally to the United States and Australia, rivalling that from Hitler's Germany' (ibid.: 487).

In fact this emphasis on that which is potentially profitable, and the dislike of 'concepts' such as 'society' and any ideas which are considered 'airy-fairy', along with the belief that there is nothing other than the individual, is not too dissimilar from the relativism and anti-foun-dationalism of some post-modern thinking which also promotes the obsolescence of such 'big' ideas. The effects that these policies have had on the way the past is presented and studied will be considered more extensively in subsequent chapters.

It is apparent that despite a declared desire to reduce centralized authority the New Right has in fact increased it. There are many fundamental contradictions in the thinking and practice of New Right politics, none more so than the declared desire to improve the lot of the individual, whilst surreptitiously increasing the power of central authority.

The radical individual is expected to accept the dominant values of the ruling Government, in return for what that Government perceives as the privilege to operate in the unfettered market. And while politicians of the New Right pronounce that there is no such thing as society, we as individuals are forced to operate within political, economic, and cultural contexts controlled by an ever increasingly powerful central government. The supposed democratization of access to council housing and education, along with other public services including museums, through the market, serves to detract from the potential centres of local political discourse and debate. As liability for education and housing, and indeed most other public services, is removed from the elected representative, and re-placed in the market, it is only the market, an undefinable surreal invention of the First World, which can be held accountable. The values of democracy and professionalism are values based on an idea of public service and accountability, which although a modern form of institutionalized power (see chapter one), does offer a greater potential for democracy than the market-place.

Briefly, the characteristics of New Right philosophy can be condensed into the following two lists. On the one hand there are the ideas of the Neo-Liberals, whose 'heritage' is essentially Hayekian; they emphasize the following: 1) the individual, 2) freedom of choice, 3) market security, 4) *laissez-faire*, 5) minimal government. On the other hand there are the Neo-Conservatives, with their belief in: 1) strong government, 2) social authoritarianism, 3) a disciplined society, 4) hierarchy and subordination, 5) the nation. These sets of priorities are in no way mutually exclusive. Thatcherism (which still exists in the 'post-Thatcher' world) in fact would seem to be a combination of these two sets of priorities. It will be argued later that there are in fact two manifestations of heritage, one which emphasizes the traditional conservative heritage, and the other, a heritage which has developed as a consequence of the New Right's emphasis on entrepreneurial activity, often combined with a disregard for the role of the professional or 'expert'.

Essentially, the New Right would appear to mix a kind of economic liberalism, with a more traditional conservative authoritarianism. This was well summarized by Stuart Hall and Martin Jacques when they stated that 'Thatcherite populism ... combines the resonant themes of organic Toryism – nation, family, duty, authority, standards, traditionalism – with aggressive themes of a revived neo-liberalism – self-interest, competitive individualism, anti-statism' (Hall and Jacques quoted in Levitas 1985: 2).

There is therefore a 'liberal' wing, which has tended to emphasize the idea of a natural order, which will ensure the benevolence of policies which will establish some future utopia, based on the rights of the individual acting within a benevolent market. There is also an authoritarian element. This is possibly unable to consider a future utopia, as it has tended to utopianize the past as it exists in the present through an emphasis on the idea of historical nation, authority and tradition. The British New Right luminary Roger Scruton, in *The Meaning of Conservatism*, asserts that

> The Conservative, unable as he is to appeal to a utopian future, or to any future that is not, as it were, already contained in the present and past, must avail himself of conceptions which are both directly applicable to things as they are and at the same time indicative of a motivating force in men.
>
> (Scruton quoted in Levitas 1985: 6)

He continues, 'There is a natural instinct in the unthinking man ... to accept and endorse through his actions the institutions and practices into which he is born. This instinct is rooted in human nature'. A strong state is required therefore, to maintain the 'Free Market'. On the one hand an attempt is made to convince the population that everything is as relative as one individual is to another, and that we can all be free spirits in the market-place. However, on the other, synchronous with this project of radical individualism is the legitimation of a *traditionally* strong authoritarian government. The marketing and promotion of the 'heritage' is a part of the hegemonic project that has been necessary for the legitimation of New Right thinking. This will be considered at greater length in subsequent chapters.

The development of the service sector

Throughout the 1980s and into the 1990s, New Right economic policies had a dramatic effect on economic structures, not just in those nation-states which have elected Neo-Conservative governments, but in many other states as well. In Britain especially, there has been an explicit attempt to rationalize the industrial base of the economy, and consequently promote a new economic and employment structure. The resulting economic structure is very much reliant on an expanded service sector.

Services, in the context of this analysis, are those economic practices which do not actually produce anything which is strictly tenable and concrete. The service sector provides consumers with facilities. Such facilities range from banking and insurance, to catering and leisure services. The service sector is by no means a new economic phenomenon, and has its origins in nineteenth-century economic expansion, but what is important is the degree to which the service sector has expanded during the last ten to twenty years, whilst the more traditional economic base has contracted.

The underlying trend towards an economy dominated by services has existed since the mid-nineteenth century (Allen 1988: 97). The real shift, however, took place during the post-war period. Overall there was an increase in service-sector employment during this period, although some areas shed jobs. For example, during the period 1959–81 there was a 44.3 per cent reduction in employment in the public passenger transport sector. During the same period there was a 70 per cent increase in financial services and a 40.2 per cent increase in leisure and recreation services (ibid.: 99).

During the post-war period, Britain changed from a country that had one of the highest proportions of population engaged in manual labour, 70 per cent during the inter-war period, to a country that, by the end of the 1980s, had one of the lowest proportions of manual labourers. The level was below that of Japan, Sweden, France and Germany (Lash 1990: 27).

It would be wrong to argue that the latest trend towards a service-based economy was entirely the result of New Right strategies: according to Wells, the start of the trend can be dated to 1973–4. The decline of the manufacturing base in Britain is undeniable: 'manufacturing output is now [1989] only slightly ahead of its previous peak annual and quarterly levels (recorded in 1973 and 2Q 1974, respectively)' (Wells 1989: 32). The suffering of the manufacturing sector has quite clearly not been mirrored in the service sector where, since 1973, output has increased by 43.5 per cent.

The transition from a manufacturing-based economy to a service economy has been going on for well over twenty years, but there is little doubt that this transition was accelerated during the period of Conservative Government, more specifically since 1983.

By the end of 1988, manufacturing output was only 6.8 per cent higher than it had been in May 1979, while the output of services had increased during the same period by 28.8 per cent. Between 1979 and 1987 manufacturing employment fell from 7.4 million to 5.4 million, while employment in the service sector rose from 14.7 million to 16.7 million (ibid.: 25–6).

This restructured economy has emerged as a truly 'post-modern' economy – an economy run with mirrors, an economy which lacked a concrete industrial base, and progressively moved towards the provision of ephemeral services and an unstable employment structure. During the

1980s total spending in the UK economy grew nearly one-third faster than production (Glyn 1989: 65). The volatile nature of the UK economy, along with others, was revealed quite sharply by the stock-market crash of October 1987. The shift from manufacturing to services is a trend which would seem to be common in most Western, major industrial economies.

The service economies which have developed in the First World were born out of the realization that there were limits to the potential turnover of material goods; therefore, it made sense to produce services, that is, 'immaterialities'. This trend towards a 'surface' economy, where the element of a product which alters most regularly is its appearance, resulted in a wider awareness of ephemerality in many areas of modern life, reflected in Marshall Berman's oft-quoted assessment of the modern world where, quoting Marx, he observed, 'all that's solid melts into air' (Berman 1983). Image and style have become increasingly important. During the 1970s and into the 1980s there was a recognition of the need to promote and enhance an 'identity' in the market-place. This, combined with the perceived need to increase turnover time in consumption, resulted in a shift away 'from the production of goods (most of which, like knifes and forks, have a substantial lifetime) to the production of events (such as spectacles that have an almost instantaneous turnover time)' (Harvey 1989: 157). There has undoubtedly been a change in the modes of pro-duction, 'A shift away from the consumption of goods and into the consumption of services – not only personal, business, educational, and health services, but also into entertainments, spectacles, happenings, and distractions' (ibid.: 285). The leisure-service sector, more specifically the heritage and history-imagineering sectors, are an important part of this economic trend, and need to be understood as both a cultural phenom-enon and also as a form of economic practice. This development will be considered at length below (chapter six).

The flexible work-force

The 'flexible work-force' is a constituent part of the expanded service sector. During the latter part of the twentieth century, the employment structure in many First World countries has been developing along the following lines: first, there is a core work-force whose skills are crucial to the functioning of an organization; second, surrounding the core is a series of outer layers which consist of groups of peripheral workers. Moving outwards from the core, each layer of peripheral workers is less skilled and less important to the organization. These workers are often part-time and have little job security; their employment may well be seasonal. An example of such a peripheral work-force is that employed in the leisure sector during the summer season. It is true that this type of flexible employment has been extant as long as the leisure industry itself, but it is the degree to which it expanded during the 1980s that is important. The outer layers of the flexible work-force constitute an important part of the whole employment structure. In 1984 nearly 90 per cent of the 4.9 million part-time employees in Britain were employed in the service sector (Allen 1988: 100).

Harvey has considered in great detail the development of this new form of economic structure and considers it as a part of 'flexible accumulation', which 'rests on flexibility with respect to labour processes, labour markets, products, and patterns of consumption' (Harvey 1989: 147).

A post-modern economy?

All of the trends considered so far in this chapter do point to a restructuring in many First World economies. We should be careful, however, to avoid the implication that such changes are a dramatic departure from the economic structures which began to develop during the later nineteenth and early twentieth centuries. What the First World, and to an extent, the world as a whole, has witnessed since World War II, is an intensification, an acceleration, of change. Ever since the early periods of industrialization there have been continuing processes of distancing, processes which have contrived to remove people further and further away from the processes which affect their daily lives. At another level, people across the globe have been brought closer together, especially through telecommunication systems.

The distancing of workers from direct contact with economic processes, and many forms of commodity production, intensified especially after 1974 and the oil crisis. Since that time, and certainly during the last ten years, there has been a greater trend towards short-term contracts, job shares, job splits, and part-time work. Such a system may be beneficial for some, but for others it may require greater flexibility than can be coped with normally. Between 1981 and 1985 'flexible workers' in Britain increased by 16 per cent to 8.1 million, while permanent jobs decreased by 6 per cent to 15.6 million (ibid.: 152). A similar trend was identified in the US. Employment in the heritage industry is a part of this restructured economy and the changes in the labour-market, with its obvious demand for seasonal employees.

The 'fluidity', or 'speeding up', of the economy has been reflected in the pace of product innovation and product consumption. The 'half-life' of most Fordist products was about 5–7 years, but in more recent years under flexible production this life has been reduced dramatically. In some high-tech industries, such as video games and computer software, the half-life is less than 18 months. 'The relatively stable aesthetic of Fordist modernism has given way to all the ferment, instability, and fleeting qualities of a post-modernist aesthetic that celebrates difference, ephemerality, spectacle, fashion, and the commodification of cultural forms' (ibid.: 156).

The advent of information technologies has also contributed to the promotion of flexible accumulation. Computer programmes can basically ensure that money works a perpetual overtime. Satellite links and computers combine to breach the once-restrictive time–space barriers. Money, essentially abstract in quality, is not affected by such barriers: 'If money has no meaning independent of time and space, then it is always possible to pursue profit (or other forms of advantage) by altering the ways time and space are used and defined' (ibid.: 229)

More so than ever before employees in the service sector are removed from the experience of final production. What is the end product of the computer software's machinations? How does a wide and varied audience receive the mass-produced spectacle transmitted around the world via satellite at the speed of light? Who is killed by the weapon made thousands of miles away from its point of destruction? As Jameson has articulated, and Harvey has illustrated, many of us are 'so far removed from the realities of production and work in the world that we inhabit a dream world of artificial stimuli and televized experience: never in any previous civilization have the great metaphysical preoccupations, the fundamental questions of being and of the meaning of life, seemed so utterly remote and pointless' (Jameson 1989: xviii).

With this distancing of the worker from the product, the experiences of everyday life have taken on a new confusion. More than ever before, the economy is literally out of our hands. Whereas the majority of people in pre-industrial societies had direct experience of their modes of production, and dealt with life within a discernible locality, workers in the industrialized world often find themselves removed from the economic mechanism; they merely make a contribution, usually to their employer's profit. This removal, or distancing, is intensified in so-called 'post-industrial' economies where even the nation-state has a limited influence over the machinations of global capital.

During the post-war period, it has increasingly been the case that exports and imports no longer take place between nations; transactions take place between different branches of multinational firms such as Ford. Nations themselves invest outside of their own space economy; for example, during the 1980s the UK was responsible for a very large level of direct foreign investment. As Harris observed, 'The UK's stock of overseas investments is second only to that of the United States' (Harris 1988: 20). Whether this was of direct benefit to UK citizens is questionable. In 1979 restrictions on financial, or portfolio investment were abolished and during the 1980s portfolio investments abroad increased. At the same time investments into the UK increased; these included the buying of 'UK bonds, securities and bank deposits' (ibid.: 21–2). During the 1980s the economies of Britain and most other Western capitalist nations developed into economies that were no longer truly 'national' economies. The globalization of capital, the situation of branches of multinationals in many different countries, the out-flow of portfolio investment from the UK to other countries, and foreign portfolio investment into that country, are examples of how national economies have been replaced by inter-national economies. This view, that the national economy and society are subordinate to global forces is known as the 'world-system theory' (ibid.: 29–32).

In this light, it may be possible to consider yet another reason for the development of heritage. It has been, and still is, a desire to maintain the only thing that nations can still call their own. In the case of Britain, the loss of power has been more difficult for some to accept than others. Britain is clearly no longer an Imperial power and the economy does not even belong to the nation. Striving for something left that was truly 'British', the heritage was recognized as a powerful economic and hegemonic resource.

Post-modern societies II

Signs. ... Signs are lost/Signs disappeared/Turn invisible. ... No sense
of harmony no sense of time ...

(From the Talking Heads album, *Naked*, 1988)

Before embarking on a more detailed discussion of post-modernity, it
should be made explicit that *post-modernism* is *not* a cogent philosophical, artistic movement. However, *post-modernity* is a condition –
one which is not an experience of radical rupture, nor so different from
modernity that the two share no characteristics at all, but rather one that
is an intensification of those experiences and processes which emerged
during the eighteenth and nineteenth centuries especially.

Post-modernity has its roots in the incongruous nature of the post-war
world, most importantly in the changes which have resulted from the
economic, political and cultural developments which have taken place
since World War II, some of which were considered in the previous
chapter. This of course implies that post-modernity is a predominantly
First World, and probably more specifically Western capitalist phenomenon rather than a universal one. To an extent this is true, but a fundamental characteristic of the so-called post-modern condition, is that it is
one which potentially affects the whole of the world, most notably in the
case of multinational capital, which seems to know no bounds in time or
space. This is also true today of the media of mass communication, where
even if television is not available, radio often will be with the BBC's
World Service and the Voice of America reaching people all over the
world.

Any analysis of post-modernity should consider its philosophical roots,
and an appreciation of its precursor, modernity.

As I have already discussed, *modernity* can be considered as the period
which had its origins in the Enlightenment, the beginnings of modern

science – the supposed discovery of *truths* and *facts*, or rather claims for the possibility of objective truth about the world and even the universe in which we live. It was during this period that the *meta narratives* emerged, discourses which implied a rigid *objectivism*, and through this a thorough analysis of our world. Such meta narratives might include Darwin's theory of evolution and Marx's analysis of capital. The Arts and Sciences were dominated (in the main) by great *auteurs*, who were an intrinsic part of the modernist scheme. Modernists also considered that there was a definite gap between high art, and low art. The foundations of the modernist view of the world began to falter with the denial of the possibility of truth and value, and the questioning not only of scientific 'fact' but also of the legitimacy of the great *auteurs* who dominated the arts, and promoted (not necessarily actively) the division between high art for those who could afford it, and lumpen art, and/or popular culture, for the rest of the population. Some might consider that post-modernism is to art and culture what post-structuralism is to philosophy. Post-modern culture might be considered as a culture where anything goes – hence Kroker and Cook's *Excremental Culture and Hyper Aesthetics*. It is an almost nihilistic and self-destructive culture; according to Kroker and Cook, the 'mood of the post-modern scene is that we are living on the violent edge between ecstasy and decay; between the melancholy lament of post-modernism over the death of the grand signifiers of modernity – consciousness, truth, sex, capital, power – and the ecstatic nihilism of ultramodernism; between the body as a torture-chamber and pleasure palace; between fascination and lament' (Kroker and Cook 1988: 9–10). Lyotard, the writer who has given post-modern anti-foundationalists some of their strongest foundations, has defined the '*post-modern* as incredulity toward metanarratives' (Lyotard 1984: xxiv).

This chapter explores what is meant by a 'condition' as distinct from a coherent set of beliefs and practices, and also considers the sense in which post-modernism is a condition, or as Jameson called it, 'the cultural logic of late capitalism' (Jameson 1984a: 52–92). In part, the development of what some may wish to label the post-modern world lay with the development of the media of modern mass communications, initially the radio and the cinema and then more importantly, during the post-war period, the television, and more recently, satellite television. These media of mass communications have facilitated the removal of many of the boundaries between high art and low art and have helped to remove difference from the varied and rich cultures all over the world. Television has helped promote the onward marching machine of Western hyper-consumerism all over the world. This is a world where the 'symbols of the free West' – Pepsi Cola, Coca Cola and the M.16 rifle – transcend almost all national boundaries. This trend towards the homogenization of culture accelerated during the 1960s, when it was observed that, 'A new form of "politics" is emerging, and in ways we haven't yet noticed. The living room has become a voting booth' (McLuhan, Fiore and Agel 1967: 22). These same commentators also observed that,

> All media work us over completely. They are so persuasive in their personal, political, economic, aesthetic, psychological, moral, ethical, and social consequences that they leave no part of us untouched, unaffected, unaltered. The medium is the massage. Any understanding of social and cultural change is impossible without a knowledge of the way media work as environments.
>
> (ibid.: 26)

The philosophical roots of what is seen as the post-modern world of the 1980s lie with post-structuralism, and its implicit denial of the possibility of discussing absolute 'truths' and 'values'. This might be concordant with the post-structuralist view of the world, largely based on the writings of Baudrillard, Barthes, Derrida and Foucault.

Much post-structuralist writing is not concerned to deny reality itself, but rather to question the foundations of Western metaphysics, and its perceived aim of defining, naming, and knowing the world.

Much of the potential for considering post-structuralism's often negative account of Western metaphysics lay with the realization of the demise of the referent. The post-structuralist world of language has been described by some as consisting of an infinite number of signifiers (words or texts) that point to a signified or a group of signifieds; this might be considered as the 'meaning effect'. Essentially, the post-structuralist conception of language implies that the signifiers are now floating around with no referents (the real objects referred to by the signifiers) to attach themselves to. Derrida writes about signifiers that point away from themselves before they are themselves, while Baudrillard believes that 'Today especially the real is no more than a stuck pile of dead matter, dead bodies and dead language' (Baudrillard 1980: 103). The most valuable point to consider is that signifiers can trigger off an infinite number of meanings to any number of people, and the meanings experienced by each person are going to be unique. The signifier has been removed from the referent, the referent being history itself; the freeplay, or intertextuality, amongst signifiers leaves the referent (history) remaining only as a superfluous notion. History is considered by many post-structuralists to be merely another element in modernism's attempt to develop rigid meta narratives which are beyond question.

The demise of the referent has been considered extensively by some writers. Barthes, for example, believes that this has important consequences for society as a whole, as without the possibility of any real meaning being attached to signs, society will be kept in a continuous state of confusion, or at least a state of blissful ignorance, where the negative takes precedence over the positive. We can know what something is not, with greater ease than we can know what something is. This is 'the tyranny of the code itself' (Harland 1987: 179). With the death of the subject, or rather, the cracking of the foundations upon which much modern thought is based, comes the most important concept of all, the demise of innovation. During the post-war period, most notably since the 1970s, Western societies especially would appear to find artistic innovation problematical. There has been an ever increasing trend towards the copying of previous styles, their remixing and calling them something new. This is what might be termed the Laura Ashley effect, after the designer who successfully marketed, on a world scale, Victorian-style patterns and prints for clothes and home interiors.

In post-modernity, this phenomenon has best manifested itself in architecture. Post-modern architecture has been seen by some as an attack on modernist architecture, and its destruction of the neighbourhood, with its imposition of utopian high-modernist buildings, exemplified by the high-rise blocks of the 1960s. This type of architecture was deemed by some to be authoritarian. The reaction against this style arrived in the form of post-modern aesthetic populism, which involved the mixing of different historical styles in a form of bricolage. Housing estates today are filled with mock mock-tudor buildings or buildings that are a combination of a number of styles. It might be possible to argue that according to these criteria, the Renaissance was a post-modern phenomenon. However, it could be argued that the Renaissance was the period when ideas were rediscovered after having been abandoned for a period of time. Post-modernity on the other hand, would appear to be the regurgitation of last year's idea or style, and its mixing with yesterday's. In terms of art, pastiche manifests itself especially well in art photography, particularly in the work of Sherrie Levine who is famous for photographing other people's photographs. Some have argued that this is deconstructive and even oppositional art.

The post-modern world is a world dominated by pastiche, best defined as parody without the humour, or as Fredric Jameson puts it 'an imitation that mocks the original' (Jameson 1983: 113). The consequence of this, and of the post-structuralist conception of language, is the 'simulacrum' – perfect copies of objects, sometimes mass produced, and placed in contexts which often conceal their original use and meanings. Such simulacra dominate societies where innovation is doomed to failure as a consequence of the death of the subject. The death of meaning facilitates the reification of knowledge, the transformation of knowledge into an object or exploitable item. Once reified, the commodification (the transformation into a consumable item) of these images is possible. During the latter part of the twentieth century there has been an emphasis on style rather than 'knowledge' and 'meaning'. This is well illustrated by *The Face*, a contemporary British magazine 'that goes out of its way every month to blur the line between politics and parody and pastiche; the street, the stage, the screen; between purity and danger; the mainstream and the "margins": to flatten out the world' (Hebdige 1988: 161). A reader of a magazine like *The Face* is, as Barthes said of the text, 'invited to wander through this environment picking up whatever s/he finds attractive, useful or appealing' (ibid.: 162).

Post-structuralism, with its regime of floating signifiers, promotes a depthless synchronic history, partly as a consequence of its destruction of the historical meta narrative. For Derrida, a perception is continually divided from the thing itself; we can never catch up with the actual moment of our contact with any text. This implies that our perception of the world is, in part, a deception. We can only hope for hazy glimpses of a past that has never really existed. This is not dissimilar from Jameson's description of the use of a kind of preterite, or past-pluperfect, that removes the process of any past actions from the present. The past is then cut off from the present and is perceived always as a completed and isolated event. All that is left is an historical surface which enhances the 'reduction of historical periods to ruling class styles that are then pastiched' (Foster 1984: 68). This development of an 'ahistory', a history that is devoid of historical forms and materials, is the mediation of the past into myth.

Thus it can be argued that the combination of post-modern hyperconsumerism and post-structuralism's floating signifiers, and the irreverence for authority, promote the development of simulacra, created from a fragmented past, regurgitated in various forms which are then ripe for reification and finally, commodification.

Jean Baudrillard, the champion of the post-modern world, has promoted post-modernism, with its simulations and simulacra, to its ultimate forms. Baudrillard moved away from Marxism in the early 1970s. This was largely due to his disagreement with Marx's conception of use value and exchange value as part of a tangible material economy, which by its very nature promotes inequalities between the two, and in its turn, obscures the exploitation of one class by another. Baudrillard was not concerned with the exchange of material products, but rather with his belief that, today, economies are concerned more with 'the operationalization of all exchanges under the law of the code' (Baudrillard 1975: 121). Baudrillard believed that this form of social control is far more pervasive than anything considered by Marx. Baudrillard implied that the one way to overcome the regime of the sign was to push this system into a kind of overdrive. Within the context of Western economies, he believed that this could be achieved through the consumption or absorption of signs. Western political systems depend on there being an element of meaning in signs, while the market provides values through their use. Since (according to Baudrillard) the masses take signs literally, there is an implication that consumers will drive the regime of the sign to its own logical self-destruction. Exactly how this will be achieved is not apparent. After the destruction of this system, there is in Baudrillard's scheme no possibility of the emergence of something better. Baudrillard is quite explicit in his belief that modern politics is nothing but a simulation or simulacrum; one political stance, whether it be left or right, is really no different from the other. This is because politics, for him, is an ambiguous discourse 'that conveys the impossibility of a determinate position of power ... this logic belongs to neither party. It traverses all discourses without their wanting it' (Baudrillard 1988a: 176). Reality is thus reduced to a collection of simulations and simulacra, 'the generation by models of a real without origin or reality' (ibid.: 166). The real is substituted by signs, which Baudrillard argues are a more ductile substance than meaning, and therefore permit the development of 'A hyperreal henceforth sheltered from the imaginary, and from any distinction between the real and the imaginary, leaving room only for the orbital recurrence of models and the simulated generation of difference' (ibid.: 167).

In *Fatal Strategies* Baudrillard argued that because society has been 'plunged into an inordinate uncertainty by randomness' it has become overconcerned with causality and teleology (Baudrillard 1988b: 189). Baudrillard considered that this had led to 'the hyperspecialization of objects and people, of the operationalism of the smallest detail, and of the hypersignification of the slightest sign' (ibid.: 189). This idea of 'hyperspecialization' is not too dissimilar from the Weberian ideas of purposive and institutional rationality considered in the first two chapters of this book. Whereas it is accepted that the increased specialization, and distancing, of professional discourses from the members of any society is potentially anti-democratic, Baudrillard's extreme criticism is not appropriate to any strategy which is attempting to enhance democratic processes. He seems content to develop a form of nihilistic hypercriticism and goes on to argue that the preoccupation with explaining everything accordingly becomes a burden which has its consequence in 'an excrescent interpretive system developing without any relation to its objective. All of this is a consequence of a forward flight in the face of objective causes' (ibid.: 189). This is the transition into the realm of hyperreality, where the nuclear arms race is justified because it has crossed the 'dead point' (an unknown moment when every system passes a limit of questioning and is absorbed into a kind of ecstatic non-questioning stasis that can never be reversed), it has passed the limits of destruction. Baudrillard considered that 'the stage for war is abolished. There is no longer any practical correlation between the potential for destruction and its purpose, and referring to it becomes ridiculous' (ibid.: 190). This is the hyperreal form of warfare which through its own ridiculousness ensures that it will never take place, unless de-escalation re-establishes the 'exchange value' of weapons.

History too has supposedly crossed the 'dead point'. Baudrillard has argued that the desire to find the point where history ceased to be real and to rectify the collapse of history is probably impossible, as the point that some seek

> ... may not even exist. It only exists if we can prove that previously there has actually been history – which becomes impossible once this point has been traversed. Outside the realm of history, history itself can no longer reflect, nor even prove its own coherence. This is why we call upon every previous epoch, every way of life, all modes of self-historicizing and of narrating oneself with the support of proof and documentation (everything becomes documentary): we sense that in our era which is that at the end of history all of this is invalidated.
>
> (ibid.: 192)

Jean Baudrillard would seem to be the post-modern prophet of doom. He has adopted some of the basic tenets of post-structuralism and taken them to their 'hyperlogical' conclusion. Society is consumed by signs which promote the nihilistic. For Baudrillard there can be no totality, no reality, no society, and definitely no history. The most society can hope for is simulations and simulacra, depthless regurgitations of signs. The accelerated overproduction and reproduction of signs is the life-blood of hyperconsumerism. 'Late' Western capitalism would seem to be the hypercontext within which anything that can be marketed will be marketed, and if it does not sell, that does not matter: put a new label on it or change its shape – round tea-bags, what will they think of next? During the latter part of the twentieth century there has been a growing emphasis on gimmicks, style and image, nowhere more apparant than with marketing of motorcars. 'Limited editions' of hatchbacks with stylish names such as 'Surf', 'City' or 'Sport', convince the consumer that they are buying something which is different, when in fact the only difference is the price.

For some, this might be a world without meaning, where certain forms of innovation seem impossible. The consequence is a society sentenced to imprisonment in a simulation of the past. Today's world is the schizophrenic's world, the world of the schizophrenic as considered by Jameson in his assessment of Lacan's writing.

Lacan's concept of language (as described by Jameson 1983: 118–120) is the orthodox structuralist one (as considered earlier), with language broken up into three elements: the signifier, the signified and the referent. The referent, as far as post-structuralists are concerned, is a non-entity, with the consequence that we can no longer talk about a reality not itself metaphysical. The other key to this concept is to see language as not naming things, but to see the importance of the relationship between signifiers in the sentence that gives us the 'meaning effect'. Jameson (ibid.: 119) describes how this meaning effect, or signified, may in fact be a mirage or illusion. According to Lacan, schizophrenia is a result of the breakdown of the relationship between the signifiers. He believes that for many people, perception of temporality, and the continuity of personal identity, are effects of language, because language has a past and future and because the sentence moves in time. As a consequence of this, we seem to have a real or experienced sense of lived time. Since the schizophrenic does not articulate language in that way, s/he does not have the same perception of temporal continuity, and therefore lives in a perpetual present. Events in the schizophrenic's life have no real continuity as the person or person's existence is discontinuous, perpetually interrupted by the other self.

A post-modernist might argue that it is the world of the schizophrenic that we, in the First World especially, live in today. Thus, many of us risk the loss of a sense of the past, or a sense of place which is partly a result of the processes of time–space compression, a compression which is the effect of information technologies and the media of mass communications. In the post-industrial economy, knowledge becomes reified in the form of information, which is *the* contemporary commodity. Information moves around the world so quickly, as does news (which is also information and therefore consumable) that production in the West becomes dehumanized. The mass media produce simulacra; their imperative is the overproduction and regeneration of the meaning effect. Marx's statement that 'it is not the workman that employs the instruments of labour but the instruments of labour that employ the workman' (Marx 1954: 399) is especially apposite today, where value is put on the speed of light exchange and reproduction of meaning. Information is transmitted so quickly, that a sense of historical perspective is in danger of disappearing. As Jameson states, we should think carefully about, 'the media exhaustion of news: of how Nixon and, even more so, Kennedy are figures from a now distant past. One is tempted to say that the very function of the news media is to relegate such recent historical events as rapidly as possible into the past ... the media seem to function as the very agents and mechanisms for our historical amnesia' (Jameson 1983: 125). During the Gulf War of 1991, CNN, the satellite news station, transmitted air-raids and other military action in the Gulf as it took place, or very soon after. Once the war was over, it was efficiently neutered by its promotion as an historical movie, effected by the release of videos.

Post-modernity and the New Right

In the previous chapter the most important characteristics of New Right thinking and practice were considered. The following section will reconsider some of these points, but with an emphasis on illustrating the similarities between the characteristics of the post-modern condition, and policies of the New Right. What is important is not that the New Right works to a post-modern paradigm, but that its thought and policies have gone some way to constituting the condition of post-modernity.

The extreme relativism of many post-structuralist and post-modern discourses is mirrored in the New Right's conception of the radical individual and the belief that there is no such thing as society. A belief in radical individualism with the concomitant assumption that there is no such thing as society is part of the post-modern denial of any form of universals. Baudrillard's belief that 'Now, where there is no other, the scene of the other, like that of politics and of society, has disappeared' is not too dissimilar from a belief in extreme atomism (Baudrillard 1988c: 210).

These positions promote the acceptance of the inability to make connections in the world; the conception of isolated individuals removed from the wider network of political, economic, social and cultural phenomena, denies the importance of communities and societies *per se*. It is in part the destruction of this individual isolationism which is, at its most base, a form of conservative selfishness, that should be the aim of any subversion of the post-modern condition.

Post-modern politics (post-materialism)

One of the main characteristics of the relativisms of post-modernism and the New Right, is the sustained attack on any form of totalizing politics, most obviously, the politics of class.

Single-class based parties no longer have a monopoly when it comes to the articulation of political positions. During the post-war period especially, a new set of single-issue groups has been established. These include, or have included: the poll-tax protest movements, anti-nuclear movements, women's movements, environmental pressure groups, gay rights movements, in fact almost any number of organizations which have responded to specific, or a set of related, issues.

Apart from the women's movement, Habermas believes that all of these movements are *defensive* of something (Habermas 1981: 34). It is apparent that the burgeoning number of single-issue, and interest groups, has included conservation, history/archaeology societies, and in more recent years, heritage organizations. The emergence of these groups will be considered in the following chapter.

One of the main reasons for the movement away from class politics towards single-issue politics is the development in the First World of a so-called 'post-materialist' culture. This culture has been scrutinized by a number of researchers, notably by Ronald Inglehart, who was sponsored by the EEC to undertake a six-nation study of social attitudes. He remarked upon the decline of class alignments in political party choice, the emergence of new political movements, such as feminism, and the development of a concern with *lifestyle*, and consumer-issue politics. Inglehart argued that because the basic material needs of most people had been met during the post-war period, a new post-materialist set of values had emerged, defined as needs for 'self-realisation, self-esteem, affection, a better quality of life and improved social relationships' (Gibbins 1989: 9).

During this post-war period, new forms of political expression also appeared: ethnicity, environmentalism and peace. Inglehart later argued that there had been a development of 'relative deprivation'; people were only happy if they had recently become materially satisfied. Essentially, people began to wonder if there was more to life.

De-differentiation and the homogenization of culture

As mentioned in the previous chapter, it is my belief that many people, in Western societies especially, have been increasingly removed from the mode of production; they are also required to be more flexible in their daily lives. Such flexibility has demanded that people be far more mobile, thus losing the identity associated with place. This flexibility, combined with the globalization of capital, has led to what some commentators have identified as de-differentiation, or an homogenization of culture. Cultural identity is supposedly becoming more uniform, and this is intensified through commodification on a world-wide scale: a McDonald's burger in Tokyo tastes no different to one bought in Paris, or Birmingham, and is purchased in surroundings which are usually identical.

De-differentiation manifests itself in a number of ways. There is the destruction of the division between high and low art, the end of auratic, or rather, the end of the provision of auratic spectacles solely for consumption by a social élite. The de-differentiation of culture also results in the incorporation of culture into the everyday political economy. This commodification and purposive rationalization of culture had already been identified and damned by a number of modern critics, most importantly Adorno and Horkheimer (1979). Lash identifies the disintegration of the author, and the contingent blending of the writer with her work, symbolized by 'the tendency of some types of theatre since the mid 1960's to include the audience itself as part of the cultural product' (Lash 1990: 11). Lash also points to the de-differentiation of the pop-video and the advert and the difficulty in identifying where 'the commercial institution stops and where the cultural product starts' (ibid.: 12). Modernity considered that reality was representable, or rather there was a problem that could be solved. For example, a modernist might have contended that a display of archaeological artefacts in some way reflected the society that created them, and that it was the legitimate function of the expert to interpret and articulate that reality. Post-modernity, or rather, that brand of post-modern thought steeped in the discourse of deconstruction, questions the possibility of representing the real, as well as the possibility of intersubjective communities, where some kind of broad agreement can be reached, and consequently a united position regarding a problem achieved and maintained.

Kellner says of the Critical Theorists of the 1930s and 1940s, that they

> came to see what they called the 'culture industries' as a central part
> of a new configuration of capitalist modernity, which used culture,
> advertising, mass communications and new forms of social control to
> induce consent to the new forms of capitalist society. The production
> and transmission of media spectacles which transmitted ideology and
> consumerism by means of allegedly 'popular entertainment' and
> information, were, they believed, a central mechanism through which
> contemporary society came to dominate the individual.
>
> (Kellner 1989a: 130)

This analysis still holds true for the so-called post-modern world. To argue that there is a radical difference between the middle of the twentieth century, and its end, is difficult; the differences are of a degree. In the mid-twentieth century the development of hyperconsumerism was confined to a relatively limited number of cultural products, and in a relatively limited geographical area, that is, the United States and the wealthier parts of Europe. The post-war period has seen a quantitative, and perhaps qualitative, expansion in hyperconsumerism, over an increasing geographical area. Free marketeers would perceive this as the inevitable ascendancy of consumer capitalism, its insatiable appetite, if you like, its supreme talent for commodifying anything and everything. The indictments made of consumer society have had very little effect politically. The fact of the matter is that people enjoy consumption, whether it be literally of food and drink, or of spectacles.

Adorno and Horkheimer coined the term 'culture industry', and referred to the Enlightenment as 'mass deception' (Adorno and Horkheimer 1979). They wished to make it quite explicit that they believed that the products of mass culture did not emanate from the people themselves. The products were part of a culture which was administered by a central hegemonic authority; very rarely has the culture industry offered consumers the potential for self-realization and development. Almost without exception, the culture industry has served the needs of central authority through the legitimation of its ideology. Adorno and Horkheimer saw both the culture industry and the advertising industry as contributing to an homogenization of form, and eventually the whole of society, as they conspired to 'merge technically as well as economically. In both cases the same thing can be seen in innumerable places, and the mechanical repetition of the same culture product has come to be the same as that of the propaganda slogan' (ibid.: 163).

A similar conception of the heritage industry is implicit in Hewison's (1987) analysis, not just because he refers to the production of the past as the heritage 'industry', but because he sees it as an artificial history imposed on the public by marketing managers from above.

It is quite apparent that during the post-war period there has been a move towards a rationalization, a standardization and conformity of culture. This is the case with the impact of things North American: the Disneyfication of the free world (and others). This type of uniform culture was, and still is, an attack on individuality. As I will argue in the subsequent chapters, those museums forced into the market, along with the heritage industry, rarely respond to the needs of the visitor. They merely respond to the perceived needs of an abstract element within a marketing niche, where revenue performance is the prime factor in any equation.

Post-modern consumers are identified by Lash as those members of the new post-industrial middle classes, described earlier as usually being members of the service class. They often have a good education and may possess a higher education qualification. The post-modern consumer will have had access to the cultures of the old élites: a little bit of Vivaldi, a little bit of Van Gogh, a little bit of archaeology through the good offices of television presenters such as historian/archaeologist, Michael Wood. Much of this cultural capital will have been received through media representations; the world will be known but not necessarily visited. The country house will have been visited but never owned. The heritage centre will have been patronized, but the history therein not necessarily understood or questioned. This is the culture of the gaze, or even the partial gaze. It is a culture founded on the consumption of specious events.

Time–Space compression and the 'end of history'

The final, and possibly most important, characteristic of the post-modern condition is that of time–space compression, with the concomitant experience of the so-called 'end of history'. The idea of an 'end' to history is best understood by returning to the concept of time–space compression outlined in chapter one.

The changing experience of time is important, as it is the next stage in the loosening of temporal/spatial fixity, resulting in an inability to come to terms with one's place in the world. As a result, this might be seen as the foundation of a more post-modern experience. The trend towards time–space compression does have a history, which again has its roots in the nineteenth century.

Harvey argues that towards the end of the nineteenth century the experience of an homogeneous, local time was increasingly eroded. Attempts to maintain a 'sense of place' in a world that was increasingly subjected to various forms of time–space compression (through developments in transport, communications etc.) manifested themselves in the museum, which attempted to preserve a sense of history (Harvey 1989: 272). However, the increasing intensity of modern time–space compression would seem to have thwarted any attempts at preserving a sense of place, especially for those in ever expanding cities. Consequently, an awareness of the relativity of people's positions in time has developed. As mass communications and transport systems expanded, an awareness of the existence of many other times and places grew. Such an awareness made it more difficult for people to come to terms with their place and their own position in the world once the lives of other people and other places became increasingly contingent upon their own.

Around the turn of the century, many people became more concerned with their own position, relative to the rest of the world. Such an appreciation of time was articulated in Einstein's general theory of relativity. According to Einstein, time only existed when a measurement was being taken. Since these measurements varied, due to the relative motions of the two objects involved, clearly there could be no such thing as absolute time. Einstein's general theory of relativity of 1916 'had filled the universe with clocks each telling a different correct time' (Kern 1983: 19). Thus there seemed to be a move towards a greater consideration of the personal past. This shift towards the personal past is linked with the shift from homogeneous, public time to various, private times. The emphasis on private, or personal, pasts was articulated through an emphasis on nostalgia, the collection and appreciation of objects, often photographs, with which the person felt a direct affiliation. Personal pasts were of great importance, in a world which became 'smaller' and more complicated by the day.

During the latter part of the nineteenth century a number of technological innovations began to transform the experience of time and space. The 'simultaneous' experience over great distances was promoted by the development of the telegraph during the late 1880s and 1890s, by Heinrich Hertz and Gugliemo Marconi. The invention of the telegraph and telephone contributed to the erosion of heterogeneous time, and before long many began to argue for the imposition of a standard time. Possibly one of the more famous supporters of a standard time was Count Helmuth von Moltke, who believed that having a number of different time zones would hamper mobilization in times of war. This changing experience of time was illustrated by the sinking of the *Titanic*. This disaster, or rather, the transmission of the news of it, symbolized the impact of the wireless on world communication, and consequently, people's conception of the present. At 12:15 a.m. on 14 April 1912 the *Titanic* sent its first distress call; by 1:20 a.m. the news of the disaster was out, and being broadcast around the world.

We should be aware that the potential ability to experience so much, so quickly, must have had an impact on people's lives. An experience of synchronicity was now more of a reality of daily life than ever before. Whereas up until the nineteenth century information would have moved only at the speed of the fastest horse, by the mid-nineteenth century it travelled at the speed of a train (*c.* 60 mph); by the turn of the century information could cover great distances, and conversations could travel down telephone lines at the speed of light. It was probably these transformations in the media of information transmissions that had the greatest effect on the human experience of time and space. The development of the media of mass communications permitted a sense of synchronicity as many people consumed information from people and places, sometimes almost instantaneously.

Since the turn of the century there has been no increase in the speed at which basic information can be transmitted. But the technological foundations have been built upon, and expanded. The obvious developments have occurred within information technology, including television and satellite communications particularly. These, along with the improvements in passenger transport, particularly the aeroplane, have led to the continuous 'shrinking' of the earth. This bunching of time and space has taken us to the position where 'time horizons shorten to the point where the present is all there is (the world of the schizophrenic), so we have to learn how to come to cope with an overwhelming sense of *compression* of our spatial and temporal worlds' (Harvey 1989: 240).

The post-modern experience of time is one which has its roots in nineteenth-century developments. The difficulty in developing a sense of place has its origins in the modern epoch. The post-modern experience of time–space compression is not one which is different in form from the modern experience, but it is different in intensity. It has been a continuing struggle to maintain a sense of place since the nineteenth century, and even before.

Such disorientation in the world is part and parcel of the idea of an end to history. Such a position, questioning the idea of history, was taken by Francis Fukuyama, one of George Bush's aides in 1989, in his now infamous article 'The End of History'. Here he contended that we should expect centuries of boredom now that history is over. This position is largely born of an idea that the capitalist West has attained a position of unparalleled supremacy in both time and space. The collapse of the Eastern bloc is seen as justification for this position. History is therefore of little value as a source of lessons for the present as many right-wingers declare that the American Dream is now a reality.

The idea that history is over, and that all we should do now is exploit the styles and images of the past, is symbolized by Kenneth Clarke's (the British Secretary of State for Education) declaration, in a circular to history teachers in January 1991, that teachers should not cover the Gulf War in their classes, as history has nothing to do with current events. The study of the Middle East in British schools tends to come to an end in 1967. It is this idea of history as that which is dislocated from the present, which is the key to an understanding of Western rationality *vis-à-vis* the past.

The questioning of history is also linked to the wider attack on the modernist meta narrative. The post-modern denial of the legitimacy of the modern historical narrative, combined with the Neo-Conservative emphasis on tradition, together promote an emphasis on certain 'traditional' institutions or *styles*. These styles have been severed from their actual historical contexts. As far as the Neo-Conservatives are concerned, such 'traditions' are articulated through policies which emphasize the role of the family and a Victorian form of morality. These ideas are imposed without a justification of this position, other than through its founding in some spurious, detached recollection of mythical 'Victorian values', which very few people are likely to remember.

> It is with regard to this return to tradition (in art, family, religion ...) that the connection to neoconservatism proper must be made. For in our time it has emerged as a new political form of antimodernism: neoconservatives like Daniel Bell charge modern (or adversary) culture with the ills of society and seek redress in a return to the verities.
>
> (Foster 1984: 70)

Conclusion

> ... a heritage is something we have possession of after the death of its original owners, and we are free to use as we choose. The fine Victorian mahogany commode, designed as a useful receptacle for excrement, now comes in handy as a cocktail cabinet; and so history-as-heritage simply offers a challenge to the ingenuity of its new owner.
>
> (Raban 1989: 24)

The achievement of the teleological project of capital is, in part, supported by the progressionist nature of many museum displays, and is condoned by the ahistoricism of modern heritage. Instead of history we have heritage. History is reduced 'to the mere dimension of temporality, the mere aggregate of events in temporality or cluster which in itself is meaningless' (Heller and Fehér 1988: 5).

This intensification of the experience of synchronicity, and the con-comitant destruction of diachrony – the loss of a sense of the past – are promoted by the heritagization of history. There is little left to do but to recycle old ideas and repossess all our pasts, and manipulate them for profit and hegemonic designs. The only totalizing project of post-modernism would appear to be a kind of anti-imperialism. History is not just at an end, but is in fact negated as part of this project.

The condition of post-modernity is largely an experience constructed through a number of different phenomena. Most important is the development of industrial society, and the emergence of technologies which have contributed to time–space compression. The consequent experiences have increasingly intensified, especially during the post World War II period.

Although the discussions in this chapter and the previous have been concerned with events in Britain and the United States, and the emergence of the New Right in both of these countries, it should be made apparent that the experiences of modernity, and more importantly, post-modernity, are not peculiar to these countries.

4 | *Conserving a past*

Conservation, the preservation of the historic environment, as the term implies has been essentially a traditional, conservative phenomenon, concerned with maintaining that which conservatives consider to be 'traditional', worthy of representing that which best signifies the idea of nation.

Conservation, or preservationism, has its roots in the nineteenth century but increased in intensity during the latter half of the twentieth century, and especially during the mid-1970s and after.

Fundamental to this critique of preservationism is a belief that such a concern with the heritage and its conservation is not necessarily an interest in the study and understanding of the past, but rather a concern with the maintenance of historical surfaces, where importance is attached primarily to an aesthetics of tradition.

Early preservationism

Preservationism did not start in 1945; in fact its roots go back to the Middle Ages. However, the foundations for the current trend of heritage conservation, as with the establishment of museums, lay in the nineteenth century.

One of the earliest governmental conservation bodies established in Europe was the Danish Royal Commission for Antiquities, established in 1807. 'The history of preservation in Scandinavia leading to the establishment of the Danish Royal Commission in 1807 demonstrates the early association of prehistoric ancient monuments with national identities and aspirations in that part of Europe' (Murray 1989: 59).

In Britain, the move towards the establishment of a governmental body responsible for the historic and archaeological environment was a gradual one. One of the main reasons for the Ancient Monuments Protection Act (1882) taking so long to become law (ten years) was the fact that it was perceived by many Tories and Whig Liberals as an attack on the rights of private property. According to Murray, this group of right-wingers argued that such monuments were already well protected by landowners, and if a monument was not protected then such a monument was clearly not of great importance.

During the discussion surrounding the Ancient Monuments Protection Bill, a form of institutionalized racist rhetoric emerged; some argued against the preservation of ancient British and Celtic remains as they were not deemed as worthy of preservation as those monuments which might be defined as 'English' (ibid.: 61). It should be remembered that an issue which was contemporary with the Ancient Monuments Bill was Irish Home Rule; in the end, Irish monuments were excluded from the Act. Also, the Act ensured that the Government retained control over the listing and assessment of ancient monuments, despite Lubbock's desire for an Independent Board of Commissioners.

In Scotland, monuments were to be administered by the Inspector appointed by the Government in London, and not by the Society of Antiquaries of Scotland, 'The aspirations of the Scots to control their own national history were not accepted by the government in Westminster' (ibid.: 61). This attitude towards Scotland still persists today, and will be considered towards the end of this chapter.

The growth of preservationism

Preservationism grew during the second half of the nineteenth century, especially amongst the middle classes. Membership of the Society for the Protection of Ancient Buildings, established in 1877, increased greatly during this period. In fact, the latter half of the nineteenth century produced a number of conservation groups, including the Commons, Footpaths and Open Spaces Preservation Society (1865), the Monumental Brass Society (1887), and most importantly, the National Trust, which was established in 1895. In 1907 the Trust was given the legal powers to protect sites and 'preserve them for the nation'.

Contemporary with the establishment of these conservation groups was the emergence of a number of photographic record societies. In 1890 the Scottish Photographic Survey was formed, and in 1897 an English equivalent was established. The National Photographic Record Association took photographs of 'scenes of interest' and placed them in the

British Museum. Other similar societies emerged in Belgium, the US and Germany. Photography was soon perceived as the medium which could truly 'preserve the past', as it was not only concerned with preservation through the recording of the built environment, but could obviously record scenes of human interest as well. 'Pictures along with print enhance knowledge of the past and diminish needs for recall. ... Photography made such images accurate and ubiquitous, replacing not only the tangibly antique but history and memory as well' (Lowenthal 1985: 257).

In France an equivalent law to the Ancient Monuments Protection Act was passed in 1905, while a year earlier the *Heimatschutz* had been created in Germany to protect both natural areas and historical monuments. In the United States, the federal government, through the National Park Service which was established in 1916, subsequently took on responsibility for the historic environment with the Historic Sites Act of 1935.

Throughout the first half of the twentieth century the number of con-servation societies gradually increased. The experiences of modernization were taking their toll. There was a desire to compensate for increasingly accelerating change, a desire to 'slow down' transformations, especially in the urban environment. Part of this desire had its roots in a wish to maintain traditions which the upper and middle classes associated with the nation, specifically, England. Certain types of heritage, especially the castle and the country house were considered to possess the qualities which could maintain and promote the historical identity of the nation. Even before World War II, some people may have recognized a trend towards globalization – the potential for cultural homogenization – and thus saw a need to protect and promote that which stood as a metaphor for the characteristics of the nation.

In Britain, the 1920s and 1930s saw the establishment of the Ancient Monuments Society (1921), the Council for the Care of Churches (1922), the Council for the Protection of Rural England (1926), the National Trust for Scotland (1931), and the Georgian Group in 1936.

The threatened nation

World War II served as a catalyst, not just in political economy, but also for many people's attitudes to the past, or rather the historic environment, and what it represented in terms of the nation's 'heritage'. Once the direct threat of invasion appeared to wane after the Battle of Britain, there developed a wider concern about, and awareness of, the nation's past, or images of that past. To an extent, this was reflected in the boom in arts sales during the war, which 'supports the thesis that amid the catastrophe of war there is a turning of minds towards the precious elements of civilization' (Marwick 1990: 85).

During the war, in Britain there had been a flirtation with socialism on the home front, but once the war was over traditional mandarin values reasserted themselves:

> Having abandoned the mild socialism that had given Bloomsbury a radical edge up to 1945, the intellectual aristocracy fell back on a system of values that was more appropriate to the function they performed, and the caste from which they came. These values were truly aristocratic in origin, in that they were conservative of tradition, pastoral as opposed to industrial, and most detectable when it came to nuances of class.
>
> (Hewison 1981: 64)

The war had threatened the status of the English ruling classes, but when the war was over, it was apparent that in one form or another, they had lived to rule for another day. Weakened by the war, and threatened by the spectre of welfare-socialism, an urgent need was felt for an emphasis on the preservation of that for which they stood.

As discussed in chapter two, despite the war, Britain emerged in 1945 as a nation which was still fundamentally divided upon class lines, although these lines would become more blurred over the decades. Its strength as a world power had been enormously undermined, and the retreat from Empire was soon underway. The nation needed to look inwards for a strength through its own identity. To an extent, this identity was found in the Royal Family, whose journey to unparalleled high public profile and popularity began after the war. As David Cannadine has illustrated, the tradition of royal ceremony as a public spectacle was an invention of the nineteenth century, and gradually increased in popularity as the trappings of ceremony took on the appearance of antiquity. For example, as cars appeared on the streets of London, the sight of the old state landau appealed to a population yearning for firmly established historic tradition (Cannadine 1983).

The wedding of Princess Elizabeth and Prince Philip in November 1947 improved the popular image of the Royal Family. Between July and October of that year, the proportion of people supporting the wedding rose from 40 per cent to 60 per cent. There is no doubt that the event itself was extremely popular. The invented tradition no longer appeared an invention, and has increasingly been perceived since, as part of the nation's long and proud history. On the occasion of Elizabeth II's coronation, the Royal Family attained a new height of popularity. Over 32 million people either watched the coronation on television, or listened to it on the radio, while 2 million people actually went out onto the streets of London; 'the coronation was associated in many people's minds, however vaguely, with the idea of a new Elizabethan age in which, through the Commonwealth, if not through the Empire, Britain would still retain a glorious place in the world' (Marwick 1990: 105–6).

As well as the developing interest in preservationism, there was also an expansion of interest in the study of the past. During the 1940s and 1950s history developed a new popular appeal. This was partly thanks to the writings of G. M. Trevelyan, and the publication of the *Pelican History of England* series (ibid.: 90). Improvements in education, especially the expansion of higher education, including the establishment of the Open University at the end of the 1960s, also had an important role to play in the developing of people's interests in history and archaeology. As well as the improvements in education, television, especially with programmes like *Animal, Vegetable or Mineral*, increased the popularity of the past. This was reflected in the increasing number of local history and archaeology societies founded during this period. According to one survey on the historical and archaeological societies in Britain, 58 per cent of those established between 1707 and 1990 were founded during the 1950s and 1960s (Selkirk n.d.).

The growth of heritage conservation

During the post-war period, there has been a move away from traditional, class-based politics towards the establishment of single-issue groups or pressure groups. A characteristic of many pressure groups is that they are often established as a response to local threats. British local government, even before the 1980s, has never been ideally democratic. Local people were more often than not disenfranchized when it came to making decisions that affected their locality.

But during the 1960s there was a trend towards the organization of middle-class, single-issue pressure groups, which would probably be defined today as part of the NIMBY (Not In My Back Yard) movement – groups of people who object to developments which may detract from their quality of life, but do not object if the development takes place elsewhere. As far as many are concerned, the first great conservation clash was over the archway at Euston Station in 1962, a battle which was lost.

Marwick identifies 1965, and the successful protest against a local development by a group in Barnsbury, Islington, North London, as the watershed in terms of pressure-group development (Marwick 1990: 150). This group managed to prevent the London County Council from carrying out a development order. The success of this group was followed by others elsewhere. Also, we should consider the fact that, during the war due to enemy bombing, and during the first 25–30 years of the post-war period due to extensive demolition, the destruction of the historic environment must have led to a sense of placelessness. For example, during the 1970s about 350,000 dwellings in England and Wales were demolished. Places such as Newcastle, under the aegis of the infamous T. Dan Smith, had their historic hearts ripped out, on the road to a rather radical and philistine form of modernity.

During the 1960s, the Government in Britain became aware of the threat to the historic environment. In 1966, the Government commissioned studies of York, Chester, Chichester and Bath, which considered the state of their historic areas. In the US there developed a similar concern. Here the emphasis was on historic areas. In 1931 there were only two cities with such areas; by 1975 over 200 areas within a number of cities had been designated heritage areas (Relph 1987: 221). Also in the US, the Historic Preservation Act was passed in 1966, while a year later, the Civic Amenities Act was passed in Britain.

Of the conservation-related groups that have been identified in Britain, nearly half of those established since 1865 were established after 1970. Such societies include Heritage in Danger (1974), the Society for the Interpretation of Britain's Heritage (1977), the Thirties Society (1979), the National Piers Society (1980), the Heritage Co-ordination Group (1980 – an umbrella organization which promotes communication between these various organizations) and the Railway Heritage Trust (1985). There are of course many more societies which have some interest in the preservation of the heritage.

It should be apparent then, that the development of historic conservation is one that has its origins in the industrializing societies of the nineteenth century, and during the latter half of the twentieth century it has expanded apace to its current position, where there is a conservation body for everything from warships to dovecotes and fountains.

The cult of the country house

There is no doubt that it is the country house which for many people symbolizes the idea of the 'heritage' in Britain, or more specifically, England. It is this type of heritage which should be defined as State heritage, and is clearly a part of a wider hegemonic struggle on the part of the traditional Conservatives to maintain their position in British society.

Again, it was the impact of the last world war which acted as the catalyst for those concerned with the future of the English country house. For many, the metaphor for an England that existed before the war was the country house. Evelyn Waugh's *Brideshead Revisited*, published in 1945, implies that,

> The country house stands for a pre-war society of established values and social relations; its very fabric is the product of a uniquely English artistic tradition, and its occupants, in their family relationships, employment of servants, and ownership and rule over the surrounding countryside, reflect a secure social order.
>
> (Hewison 1981: 65)

The fear for the landed classes was that this tradition would be lost for ever, especially now that the ugly spectre of socialism haunted the corridors of Whitehall. But they need not have worried. Much of that first post-war cabinet had been public-school educated, and although ruling-class values were challenged in many areas, stately homes were viewed more as the residences of 'distressed gentlefolk' than symbols of ruling-class elitism.

In 1946, Hugh Dalton established the National Land Fund with an initial grant of 50 million pounds. This fund was in fact later plundered by a Conservative Government to the tune of 50 million pounds, leaving 10 million, which had been accrued over the eleven years of its existence. This fund enabled country houses to be accepted in lieu of tax, and then handed over to the National Trust. Among the first houses that were given to the trust in this way were, Hardwick, Sudbury and Saltram, but despite the initial efforts made to preserve country houses, no less than 629 were demolished between 1945 and 1974.

If we consider the Conservatives' emphasis on tradition, a strong State and authority then the strategies followed by the heritage movements have been appropriate to their objectives.

Despite the New Right's declared strategy of creating opportunity for all individuals in spite of their class, the promotion of certain forms of heritage has undeniably gone some way in promoting certain ideas of tradition and authority, along with a disdain for post-war collectivism, welfarism, and the perceived immorality of the 1960s.

The New Right wanted to destroy the 'Old England' nostalgia that posed a threat to its form of modernization. At the same time, it desired a return to what was perceived as nineteenth-century economic dynamism, and thus the retrieval of the political status of Britain as an international force by improving business enterprise. However, the aim was to destroy the 'Old England' of the working class, and to save the images of heritage that belonged to the ruling class and the legitimate nation.

The ultimate aim of the New Right has been the destruction of traditional militancy, and the way in which workers defend their trade. This was illustrated by the manner in which the miners' action in Britain was viciously and vindictively dealt with, or, in the US, Reagan's position regarding the air-traffic controllers. At the same time, however, there has been a desire to maintain the more acceptable and harmless, some may say quaint, aspects of working-class culture.

The foreword by Sir Roy Strong in Patrick Cormack's *Heritage in Danger* really marks the beginning of the post-modern heritage movement in Britain:

> The glories of our Royal Palaces and great houses, the splendours of our cathedrals and larger churches, the modest charm of the village church, the old manor house and rectory, the sweep of the downland or the rugged moors, the fragrance of an English garden or the heady exhilaration of cliffs and coastline – these are just some of the assaults on the senses which we categorise as our heritage. And within this word there mingle varied passionate streams of ancient pride and patriotism, of a heroism in times past, of a nostalgia too for what we think of as a happier world which we have lost. In the 1940s we felt all this deeply because of the danger from without. In the 1970s we sense it because of the dangers from within.
>
> (Strong in Cormack 1978: 10)

National conservation bodies

Throughout the 1980s in Britain, there was the development of a set of policies which were designed to guarantee a more unified and ordered approach to the conservation of the historic environment. In the following discussion, it should be borne in mind that there is no objection to the conservation of the historic environment *per se*, but rather an objection to the systems of allocation of resources, and the undeniable bias in terms of what is defined as the 'heritage'.

The Conservative Government which came to power in 1979 was, as discussed in chapter two, a Government of the New Right. But this did not entail the destruction of traditional Conservatism, and in fact in many areas of government there has been a curious blend of Old and New Right thinking. It can be argued that this blend has been nowhere more apparent than in policies, both direct and indirect, pertaining to the heritage.

English Heritage, or the Historic Buildings and Monuments Commission (HBMC), the body established under the National Heritage Act 1983 with responsibility for the protection, and the promotion of public enjoyment and understanding of the historic and archaeological heritage, has contributed to this hegemony through its emphasis on the authority of the landed classes, and a more than remarkable propensity for organizing mock battles.

What is important about HBMC is the way in which it has developed since 1984. In one way, it symbolizes many of the contradictions inherent in Neo-Conservatism. The majority of its stock of buildings represent the heritage of the land-owning aristocracy, and thus represent the 'tradition' of the nation. However, English Heritage, established as a body now removed from direct government control, was set up with the explicit task of 'making the heritage pay'. Section 35 of the National Heritage Act 1983 is quite explicit in its provisions allowing the organization to promote the sale of souvenirs, catering facilities, and much more. Although quite innocuous as a paragraph in an Act of Parliament, what this section represents is the placing of the heritage in the market-place. The provision of education relating to the historic and archaeological environment for the wider public is not a public service, but is in fact a marketable commodity. (It should be noted that HBMC does have an education section, which amongst other important services, guarantees free access to monuments for school parties.) The principles of New Right free-marketeering were foisted on the heritage, in the same way as they have been elsewhere (see chapter two). The contradiction lay in the fact that the transformation of the historic environment into a marketable commodity is partly an attack on the conservation ethos developed during the 1970s. There is a growing fear that the impact of tourism will do far more harm than good to the historic environment.

Although HBMC was still struggling after six years to make any kind of profit in terms of trading (see Historic Buildings and Monuments Commission 1989) this has not prevented its involvement in some rather bizarre schemes, including the Marble Hill development in West London. Here, English Heritage wanted to do away with the popular municipal playing fields, and replace them with landscaped gardens from the 1720s. The fact is, there is no historical basis for such landscaping at Marble Hill. As one journalist has put it, 'the park represents two ghastly solecisms. It is municipalised and popular' (Hale 1989: 11–12). This conservation body may be considered as refusing to spend the public's money in a way that the public want it spent.

As a quasi-autonomous non-governmental body (quango), the organization receives most of its financial support from the Government, whilst, in theory, being free to run its affairs without direct government influence. The fundamental ethos behind this development was that of situating what should be a public education service, in the market-place. True to the thinking of the New Right, monuments, including Stonehenge, castles, abbeys, and the like, were to be marketed. Crucial to the marketing strategy was the membership scheme which gave free access to English Heritage properties, as well as a regular newsletter. This emphasis on marketing should be kept in mind, and will be considered in subsequent chapters (especially chapter six).

The definition of the 'heritage' is enshrined in an Act of Parliament. The Act defines who can decide what an ancient monument or historic building is, and what can be done with it. In section 33 (8) of the Act, such decisions are placed in the hands of the 'Commission'. The Commission is constituted by a group of committees and 'eminent persons'. These persons and committees make decisions without recourse to the general public whose heritage they are preserving and presenting. Such a system serves to define what is deemed to be real history. By its very nature, selectivity is a political act.

Such a centralized process, placed in the hands of an unelected body, results in the creation and maintenance of a heritage which, by its very nature, is constituted anti-democratically, and thus represents the past of a favoured fragment of society. There would seem to be an assumption on the part of such organizations that they spend the public's money in a manner that the public would not object to, an assumption based on a premise that everybody is white and middle class. The public heritage is undoubtedly an extremely narrow and selective concept founded on a dismissal of the richness and variety of what different groups consider to be *their* heritage.

Such a narrow perception of what is *good* heritage has been symbolized by the debate over the reuse of barns. In 1990 HBMC declared that planning permission should be denied to anyone who wished to convert a listed farm building. It was argued that conversion is by its very nature destructive, and that archaeological deposits may be destroyed by new drains or swimming pools. This blanket decision, preventing the reuse of certain buildings, is an example of the anti-democratic nature of many heritage bodies. HBMC argues that converted buildings automatically have to be de-listed, thus losing their official 'historical' status, as defined by the Commission. This should not be seen as an argument for the wholesale unsympathetic conversion of historic properties, but rather one for the recognition of the need for each case to be considered in the light of local needs and wishes. A building should not lose its history because it develops and its use changes.

A heritage would appear to be that which only seems to be 'something', an image, an historical surface, rather than a building or object which possesses a history, something which develops through historical process, that is, *changes*. The aim of heritage would appear to be to select only that which pleases the sensibilities of a narrow group of people. Those who decide what is worthy of preservation and how it should be preserved, are basically deciding what is worth remembering. In Britain, the collective long-term historical memory is controlled and produced by a small number of quasi-autonomous unelected bodies. They include CADW (the Welsh equivilant to HBMC), Historic Scotland, English Heritage, the Royal Commission on the Historical Monuments of England, as well as charitable organizations such as the National Trust, and the National Heritage Memorial Fund. These organizations have control over a great part of the collective memory of the population. Through this definition of what is worthy of the nation, they concurrently maintain an idea of nation which is actually an artificial creation of the nineteenth century.

At a conservative estimate, at least 60 per cent of English Heritage's annual budget has been spent on historic buildings in one way or another, the majority of this in the form of grants. This compares with maybe as much as 20 per cent being spent on archaeology, and only a part of this being spent on sites dating earlier than 1066. These figures show that 60 per cent of English Heritage's budget is being spent on 0.05 per cent of England's past.

Not only is there a period/class bias, there is also a regional bias, illustrated by the proportions allocated to properties in care in 1988/9. Of the total amount spent 55 per cent went to the Thames and South-East, whilst the North and the Midlands received 22 per cent each. In fact, according to a survey carried out by the British archaeological pressure group, RESCUE, on the *total* funding in British archaeology in 1987, over 54 per cent of funds allocated to England, Scotland and Wales went to the counties in England below the traditional north–south divide (the Wash/Severn estuary line). Also, in the same year, grants totalling 5.3 million pounds went to ecclesiastical buildings, and one-third of the total of these went to London, Suffolk and Norfolk (Plouviez 1988).

It should be pointed out that the projected expenditure plans suggest that the regional imbalance as far as properties in care are concerned may be redressed to a certain extent during the 1990s.

Another important source of funding for the heritage in Britain is the National Heritage Memorial Fund. The NHMF is the re-establishment, via the National Heritage Act of 1980, of the National Land Fund, which had been plundered during the 1950s by a Conservative Government. This Act created new provisions for accepting property 'in satisfaction of capital transfer tax and estate duty; to provide for payments out of public funds in respect of the loss of or damage to objects loaned to or displayed in local museums and other institutions' (HMSO 1980: 1). The fund would not seem to be purely concerned with the preservation of ruling-class style. It does in fact give aid for the purchase of a varied selection of 'heritage' items. But as with English Heritage, the NHMF is a highly centralized organization run by a very select group of 'experts' 'who have knowledge, experience or interests relevant to the purposes for which the Fund may be applied' (ibid.: 2). These experts, or trustees, are appointed by the Prime Minister. The trustees are allowed to make grants out of the fund for any part of the heritage (buildings, objects, land) 'which in the opinion of the Trustees is of outstanding scenic, historic, aesthetic, architectural or scientific interest' (ibid.: 2). Again, this body is essentially undemocratic – the definition of 'outstanding' is left to a group of unrepresentative people who are not required to consider the opinions of the wider public.

The NHMF is chaired by Lord Charteris of Amisfield, who for 30 years was in the Private Secretary's office of The Queen. He then became the Provost of Eton during the 1980s. The National Heritage Memorial Fund spent 100 million pounds in an eight-year period. The Government in 1988 alone gave the National Heritage Memorial Fund 20 million pounds.

Most money is spent on stately homes and works of art, although some grants are given to other causes, such as the restoration of Brighton pier. Lord Charteris too, echoes the sentiments of Sir Roy Strong, Patrick Cormack and David Pearce, when he says: 'I would argue that the country house, with its contents, with its park, with, if you like, the world of letters and politics of the people who've lived in it, is Britain's supreme contribution to civilisation' (Lord Charteris in G. Norman 1989: 5). Commenting on the purchase of Kedleston Hall, Derbyshire, for 13.5 million pounds, Lord Charteris asserts, 'I think that £13.5m of public money for assuring Kedleston and its contents for all time is a bargain' (ibid.: 5). Rescue archaeology in England during the late 1980s received a total budget of about 7 million pounds per annum, for *all* periods.

Lord Charteris attempted to imply a balance in the type of heritage with which the National Heritage Memorial Fund has concerned itself. It purchased some trade union banners, which Lord Charteris believed to be 'beautiful'.

It is perhaps wrong to object to the allocation of such vast amounts for the preservation of buildings and objects *per se*, but what is highly questionable is the fact that these amounts of money vastly outweigh the allocations made for the preservation and *study* of other aspects of history and archaeology.

If the point needs to be reiterated, below is a sample of varying allocations of grants made during the 1980s: 9 million pounds for Belton (a country house), 4.5 million for Calke Abbey (a country house), 3 million for Fyvie (a country house); 85,000 for the Bluebird car (this grant given with the condition that the car remain at the Motor Museum at Beaulieu, the home of Lord Montagu, the Chairman of English Heritage); 25,000 pounds for the Loch Ness Wellington bomber; 189,500 pounds for the papers of Field Marshall The Earl Haig; 15,000 towards the conservation of the sculptures from St Paul's, Jarrow; 14,500 pounds for the Achavrail armlet; 1,000 pounds towards the purchase of the Freston pendant; 1.4 million towards the restoration of Painshill Park, Surrey (a landscaped garden); 30,724 towards the cost of an eighteenth-century viol; 7.7 million for Weston Park, Shropshire (a country house); 30,000 pounds contribution to the Big Pit coal-mine, South Wales (National Heritage Memorial Fund 1988).

Such forms of heritage conservation are primarily concerned with the maintenance of a particular ideology through the promotion of images of ruling-class style. The emphasis is on the shallow representations of very specific forms of 'traditional' lifestyles, lifestyles which the visitors to the country house can now 'appreciate', as they are further encouraged to consume and respect these signifiers of a way of life which has been transformed into a mode of spectacle consumption. The mode of consumption is a part of an expanding service class culture (see chapter six).

Another organization which has underpinned the heritage conservation movement is SAVE Britain's Heritage. Initially this organization set out to enlighten the public as to the plight of the country house and its beleaguered owners. The introduction to *The Country House: To Be or Not to Be* informs the reader of the tragic fate of many country houses (Binney and Martin 1982: 5). As with most SAVE publications, the emphasis is on conservation without the history. They justify conservation on the basis of aesthetics, and the belief that preservation pays. There is no doubt that in many areas the insistence on the maintenance of the historic environment is preferable to its replacement by a post-modern pastiche. However, SAVE believes 'that the current reaction against stereotyped accommodation – be it houses, shops, offices, hotels, pubs or restaurants, is part of a more fundamental and enduring appetite for buildings and places with character and individuality' (Hanna and Binney 1983: 1). The writers here have in fact hit upon an important point, but at the same time as arguing for the maintenance of a sense of place, they implicitly deny the importance of historical understanding.

The end of modernity, and industrial conservation

It would be unfair to argue that all heritage conservation is concerned with the preservation of ruling-class styles. In fact in recent years there has been a boom in the preservation and marketing of industrial heritage.

There is no doubt that many buildings which represent past industries must be conserved as historical and archaeological resources. They undoubtedly represent the greatest transformation in human society since the transition to farming in the Neolithic. However, there is a danger that while such *buildings* are being preserved, the history of the people who worked within them is being progressively lost. Take for example the declaration of the authors of *Bright Future, The Re-use of Industrial Buildings*: 'Until very recently people have tended to judge industrial buildings by what they represent, rather than what they are' (Binney, Machin and Powell 1990: 9). Here again, there is a plea for shallow aestheticism, a pretext for the promotion of our historical amnesia. What these industrial buildings are, is a valuable resource which can help people understand the processes which led to the exploitation of millions of people world-wide, but at the same time, laid the foundations for what for most people in Europe is a comfortable lifestyle. Such buildings are also monuments to the suffering of people, as are the war memorials in every town and village. Frequently however, the conservation lobby wishes to transform these buildings into images of grandeur, symbols of a magnificent past. Perhaps there is a wish that the public will forget what they represent, and thus consider them in the same light as 'medieval churches or Georgian country houses have been for generations' (ibid.: 19). The authors argue for the reuse of buildings, which in itself may be commendable. However, nowhere in their consideration does there appear to be any discussion of how the history of these places can be preserved, or more fundamentally, how a sense of place can be promoted.

This kind of preservation of a building serves to define its location somewhere, but nowhere specific, in the past. The (post-)modern sense of history is one which promotes the past as that which is over. The preservation or conservation of a building seems to remove or erase its historical position; it serves to promote a disregard for its original use and history. Take, for example, the survey by the Royal Commission of English hospitals, which 'have outlived their usefulness and are now redundant as a result of changing medical practice and government policy' (Royal Commission on the Historical Monuments of England 1990: 2). Short of demolishing such buildings, the best way to relegate the history of their actual use to a distant memory is to carry out an architectural survey, and thus put them to rest.

A sense of place is reliant on that place possessing characteristics which reveal temporal 'depth'. But, the combination of certain forms of conservation and post-modern architecture work together to undermine a sense of place. Preservationism is concerned with preserving that which is deemed to be aesthetically pleasing or acceptable to a very narrow group of people. The aim would seem to be the conservation of 'traditional' sensibilities through the denial of historical contexts, while attempting to maintain an idea of ruling-class strength and eminence. An attempt is made to integrate emerging service-class sensibilities, with those of the old ruling classes, through the participation of the service class in the consumption of images of tradition. This is the aim of the 'traditional' Neo-Conservative. However, the selective conservation of certain buildings is akin to removing one's favourite quotes from a wide and varied selection of books and imposing them in a new and artificial context. At the same time, the promotion of our historical amnesia is compounded by so-called post-modern architecture.

Post-modern architecture

> This return to the eclecticism of the previous century is due, as it was then, to compensatory needs. This traditionalism conforms to the pattern of political neoconservatism in that it redefines problems that lie at a *different* level as questions of style and thus removes them from public consciousness. The escapist reaction is linked to a move toward the affirmative: everything *else* is to remain as it is.
>
> (Habermas 1989: 19)

Post-modern architecture with its unreferenced quotation of historical styles, is in essence a form of historical plagiarism. It is the 'writing' of the built environment from misquoted sources, devoid of any historical order. In the context of the uncontrolled market, there is no doubt that the uncontrolled misquotation will continue unhindered.

The quotation of historical styles in architecture is of course nothing new. According to Kern, 'No group of artists was more acutely aware of the dead weight of the past than the architects, who quite literally could see it lining the streets of European cities' (Kern 1983: 56) The Ringstrasse in Vienna is an excellent example of such a group of buildings. It was constructed between the 1860s and the 1890s. Each of the buildings was designed in an historical style that was deemed appropriate to its function: the Parliament was classical Greek in style, the City Hall was Gothic, the University Renaissance, and the Burgtheater Baroque (ibid.: 56). It is possible to consider this as a post-modern approach; however, the crucial difference is that most post-modern architecture of the late twentieth century does not consider the appropriateness of the style to be adopted in the same way as was clearly the case in nineteenth-century Vienna. A car-park today may be any of these styles, or may be even a mixture, and the same goes for any building. There is doubtless some demand for certain types of building that signify power, and therefore demand the use of classical style. The AT&T (American Telecommunications) building in New York is a good example of this.

Otto Wagner was extremely critical of this historicism. In his textbook of 1895, *Modern Architecture*, 'He speculated about what had produced such deadly eclecticism and slavish devotion to the past and concluded that while most ages had been able to adapt artistic forms to changing techniques and needs, in the latter half of the nineteenth century social and technological change had proceeded too rapidly for artists to keep pace, and the architecture fell back on earlier styles' (ibid.: 57).

The reaction against modern architecture took place during the early to mid-1970s. 'Post-modern architecture literally refers to what comes after modernism, but is largely based on self-conscious and selective revival of elements of older styles' (Relph 1987: 213). By the late 1970s whole areas were being constructed in a post-modern style. St Andrew's Village, a shopping mall near Toronto, was advertised as possessing 'the character and charm of a century old village with ideas borrowed from the past to capture the spirit of the buying public's 'Back to Roots' movement – different elevations, staggered frontages ...' (ibid.: 217–18).

Post-modern architecture, which is part of the heritagization of space, serves to impose signifiers of an uninterrupted past. The emphasis on ruling-class styles from various historical periods conditions a belief in an historical continuity and collective memory – a past without difference, or a history that has ended. Unless people learn how to differentiate between pastiche and the original, the built environment becomes a meaningless mixture of historical styles. A context of living which loses any temporal perspective. Whilst accepting that there are differing contexts of reception, and that the idea of a duped mass society is Baudrillard's problem and not ours, it is still a likelihood that generations to come will inherit a heritage of heritage – an environment of past-plu-perfects which will ensure the 'death of the past'.

There should be no doubt that the heritage conservation movement, combined with the post-modern architect, are together creating a built environment which represents the image of a number of selected pasts in the present. Such images represent an artificial ideal that aims at 'ambience enhancement' and convincing the population that they live within a society which possesses a continuous historical identity. This identity is deemed ultimate, and thus the idea of history as a process which continues in the present is rejected. This emerging bricolage-environment is one which provides an historical surface onto which the colours of the nation can be painted. Britain's demise as a world power has demanded a new form of introspection. An image which is essentially English [sic], has been reconstructed, and nowhere has the image been more promoted than through the heritage, and more specifically through the heritage magazine.

Heritage magazines

Such magazines are a product of the late 1970s early 1980s development of heritage. They continue the tradition of the well-established 'Shire' magazines as well as the national equivalents such as *The Field* (est. 1853), *Country Life* (est. 1897) and *This England* (est. 1968). All of these magazines are bursting with glossy colour images of 'our green and pleasant land' (*This England*, Summer 1990).

In the newer heritage magazines, such as *Heritage, The British Review*, published in England (est. 1984), and *British Heritage*, published in the US (est. 1979), it is almost guaranteed that in each issue of either of these magazines there will be an article on a country house. *British Heritage*, the American magazine, is probably the more interesting phenomenon, largely because it is American. This magazine clearly panders to the dreams of those Americans who have never quite come to terms with the relatively short length of their history, and therefore find security in the imagined roots of 'that England'. The magazine also acts as a 'shop window' on Britain for prospective American tourists, thus justifying the claim that Britain is becoming little more than one large heritage centre and we are all the actor-interpreters playing our part. Through *British Heritage*, the reader can order a stained-glass window depicting the 'Seven Ages of Man', the complete series of *Brideshead Revisited* on video, or a family history, as long as your surname is in the list of 'distinguished American families'. For $19.95 you can 'buy Britain' – video tours that mean you never have to leave the comfort of your own armchair. For those with a military bent, there is 'The D-Day Commemorative .45, the first firing M1911A1.45 Pistol ever created, to honour the brave Americans who served in World War II', or if commemoration of a real event is not good enough, there is King Arthur's Excalibur, wrought of stainless steel, 24 karat gold, sterling silver, hand-set crystal cabochons, inserted in crystal-clear rock, 51.5 inches long and at a cost of $675.00. This is the past as one monumental souvenir shop, a site of conspicuous commodity consumption.

The idea of nation

> Thatcherism appears as the authentic voice of white working-class patriarchal values, preaching the importance of a strong nation and a strong family ...
>
> (Gamble 1988: 198)

This chapter has shown so far that the heritage, combined with post-modern architecture, promotes the problematization of a 'true' historical sense of place through its selectivity, and an emphasis on a narrow definition of the heritage. Through this emphasis on the conservation and representation of images of the ruling classes, and highly selective superficial images of a benign industrial past, it is attempting to construct an idea of nation, a sense of organic continuity.

The idea of 'nation' is a relatively new one with firm roots in the nineteenth century. The Conservative Party has always seen itself as the party of 'nation'. A key to the concept of British nationhood is the idea of a continued unbroken line of history. This belief is clearly espoused by Conservative MP Norman Tebitt, one of 'seven eloquent citizens in a symposium on the nation's destiny as the loom of Europe overhangs us and doubts solidify about 1992', which appeared in the 'rural' magazine *The Field* in May 1990. The section was entitled 'Fanfare on Being British'. The crux of Tebbit's argument was essentially environmentally deterministic: because the British are an island race, that results in them being a 'favoured' people: 'The blessing of insularity has long protected us against rabid dogs and dictators alike' (Tebbit 1990: 76). Tebbit viewed the arrival of invading armies during Britain's early history as 'waves of immigration'. These 'immigrants were integrated to such an extent that only the Jewish community remained identifiable and that only by a religion on which the culture of the whole nation is largely based' (ibid.: 78). Of course, the sub-text here is that these peoples became integrated because of the colour of their skins, and no doubt today they would pass the 'cricket test'. Tebbit argued that more recent immigrants have 'bruised' this England, and have been 'resistant to absorption, some defiantly claiming the right to superimpose their culture, even their law, upon the host community' (ibid.: 78). The language used by Tebbit was 'biological' in its style: the immigrants are parasites, living off the larger, superior 'host', which would only too gladly bestow its culture upon them, if they would only allow themselves to be consumed by the benign mother nation.

The other 'threat' to the sceptred isle was considered to be Brussels. Tebbit commented that, 'Even our heritage of British country sports is now threatened not so much by legislation in our Parliament but through the Brussels back-door. Indeed there is a risk of being harmonized into sterile uniformity by countries whose respect for wildlife and conservation practice leaves more than a little to be desired' (ibid.: 78).

Another Conservative MP, Michael Heseltine, revealed himself as a pundit of the 'rural idyll'; he believes that there is 'an England as she was: changeless in our fast-changing world' (Heseltine 1990: 78). This nostalgia is typical of much heritage, an attempt to preserve an image, to promote a timelessness in a place which never really existed for anyone, a desire which can only be lived by most people when they watch *All Creatures Great and Small* and *The Darling Buds of May*.

A. L. Rowse echoes Tebbit in his belief in the 'continuity' which characterizes English history. Rowse informed his readers that,

> The English are a practical people. Not theoretical like the Germans; nor dogmatic like the Russians (think of Tolstoy and Lenin); nor arrogant like the French (think of Louis XIV, or Napoleon, or even de Gaulle). Why were the British – for we must include the Scots and the Anglo-Irish here – more successful in running an Empire than anybody else since the Romans? Because they were more practical, more imaginative, and had more sympathy with peoples.
>
> (Rowse 1990: 79)

In the same issue of this magazine, retired Law Lord, Lord Denning, commented, 'To me, being British means being English, and proud of it. Proud of all that our British race have done for the world' (Denning 1990: 80). It would be most bizarre to hear a French person asserting, 'To me, being French means being German'. This quotation does actually highlight a serious point, which has been apparent in many of the statements made about 'what it is to be British'. It is quite clearly England which is perceived as 'first among unequals'.

England's domination and restraint of the Celts is an historical fact.

There is no need to discuss here the often barbaric acts perpetrated by the English against the Celtic-speaking peoples. What is important, however, is the use of heritage in the maintenance of this hegemony. Celtic peoples are perceived by the Right as peripheral to England. As with the rest of the world, they owe a debt of gratitude to the benign influence of the English. The Secretary of State for Scotland commented in *Scotland's Heritage*, produced by the Scottish Office,

> It is a natural and proper thing for each of us to take pride in our national identity and the achievements of our native country, but we should do so in a spirit which gives full recognition of the part that other countries have played in our cultural and historical development – and the contributions we have made to theirs.
>
> (Rifkind 1989: 3)

For 'other countries', read 'England'. Such a proviso has not appeared in any equivalent English publication. Rifkind finished his introduction with an echo of the previous quote. Talking of plans for the new Museum of Scotland he argued that Scots should be proud of their heritage, 'but with a proper appreciation of the contributions of other countries and other cultures' (ibid.: 4). This style was maintained in the main text of the publication as well. The reader is told how visitors expect Scottish culture to be placed 'in the wider context of Britain and Western Europe' (Scottish Office 1989: 13). It is of course crucial that all historical monuments are placed in their wider contexts, geographical, cultural, economic and political. The other important characteristic of Historic Buildings and Monuments Scotland, now Historic Scotland, is that it is directly responsible to the Secretary of State.

Heritage and Europhobia

'Don't let Europe Rule Britannia', pleaded the editor of *The Field* in the spring of 1990. A regular feature in this magazine has been the 'Don't Let Europe Rule Britannia' section. The editor's fears were articulated as follows: 'Britain may soon find itself inextricably submerged inside a United States of Europe', and *ipso facto*, 'Banners and Beefeaters ... our Monarchy, Parliament, national sovereignty, and many ancient traditions like this [quotation below a picture of Beefeaters marching] may soon be a thing of the past' (Faiers 1990: 12). The article contains quotes from right-wing luminaries such as Winston Churchill and of course, Enoch Powell. Faiers claims that 'Since our magazine purports to reflect the true nature of English people, and is totally produced by Britons young and old, we are as guilty as the rest of our countrymen in waiting until the eleventh hour before mounting a protest against something we don't agree with' (ibid.: 13). This echoes an earlier statement regarding our waiting 'until the last minute before taking action. We did it in 1939...' (ibid.: 12). The analogy between Nazi aggression and the threat posed by modern democratic institutions is a common device employed by contemporary English nationalists, and has been used elsewhere (for example Sir Roy Strong, quoted above).

Attacks on Britishness cited by Faiers included the 1971 great knitting needle disaster, when, thanks to the European Commission, 'knitting needle sizes were changed, so making obsolete all the knitting patterns collected by British women through the years' (ibid.: 13). The concern over knitting, pints, and currency, is akin to the problem surrounding heritage. It is a concern with objects treated as ephemera: there is no consideration of deeper issues, historical processes. Faiers has told his readers that 1992 is 'the biggest issue to face the British people since 1066' (ibid.: 14). It should be apparent to most people that 1066 was an invasion and occupation, not the opening up of a pan-European market. Again, this continual citation of events from history and their subsequent manipulation and perversion is all a part of the heritage game.

These commentators continually compare the development of a united Europe with World War II, or other military threats. It is the imagery of this isolated island standing alone against injustice which is the desired aim of such comments.

In an infamous interview, which lost Tory cabinet member, Nicholas Ridley, his job in July 1990, he said of German aims in Europe: 'This is all a German racket designed to take over the whole of Europe' (Ridley in Lawson 1990: 8). Mr Ridley then went on to say that, 'I'm not against giving up sovereignty in principle, but not to this lot. You might as well give it to Adolf Hitler, frankly' (ibid.: 8). During the interview implicit comparisons were made between Kohl, the incumbant Chancellor of Germany, and Adolf Hitler (ibid.: 8).

These points of views were not new; they represent an idea of nation which has been around since the nineteenth century. What is important, is that they hopefully represent a struggle for, or rather a reaction against, the welcome demise of the nation-state in the First World. Thus it is one of the major aims of the purveyors of 'heritage' to reveal this demise as untimely.

The idea of nation is one which has been, and still is articulated through a number of legitimation mechanisms, the most important of which is the promotion of the idea of continuity and tradition. Since coming to power, the Right in Britain have called for 'a continuous national history' with a patriotic orientation (Samuel 1989b: 9). Right-wing historians have argued for the development of a 'proper pride' and an emphasis on 'shared values'. It is undeniable that an ordered coherent history is appealing, a type of ordering which is apparent in the museum displays which were discussed in chapter one. Such an ordering serves to create a solid foundation which gives a certain security during times of change or instability, and is especially attractive in the post-modern world where time–space compression, amongst other experiences, serves to erode our sense of place.

In fact, most modern traditions were invented during the nineteenth century, including the current format for the celebration of Christmas. Many 'invented traditions' do however have roots which go much further back in time.

Hobsbawm defines invented tradition as 'a set of practices, normally governed by overtly or tacitly accepted rules and of a ritual or symbolic nature, which seek to inculcate certain values and norms of behaviour by repetition, which automatically implies a continuity with the past. In fact, where possible, they normally attempt to establish continuity with a suitable historic past' (Hobsbawm 1983b: 1).

New nations, or nations whose societies were undergoing fundamental restructuring as a consequence of revolution (industrial or political), needed to invent tradition in order to develop a certain level of cohesiveness. Flags or the personification of the nation in characters such as Uncle Sam or John Bull were part of this invention (ibid.: 7). When considering such mythological figures 'one is confronted not by realities which become fictions, but rather by fictions which, by dint of their popularity, become realities in their own right' (Samuel 1989a: xxvii). Even if such figures do have some kind of foundation in truth, it is usually the case that the figure has been transformed to such a great extent, that s/he bares no resemblance to the original.

The period from *c.* 1877 to the outbreak of World War I saw the height of invented tradition. For a large part of the nineteenth century the press was hostile towards the monarchy. One of the reasons for the lack of ceremony during the early to mid-Victorian period, according to Cannadine, was the fact that the people of the time 'saw themselves as the leaders of progress and pioneers of civilisation, and prided themselves on the limited nature of their government, their lack of interest in formal empire, their hatred of show, extravagance, ceremonial and ostentation. The certainty of power and the assured confidence of success meant that there was no need to show off' (Cannadine 1983: 112). Local loyalties seemed to be more important than national ones, although deference was shown to the national heroes of the time, people such as Wellington and Nelson. The Royal Family was not particularly popular, partly because it still possessed a certain amount of political power. As the real power of the Royal Family waned, ritual increased, and its role was gradually transformed. 'In such an age of change, crisis and dislocation, the "preservation of anachronism", the deliberate, ceremonial presentation of an impotent but venerated monarch as a unifying symbol of permanence and national community became both possible and necessary' (ibid.: 122).

During the late nineteenth century there was growing international competition, symbolized by the scramble for Africa. During this period there was a large-scale rebuilding of many capital cities (ibid.: 126). 'But it was not until the closing decades of the nineteenth century, when national prestige was seen to be threatened, that action was taken, converting the squalid fog-bound city of Dickens into an imperial capital' (ibid.: 127). In 1888 the LCC was established, providing the city with its first single authority.

The end of the nineteenth and the beginning of the twentieth century was the 'golden age of "invented traditions"', as the appeal of the monarchy to the mass of the people in an industrialized society was broadened in a manner unattainable only half a century before' (ibid.: 138).

During the nineteenth century the development of new efficient forms of media permitted for the first time the promotion of an idea of nation. The emerging high profile of the Royal Family as that institution which best symbolized nationhood was crucial. The ideology of nation attempted to unite regions and places in the perceived struggle with the newly emergent nations on the continent. The idea of nation was clearly one born out of economic and political expediency within the context of increasing international competition, rather than one born out of identifiable cultural similarities across many different regions and a desire within these regions to develop as one nation.

Hobsbawm argues that 'politics in the new nineteenth-century sense was essentially nation-wide politics. In short, for practical purposes, society ("civil-society") and the state within which it operated became increasingly inseparable' (Hobsbawm 1983a: 264).

A national politics does not necessarily produce a nation as perceived by the people. Even national parties and trade unions are organized at a local level. The national *is* important in certain circumstances, for example, pay bargaining and industrial action, but the local is probably of more importance in terms of the ways in which a problem is understood or perceived.

The idea of nation is not a straightforward one: 'National fictions might be considered not as reflections of ideology, whether at second or third remove, but as components in it, an imaginative underpinning, or disguise, for precepts which are the common currency of political debate' (Samuel 1989a: xix).

The New Right has created a patina of stability. By articulating a position founded on the bedrock of a supposed continuing historical tradition, the New Right hopes to find some kind of legitimation for policies which were radical, and disturbing, in all senses of the word. Through a strategy of selectivity, and a positive manipulation of the past, the recent history of the successful Welfare State was avoided as a part of a strategy which aimed to situate the 'true' history and tradition of the nation within the Victorian period. The selective quotation of certain traditional values, such as authority, morality, and hard work, aimed to reveal the 'soft underbelly' of a complacent Welfare State, typified by the immorality of the 'swinging sixties'.

The promotion of certain images of nation does in fact contribute to our historical amnesia. The emphasis on a mixed and matched bricolage of ruling-class styles from a number of periods denies an appreciation of the everyday past of the *majority* of the people. The imposition of an artificial concept of nation disguises the originality and sense of place, and the differences that exist in the pasts of different places. The final two chapters will consider a model, and techniques for, establishing a sense of place which must be based on locality. This will not deny the effect of nation on a place, but it will question the traditional emphasis made on the national past and heritage.

5 | *Simulating the past*

During the 1970s and 1980s there was a remarkable expansion in sites which purported to be representations of the past. This might be termed the 'heritage boom'. For our purposes the 'heritage boom' includes open-air museums, heritage centres which often employed new technologies to produce multi-media experiences, and certain established museums which decided to adopt some of the representational techniques developed by heritage attractions. This chapter will consider some examples of such representations, as well as their origins.

A key characteristic of many of these developments was the trend towards the promotion of heritage 'experiences', experiences produced through an often inspiring combination of sight, sound, and smell media. These media were of course expensive to develop and maintain. This expense thus gave rise to the concomitant trend towards automatic and sometimes excessive admission charges. Combined, these developments, along with restricted public finance for museums and the arts in general, led to the development of corporate images, and extensive advertisement campaigns. Such corporate images are epitomized by the Imperial War Museum's logo – the 'M' constructed by search lights, which won a prize for its originality – and the Museum of London's logo – Dick Whittington and his cat. These are all trends which characterize the placing of 'the past' in the market, and the need to make its representation more exciting if the past is to make money. It should not be forgotten, however, that many of these developments were prompted by a wider realization that many museum displays were in fact quite dull and uninformative.

The developments of the 1970s and 1980s should be seen in their historical contexts. Many of the new representations have progenitors with origins in the nineteenth century. The more recent expansion of such representations should be considered as another part of the intensification of the (post-)modern experience.

Early forms of heritage representation

Criticisms that are levelled at so-called heritage representations should not be taken as implying that museums are beyond criticism. The concern here is with certain forms of representation which some have considered to be a welcome departure from the orthodox museum, whilst others have been highly critical of most, if not all, forms of such heritage representation.

Robert Hewison, in his book *The Heritage Industry, Britain in a Climate of Decline*, concentrated on what some refer to as open-air museums (Hewison 1987). Such museums include Iron Bridge, Beamish, Wigan Pier, the various folk-life museums, and in the US, places such as Colonial Williamsburg and Greenfield Village. Although Hewison was correct to show how the expansion of heritage occurred in Britain within a climate of economic decline, there were in fact a number of other factors which influenced the expansion of heritage during the 1980s.

The folk-life and open-air museums, which are the obvious predecessors of many heritage attractions, have existed, as a form, for over one hundred years. A folk-life museum can be defined as a museum which is concerned to represent the everyday life of working people, and more often than not, rural people. In many cases such museums developed in open-air sites, and successfully catered for the growing demand for rural and historical 'experiences'. Folk-life collections have not been entirely presented in open-air museums. As traditional, indoor museums became aware of their success, they too moved towards re-creations of historic environments. The main difference between the indoor and outdoor types of re-creation, is that the open-air museums became notable for their use of 'living-history' methods of interpretation.

Proto-heritage: folk-life museums

The open-air, folk-life museums first developed in Scandinavia, as a response to the perceived threat of the Industrial Revolution, and its impact on traditional rural lifestyles. The first open-air museums were originally conceived during the last quarter of the nineteenth century. The first museum of this genre had its roots in the Museum of Scandinavian Folklore, opened by Artur Hazelius in 1873. As his collection expanded he managed to acquire a 75-acre site, and the outdoor museum opened in 1891. As with the more recent outdoor museums such as Beamish (Co. Durham, England), the collections included buildings from different places and different periods.

Hazelius' desire was 'to use the idea of heritage and understanding of the past as a steadying influence in the face of violent changes of modern life' (Alexander 1979: 85). The trend towards folk-life museums continued in Scandinavia, one example being the Danish National Museum which opened in 1901. This again consisted of a collection of rural buildings in a 90-acre park.

The folk-life genre took hold overseas also, especially in the United States. Colonial Williamsburg was founded in 1926 as an attempt 'to bring the colonial capital back to life' (ibid.: 91). The first outdoor museum in the US to be based on the Scandinavian model was the Greenfield Village at Dearborn, Michigan. This site, created by Henry Ford, contained

> a traditional New England green with church, town hall, courthouse, post office, and general store; the Scotch Settlement schoolhouse Ford attended as a boy; the Plymouth, Michigan, carding mill to which Ford's father took wool; Noah Webster's house; William Holmes McGuffey's Pennsylvania log-cabin birthplace; a 500–ton stone Cotswold Cottage; and the Sir John Bennet jewellery shop from Cheapside, London, with its clock graced by statues of Gog and Magog.
>
> (ibid.: 92–3)

This list reveals a certain magpie proclivity, and indeed, this manifest bricolage, the creation of a mythical place based on the whims and dreams of the world's greatest capitalist, could be viewed in retrospect as a prophecy of post-modern heritage.

Sponsorship of open-air museums by successful entrepreneurs was not unusual in the US. As well as Ford's Greenfield, Colonial Williamsburg was sponsored by John D. Rockefeller. The Wells brothers, of the American Optical Company, sponsored Old Sturbridge Village (Leon and Piatt 1989: 65). It should not be surprising then that such establishments may not be inclined to be critical of the socio-economic system which established them.

Rockefeller alone contributed 79 million dollars for the development of Colonial Williamsburg, a development which included the destruction of more than 700 post-1790 buildings in order to fabricate the late eighteenth-century ambience. From its very beginnings, Colonial Williamsburg, along with Greenfield, was constructed as an artificial place: 'Williamsburg helped enshrine the colonial era as one especially appropriate to museum restoration projects' (ibid.: 67).

There is no doubt that such places do act as 'breathing spaces' in the (post-)modern world, which for many makes increasing demands on their stamina. In many open-air museums there is an emphasis on vernacular forms of industry. As discussed in chapters one and four, modern economic systems have increasingly removed people from the processes of production. More so now, in an age of information technology, than ever before, there is 'something comforting and appealing in seeing a broom, chair, blanket, or iron created by the skilled hands of the patient craftsperson. To many visitors, such demonstrations symbolized what was lost in the transition to the modern urban-industrial world and infused living-history museums with a nostalgic atmosphere' (ibid.: 67).

The earlier success of many open-air museums acted, in part, as the prompt for Walt Disney's first theme park development. There is no doubt that the development of many heritage attractions owes a great deal to Disney, both in terms of the media employed, and the style and systems of organization developed in the Disney parks. Many heritage attractions are often considered as striving to attain the 'Disney effect' – sites of fantastic spectacle, with an emphasis on titillation, rather than education. In fact, in terms of the genealogy of these different media, Disneyland could be considered as the younger cousin of the open-air museum, and the auntie of the modern-day heritage centre. However, a clear chronological account of heritage is difficult.

Disneyland was opened in 1955, and contained a number of 'history-flavoured entertainments' (Wallace 1989: 159). Disney may have been influenced by the successes of the early open-air museums, such as Greenfield and Williamsburg. As with the open-air museums discussed previously, a theme that is peddled by the heritage attraction, and was in Disneyland, is the trip back in time.

One of the main attractions at Disneyland is Main Street, which, 'ostensibly, is grounded in historic reality. It was fashioned we are told, out of Disney's recollections of his turn-of-the-century boyhood in Marceline, Missouri' (ibid.: 161). The official Disney historians have actually confessed that the recreated Main Street, 'was quite unlike the Main Streets of yester-year' (Disney official history, quoted in Wallace 1989: 161).

Both Disneyland and the vast majority of open-air museums produce representations of life-styles that are devoid of conflict and antisocial behaviour, and exist within a calming rural landscape. Leon and Piatt argue that the cost of developing an industrial open-air museum means that pre-industrial agrarian bias will dominate this genre (Leon and Piatt 1989: 72). However, in Britain, attempts have been made to represent industrial society through the form of the open-air museum. The most obvious example is Beamish; even here, however, the bucolic spirit is in no way dispensed with. In fact the site is advertised as being set within

The Representation of the Past

'200 acres of woodland and rolling countryside' (Beamish Museum 1990a). The rural idyll arbitrates in an historical representation, which should, at least in part, be concerned with squalor and a degree of adversity in life at which most of us today would balk.

Beamish is a collection of buildings and objects from all over the north-east of England. The 'town' comprises six late Georgian houses from Gateshead, the Victorian park is from another part of Gateshead, the Co-operative shop is from Anfield Plain to the east of Consett, the Sun Inn public house is from Bishop Auckland. In fact, the various buildings have come from an area of about 400 square miles, and some of the farm buildings have their provenance even further afield.

It is claimed that open-air museums are in fact a radical departure from more orthodox museums. It is often declared that they 'bring the past to life'. There is no doubt that as entertainments, as sites of spectacle consumption, many such tourist-spaces can be considered as successful, especially if crude marketing criteria are applied.

A common complaint made of museums is that they are imposing, and that they articulate power through the imposition of varying forms of private, or excluded, space. The cabinet is enclosed and removed from the visitor and certain areas of the museum are off-limits to the public. Open-air museums, it is claimed, have changed all this. This is not so. One of the most confusing characteristics of Beamish is not knowing where one can, and can not look. Some signs around Beamish are 'heritage signs'– signs from the past, which constitute a part of the display. Other signs are modern, in that they convey information which is necessary for the organization and control of the museum. Buildings which appear to be part of the museum turn out to be locked and 'No Admittance' notices turn out to be 'real'. This is certainly the case with the Heapstead building at the colliery. The entire site is replete with contextless objects without labelling. Of course, in order for the place to be promoted as 'the real thing', labelling would itself be incongruous to this end. However, if the visit is to be a learning experience, and no guides are available, the visitor is left to admire the 'thingyness' of the object for itself. To understand, or appreciate the site, a certain amount of cultural competence is required. The museum relies heavily on the promotion of selective memory or nostalgia.

The site is successful because the visitor is placed in an environment of nostalgia-arousal: 'The past went that-a-way. When faced with a totally new situation, we tend always to attach ourselves to the objects, to the flavour of the most recent past. We look at the present through a rear-view mirror. We march backwards into the future' (McLuhan, Fiore and

Agel 1967: 74–5). Most of the buildings, objects, advertisements etc. were extant long after the period in which the museum is supposedly set. The visitor participates and promotes the nostalgia effect: 'that's just like the iron we used to have!', or, 'this living room looks exactly the same as Grandma's!'. There are of course multiple contexts of reception. Each exhibit, or re-creation, is reinterpreted in different ways by different people. Those visitors who have worked in mines will doubtless remember the less representable aspects of industrial life – the danger, the unemployment, and the fact that their village was not set in idyllic, rolling rural surroundings between two farms. Such representations are occasions of partial recall. The most dangerous consequence of this type of museum is its effect on those who can not remember. For them, their nostalgia is often second-hand. Their parents or grandparents can pass on their own nostalgia, and before long, a generation will exist whose heritage lies with the heritage industry. The consequence of this form of mediation through an emphasis on historical surfaces, set within the eulogized, and almost universally desired, rural idyll, 'is that the story of industrial development in the north-east, rather than being told as one of ruptures, conflicts, and transformations, emerges as a process that is essentially continuous with the deeper and longer history of the countryside in which the power of the bourgeoisie has become naturalized' (Bennett 1988: 69).

The exploration of nostalgia is not necessarily a bad thing; people's emotional attachment to that which they remember is of paramount importance. This natural interest in the past should however be used as a kind of preface to a more critical engagement with the past and its links with, or contingency on, the present.

This idea of historical processes directly affecting the present is something which will be negated, or perhaps even lost once Beamish concentrates on one specific year: 1913. For most of its existence the Beamish buildings represented a period from the 1790s to the 1930s, and the interpretation concentrates on the period from about 1890 through to the 1930s. Beamish does not, however, attempt explicitly to impose the idea that the created place is in fact a unified place. Each different area of the museum represents a different aspect of the 'regional heritage': the middle-class town, the working mine and cottages, and the rural economy. In a way, Beamish is meant to be a microcosm of the north-east, rather than a specific place. Also, it does actually make an attempt to represent historical process in some form, most obviously in the miners' cottages. Each cottage is representative of a different decade, ranging from the 1890s to the late 1930s. However, this is about to change (1990/1); a decision has been made to place the entire site in the year 1913, the most productive year in the history of north-east England's industry, and the year of greatest coal production nationally. It might be asked, why was the year of the

General Strike, 1926, not chosen? It is as if the directors feel that Beamish has become accepted as an artificial place, and that any representation of historical process is no longer necessary. Thus the creation of an artificial and isolated place, removed from the everyday experience of process through time and space, is now acceptable to the visitor. More so than ever before, Beamish will exist as a fantasy island, taking 'time out' from history.

By the end of the 1980s there were nearly 500 museums which contained industrial material; about a third of these had been established since 1970. The presentation of industrial heritage has become a celebration of an escaped and completed past. The industrial 'experience' as served up at Beamish and Ironbridge serves not only to beautify an often terrifying past, but also to promote its relegation into a more distant past. This relegation is cultivated through the removal of the industrial heritage from real places and its re-placement into those which are artificial.

Perhaps more disconcerting than many of the open-air museums are attractions like Littlecote, 'The Land that's Trapped in Time', which opened in 1986 and closed in 1990, reportedly to be replaced by a golf course and a 90-bed hotel with conference facilities.

Such attractions fall into an almost undefinable category; they are not theme parks, in the Disneyland or Alton Towers mould, neither can they be considered didactic experiences. Littlecote was bricolage at its most extreme. The public were offered a Roman villa and mosaic where they could 'imagine the life led by these 4th century colonists' (Littlecote publicity leaflet). We might question the use of the word 'colonists'. At Littlecote the visitor was also invited to experience, 'lusty knights do combat with lance, sword and mace. And when stillness falls, magnificent falcons soar high in the skies to swoop at man's command'. Following this the visitor was then invited to go on to witness 'The Splendour of the Tudors' at Littlecote mansion. After this, they could move on to the Civil War, and witness the waxwork protagonists 'held in time'. Meanwhile, life goes on at Littlecote as 'craftsmen ply their trades in the village street – selling their wares to passers-by' (ibid.). The penultimate potential time-trip was then a visit to Fort Littlecote, where the struggle between red-coated soldiers and Red Indians is 'echoed'. Finally, 'from the romantic age of steam, the Trans-Littlecote Steam Railway crosses the length of the land' (ibid.). Littlecote was little more than a series of representations of sets from *Dr Who*, or the *Time Tunnel*. However, such sites should be taken seriously, as for some people they may have been the nearest they get to learning about the past. This should especially be the case, as in 1987 Littlecote won the British Tourist Authority's prize for the best commercial tourist attraction.

Empathy and first-person interpretation

The heritage spectacle, which is responsible for the numbing of our historical sensibilities, does so through a combination of different media. Common to many heritage representations is the idea of empathy, a promotion of the idea that we can travel back to the past.

The early open-air museums tended to opt for third-person interpretation, where there was no pretence, and history was interpreted as those traces of past societies which exist in the present only. But, 'Over time, a different interpretive style, first-person interpretation, developed. Its roots were partly in the theatre, but it also emerged naturally, and sometimes unwittingly, from the conversations staff members had with visitors, especially in craft shops' (Leon and Piatt 1989: 86). The quest for accuracy, and thus true empathy, reached its probable limits at the Plimouth Plantation, where the actor-interpreters were trained to speak, not only in the first-person, but also in the dialects which existed in the early seventeenth century. The staff were now considered as informants, and the visitors, interpreters. For many visitors this method of presentation proved daunting: the actors' use of strange speech and their refusal to acknowledge anything after 1627 was also disconcerting (ibid.: 88).

Part of the revision at Beamish open-air museum will also include a move from third-person to first-person interpretation. First-person interpretation is no new thing in Britain, and some places go to extreme lengths to produce the 'authentic' experience. At Kentwell Hall, Suffolk, each year, the owners recruit some 200 volunteers to dress up and pretend to be Tudor folk. The owner of Kentwell claimed that he wished 'to know everything about the daily lives of people of all stations of life'. He also asserted that it is possible to illustrate daily life to all of the senses: 'You can see and touch clothes as they were in XVIth century, you can eat Tudor food, you can listen to Tudor speech patterns, songs and music, use Tudor tools, walk around Tudor buildings, smell Tudor herbs'. Luckily for the author he happens to live at Kentwell. He tells us that he is surrounded by open countryside 'and nothing from the 20th century obtrudes' (Phillips 1984: 10).

The re-creation takes place in some of the buildings around the manor. The 200 volunteers take on jobs that would have been going on, in and around the area. 'We strive for authenticity in all we do and to eliminate anachronisms'. The re-creation is aimed at school-children. Phillips tells us that, 'Few boys between, say, 12 and 16 have no interest in seeing, say, armour being made or a plumber making lead. Most girls are sufficiently interested in cooking, baking, spinning, sewing etc. to want to see how it was done previously without modern aids' (ibid.: 10).

The Representation of the Past

This type of re-creation is clearly very popular with the 20,000 school-children visiting per season. But, popularity is not an acceptable criterion alone for judging such a representation. When considering such an attempt at empathetic re-creation, we need to consider the degree to which any kind of empathy is possible. In fact it is quite clear that this kind of unquestioning empathy can be dangerous. As noted above, the director of the Kentwell project seemed to have no qualms over the presentation and promotion of sexual stereotypes. The whole approach falls short of competent history, which should be concerned with the contrasting of the past with the present. It should surely look for links that are common to different historical periods, and reveal and throw into sharp relief the injustices that once existed, and those which may be still there, but in a different form. The inequity of a patriarchal society is one of these links or themes.

At a fundamental level, the desire to escape the present, and the experiences of modernity and post-modernity, should not surprise us. But it is the promotion of empathy, and its concomitant denial that the past, and places, exist in the present, which is in part responsible for the destruction of a sense of place. The promotion of the idea that we can travel back in time implies that the 'expert', or providers of heritage, 'know' the past, and therefore, belies the fact that all our pasts are constructed in the present. Even if a time traveller could witness events in history first hand, they would not know, or understand the past – it would be merely one person's perception of that event. A member of Tsar Nicholas II's family would quite likely perceive the events in Russia in 1917 differently from a member of Lenin's family, if they were to both travel back to that time and space. (For an extensive discussion of the idea of history, empathy, and time travel, see Lowenthal 1985: chapter one.)

Another form of empathetic re-creation is the mock battle, or historical re-enactment. Such events have been staged for many years, but, as with the heritage industry, the last decade or so has seen an increase in demand for their services.

Each summer, English Heritage organizes an extensive programme of special events. In 1989 49 per cent of events were military. These events were a mixture of Medieval combat, 155 mm howitzer salutes, Fort Cumberland guard displays and American Civil War living-history garrisons, and many more.

The Chief Executive of English Heritage has argued that these events are a 'taster', and that they invite people to investigate further these aspects of English history. In fact it may be considered that these events are nothing but mere titillation, meaningless amateur dramatics promoting

the post-modern simulacrum, a hazy image of a manipulated and trivialized past. The most ridiculous was the American Civil War garrison
at Fort Brockhurst, Hampshire. This along with the 'Napoleonic battle
spectacular' with music by Hautbois, is what some would ascribe as
the quintessential post-modern ferment. History is decontextualized and
mixed with non-history in a promotion of pastiche. English Heritage has
argued that because these so-called re-creations are popular, that makes
them acceptable. Popularity is hardly any guarantee of its own quality,
as any inspection of newspaper sales will testify.

Discussion

Common to these forms of heritage representation is a certain form of
artificiality – not just an artificiality caused by the fact that some of them
do not, or can not employ real buildings or artefacts in their 'real'
locations, but one that is based on the construction of 'unreal' places.
What Disneyland and many contemporary heritage attractions do, is to
use images from the past to create a spectacle, an environment that is
different, but to a certain extent remains familiar and safe. Such attractions vary enormously in their emphasis on the education/entertainment
ratio. There are the Disneylands, the Alton Towers, the Camelots and
the American Adventures, which, like post-modern architecture, are concerned with imagineering [sic] projects in their most basic form – the
development of an environment constructed through historical surfaces,
a context of superficial spectacle-consumption and entertainment. These
in their own way contribute to our historical amnesia through a quotation, or rather, a misquotation, of historical styles, and the creation of
artificial places, and they therefore merely compound the historical
mélange established by the conservation bodies and post-modern archi-
tectures considered in the previous chapter.

The heritage site is often a spurious simulacrum; Beamish, Greenfield
Village, and, to a certain extent, Colonial Williamsburg, are artificial
places, in that they are constituted by buildings and artefacts from a
number of different places and different times. Unlike real places these
heritage environments are not historic environments which have
developed 'naturally' over time as the town, village or city has developed.
Heritage sites are constructed as 'time capsules' severed from history,
islands of mediated image, sites of out-of-town heritage shopping. These
life-sized 'time capsules' need to be considered carefully. In many ways
they represent a form of historical bricolage, a melting pot for historical
memories. So many places and so many times represented in a contrived
place, may in fact contribute to a sense of historical amnesia, rather than
the desired aim of maintaining a sense of the past, or tradition.

The Representation of the Past

This trend towards the creation of artificial heritage space is well represented at Beamish, and has been discussed frequently (Bennett 1988; Shanks and Tilley 1987: 83–6). Such places are literally on a road to nowhere. Part of the display at Beamish includes old road signs which point to places in the north-east, but the signs point in the wrong direction, and obviously, display the incorrect distance; thus Beamish is located in a mythological map of the mind, and exists only in a form of hyperspace – abstract space which is unmapable. This contrivance encourages a universal sigh of relief from those who witnessed these processes of industrial capital. And for those of us who were not there, we can say, 'well, it wasn't that bad was it?' We can then return to lives in the service sector, and happily forget that the processes of industrial capital have been moved to the Third World. The relegation of heavy industry into a dim and distant heritage-past is an element of the wider attempt to dislocate us from historical processes and de-politicize the past.

Artifice and the denial of the contingency of the past on real places is also promoted by those sites which attempt empathetic representations. Empathy or first-person interpretation denies the existence of history as process, which moves from the past through the present and into the future. It promotes synchronous pasts, where all our pasts exist as assets to be stripped and exploited purely for their surfaces. First-person interpretation often prevents the interpreter from considering historical and archaeological explanations which post-date the period which they are supposed to be acting within. This mechanism permits the heritage marketeers to stave off the more radical and investigative debates that have taken place in more recent years. In short, the idea of time travel, or empathy, is one of the most dangerous and anti-critical modes of representation available, and if used at all, it should only be employed as one technique amongst many.

The recreated event also achieves a similar effect. Many such events may contribute to the destruction of place. More often than not the events will not depict occurrences from the past of the locality being used, but there will be, perhaps, a set piece, an imaginary battle that moves from one locality to another each weekend. As mentioned above, an example which symbolizes this problem is the appearance of the American Civil War garrison at Fort Brockhurst, near Portsmouth, Hampshire, England. The historical identity of such a place is eroded by the placeless mock battles and re-creations that occur all over the country. Such 're-creations' of history are acted out in places that have little or no connection with the events depicted, and sometimes the re-creations are in fact completely spurious. Such living-history events do nothing but promote a sense of schizophrenic place.

A place will have its 'true' identity based upon its perceived historical position, constructed through the perceptions and understandings of people who live in and know that place. But today places are subjected to the whims of marketing directors, who have little or no real knowledge of them. Visitors will come from miles around to witness the destruction of place, through the acting out of events that have had no part in its construction.

In many cases of post-modern heritage, the emphasis has been on re-creation through technical artifice. Many such representations have repressed a sense of place, as much as they have encouraged a nostalgia for a less frenetic world.

Heritage centres

As well as the increased demand for the outdoor historical spectacle, there has also been a burgeoning of the indoor heritage attraction. Such attractions should not be considered as a dramatic departure from more traditional museums. The heritage centre usually attempts to represent some part of a place's past through more 'post-modern' media: sound, light, smell, and even heat. A heritage centre may in fact employ didactic methods which are quite similar to those found in many museums; there is an emphasis on the use of objects, or replicas of objects. This is usually combined with some form of narrative, either written, or played over a sound system of some sort. However, most heritage centres tend to concentrate on one specific theme of a place's past, often a theme which is in part mythological, or a theme which can at best be described as pseudo-historic. Also, the heritage attraction tends to emphasize its medium of representation, or the spectacle that it has to offer. Often this seems to be more eminent than the historical event or message. The medium of representation has become all important in a marketing niche where entertainment has often drowned out the educational aspects of the representation. This trend has been such an important one that many museums, in order to compete with such attractions, have felt that they too should adopt similar representational strategies.

The emphasis on spectacle, rather than education, is not a new phenomenon. There has always been a fundamental problem in knowing when the entertainment stops, and the education starts. That is not to say that the two are necessarily mutually exclusive, but rather, that there is a clear problem with the medium of representation 'drowning out' the intended educational information, where the medium becomes the *massage* [sic]. The heritage centre's emphasis on the spectacle is not a new departure;

the 'heritage', or chronology, of (post-)modern heritage is not straight forward, and goes back much further than Disney.

Charles Wilson Peale, the creator of the Philadelphia Museum in the early nineteenth century, attempted to place objects in their contexts by locating them in front of painted backgrounds, representations of the natural settings of the animal or object. 'For a time, he employed "Moving Pictures" (or "Perspective Views with Changeable Effects"), experiments in light, sound, and clockwork motion, offering his visitors views of nature, technology, naval battle, and scenes from Milton's *Paradise Lost*' (Kulik 1989: 5).

A lesson for modern museums lies in the fact that after Peale's death in 1827, the museum failed to raise public funds, and 'was incorporated as a joint stock company' (ibid.: 5). Profit, now a prerequisite for the museum's survival, led to live animal shows, 'to Siamese twins, to the "Virginia Dwarfs," to the "Big Children" (two large unfortunate girls from Poughkeepsie), to the "Belgian giant" and the "Automation Musical Lady"' (ibid.: 5). The museum became the property of P. T. Barnum in 1850. Barnum 'blurred the boundaries between museums and carnival sideshows, between the theatre and the circus, between the real and the contrived' (ibid.: 5). Also, a Panorama Craze developed towards the end of the eighteenth and the beginning of the nineteenth centuries in both Europe and America. The diorama was developed in 1823 by Louis J. M. Daguerre and Charles Marie Bouton. This type of diorama consisted of a painted gauze and moving lights; these combined could change scenes and give the impression of movement. According to Alexander, 'No more spectacular panorama ever existed than Colonel Jean-Charles Langlois's *Battle of Navarino*, shown in the Champs Elysées Rotunda in 1830' (Alexander 1979: 82). This spectacle included wax representations of dying sailors and sound effects. We must question the assumption that the society of the post-modern spectacle developed after World War II.

The heritage centre developments of the late twentieth century were not radically new developments, but as with many post-modern phenomena, they represented an intensification and expansion of a medium.

An example of a heritage venture which combined the use of the ultra modern technological experience with the promotion of a 'traditional' heritage was Royal Britain, a heritage centre adjacent to the Barbican centre in London.

The message of Royal Britain was undoubtedly patriotic. The 'story' was concerned to highlight 'The colourful personalities and exploits of Britain's Kings and Queens' (Royal Britain 1989: 1). The media employed included life-size reconstructions of building interiors, music, recorded voices, lighting effects, projectors and life-size manikins of the Royals. According to the owners, the exhibition used 'the most up to date technological magic to bring to life the "feel" of each period' (ibid.: 1). However, this attraction was one of the few notable heritage failures, and was closed in 1990.

In many ways Royal Britain gave much of the information that many visitors would have demanded. This included the genealogy of the various royal families, their most famous exploits, who was doing what to whom, and how they were doing it, and what were their little quirks. For example we were told that William I's favourite punishment was to have his enemies' hands and feet chopped off. Such facets of certain Royal's characters were represented through 'witty' cartoons. The murder of Edward the Martyr (975–9) by Elfrida his stepmother, was one such cartoon. We are told how Henry I snored loudly, and that Stephen (1135–54) had piles. It is good to know they were human, but no such tales were told of the current incumbents.

Royal Britain was essentially an uncritical multi-media experience. Uncritical because it failed to ask questions; it never challenged the actions of some of the more dubious rulers. There was some problem solving: the visitor was asked to vote on the innocence or guilt of Richard III (1483–5), and to declare 'true or false' as to the fate of each of Henry VIII's (1509–47) wives. Were they divorced, or beheaded, did they die young or survive him? Royal Britain represented the royal past as characterized by continuous success and glory, 'Warrior, saint, diplomat, law-giver, crusader, statesman [sic], peace-maker and symbol of unity. Over the last thousand years the British sovereign has been all of these and more' (ibid.: 53); the 'more' might have been considered with greater reflection!

Possibly the reason for the failure of Royal Britain was that it was a post-modern media representation of something which could be experienced for 'real' at Westminster Abbey. Also, such a crass commercialization of what is undoubtedly a much-respected and revered institution was perhaps not what visitors wanted.

Another heritage centre which is concerned to represent the history of another 'safe' and revered institution is situated in Oxford, England. The Oxford Story, produced by Heritage Projects Limited, most famous for the Jorvik Viking centre in York, purports to present the history of Oxford University. Seated at a moving desk the visitor is taken on a circuit, through a series of exhibits which contain life-size manikins of teachers and students at work and play throughout the history of the University. The great historic smells of this austere institution are also an important element of this representation. The Oxford Story is a trip through time; 'Space travel is an invention of our century, time travel is always possible because human beings have an imagination' (Oxford Story narration). At least here there is an emphasis on the imagination, but the emphasis is still on the possibility of 'knowing the past' through empathy.

The admiration of the University as a venerable institution is the dominant message of The Oxford Story. The University is described as 'a place where our most able young men and women come for the training of their minds' (ibid.). It concerns itself with informing the general public that such an institution has a monopoly on producing the good and the great from Roger Bacon to Margaret Thatcher. The University is treated in isolation, a temple of excellence removed from the rest of the world. Oxford in the eighteenth century was 'a peaceful backwater', and this period was, 'a time of relaxation' (ibid.). Entire historical periods are summed up in throwaway epithets, such as, the medieval period being 'an energetic but violent age. . .due to too much beer' (ibid.). Again, there is a denial that place is constructed through time, and under the influences of other places. The most worrying aspect of The Oxford Story is that the representation even denies the existence of the surrounding city. The most notable exception to this is the recalling of St Scholastica's Day: in 1355, a riot took place, a consequence of 'friction' between the town and the University. The friendly voice of our narrator, Sir Alec Guinness, informs the time traveller, that as a punishment for this, the citizens had to pay a fine every year for five centuries. It does not mention that 63 people were killed. We are not really told who was to blame for the riot, but the narration implies that the University was wronged, and thus, the town's people were justly fined.

The treatment of places in isolation is typical of much heritage. The Oxford Story would seem to be one of the most extreme, as it concentrates on a very particular aspect of a city. The University is thus set in some kind of dimensionless place; in a way it is promoted as an almost fabulous, or legendary place, with the strength to exist outside of the real world. This surreal image is reiterated through the declared connection with Lewis Carroll, and *Alice's Adventures in Wonderland*, the Rabbit and Alice often appearing on publicity for The Oxford Story.

The ability to concentrate on isolated, and sometimes, historically unsubstantiated phenomena, is an important characteristic of much heritage. The Oxford Story is but one example; the Canterbury Tales, located in that city, is another. In Nottingham, this form of pseudo-history is represented by The Tales of Robin Hood. Here, the legitimation of an undoubtedly attractive myth, and its mediation into a well-packaged quasi-historical narrative, coupled with the emphasis on the always seductive heroic (male) individual, obviates any requirement of discussion of 'real' history – what life was really like in Norman Nottingham. Here, history is almost twice removed, a distant second cousin of the heritage representation. Not only is the subject of representation treated in isolation from the place of Nottingham, the emphasis on a mythological character removes the entire spectacle from the usual contexts of time and space.

The heritage industry has often been discussed with reference to a few well-known and spectacular examples. This trend belies the fact that the heritage representation has successfully expanded into many places, employing greatly varying levels of media sophistication. An example of a more mundane experience is Bygones, a Victorian experience in Torquay, Devon, which opened in 1987. 'When you walk into *Bygones* you are transported back in time about 100 years to the reign of Queen Victoria' (Bygones 1987: 1). The first experience at Bygones is a Victorian street scene, which is very similar to those that were established in a number of British museums earlier this century; the most famous is 'Kirkgate' in York Museum. The main difference with Bygones is the sounds and smells.

The rest of this heritage centre concentrates on the interiors of middle-class Victorian homes. The rooms include the bedroom, the bathroom, the kitchen, and the parlour. The final part of this heritage centre is the most bemusing. It is called 'Fantasyland', and consists of a model fairy-tale town and a train set. 'Fantasyland' includes a model of Buckingham Palace which is adjacent to what looks like a model of the Taj Mahal. The rest of the town includes models of buildings, or rather styles of buildings from all over the world, and quite clearly also, from someone's vivid imagination. Behind 'Fantasyland' is a display of *real* military memorabilia, including medals and photographs.

The Spectacle in the Museum

What has been described as the heritage spectacle did not suddenly develop during the 1970s and 1980s. As was illustrated earlier, the reconstructed historic scene has been with us for at least a century, and probably a lot longer. As the differences between the heritage spectacle and the museum exhibition have to a certain extent always been indistinguishable, during the later twentieth century there has been a growing lack of distinction between the heritage experience and some museum displays. During the 1980s and the early 1990s some museums reacted to the success of heritage, and the need to survive in the market-place, by mimicking the heritage spectacle, rather than attempting to provide a service that sets the museum apart from the all too common multi-media experience.

An early reaction to the success of the open-air museum manifested itself as the reconstructed street scene, especially the Victorian variety. In fact its current format in Bygones and the recently opened Waterfront museum in Poole, Dorset, owes its existence to earlier museum reactions to the open-air, or, folk-life, movement which developed earlier this century. The Waterfront museum at Poole has as its first exhibition a reconstructed Victorian street, complete with smells.

John Kirk's 'Kirkgate', a reconstructed street exhibition, opened on St George's Day 1938. This street was reconstructed with façades from a number of different places, including York, Bath, and Stamford. The buildings were also from a number of different periods – the fifteenth, eighteenth, and early nineteenth centuries. This again begs the question, have the characteristics of post-modernity been with us for a lot longer than seems to be currently accepted?

Brears and Davies believe that, 'To a public accustomed to traditional glass-cased museums, *Kirkgate* proved to be a magical experience: the feel of the cobbles underfoot, the soft glow of the lamps, the sparrows on the window ledges and the daffodils in the window boxes all uniting to give the impression that visitors really had "stepped back in time" to an early Victorian town' (Brears and Davies 1989: 76). A number of other museum streets opened in the north of England during the post-war period. In Leeds, Abbey Fold opened in 1954, and in 1964 the new Doncaster museum opened, which also boasted a series of period shops.

In the same way that the museum sector reacted to the folk-life movement, through a not unsuccessful attempt to mimic it, museums in more recent years are reacting to the heritage industry in similar ways. The problem is that often they are merely aping the heritage industry, and in some cases, are not producing anything which is radically different. There are notable exceptions, which will be considered in chapter eight. In many cases the spectacle is used by the museum to attract customers who will hopefully move on to the more didactic experiences once the spectacle has been consumed. There is though a danger that the titillating spectacle will engulf the visitor's perception of a museum and consequently negate the potential impact of the didactic presentation.

A major British national museum which completed its redisplay in 1990, with no doubt, the thought of competing with the heritage industry in mind, was the Imperial War Museum, London. Most of the displays are still the orthodox object and text displays, as well as plenty of audio-visual media. The centre pieces of the new Imperial War Museum are the two 'experiences': the 'Blitz Experience', and the World War I 'Trench Experience'. The first opened in 1989, and the second in 1990.

Probably the most telling point about the 'Blitz Experience' is that I voluntarily went through it twice. I do not believe that I would have rushed to London in 1940 to experience some bombing! The two experiences include both sight, sound, and smell sensations, and in the case of the Blitz, earth-moving experiences. The visitor sits in an air-raid shelter and listens to ex-soap star, Anita Dobson, whose voice is immediately recognized by schoolchildren, who in turn tend to giggle all the way through this experience. The chirpy cockney tells us how they are not worried by the bombs; the fortitude of the beleaguered, but loyal and patriotic English working class, is an important theme. After the raid is over, the visitor is taken into a smoke-filled room, which is supposed to be a devastated East End. In the distance, the lights flicker around a model of St Paul's, supposedly representing the flames threatening this national monument. Here, an ability to suspend disbelief is a prerequisite.

It has been said of the 'Trench Experience' that, 'The installation invites the public to relive a moment of history. ... Once inside each visitor feels the full impact of the battlefield with gun flashes, smoke, sound re-enactment and authentic smells' (*Museums Journal* 1990: 21).

At the opening of the 'Trench Experience', one veteran from the Great War is reported to have commented, 'Much safer than any trench I've ever been in' (Colonel William Taylor, reported in Kennedy 1990). 'It's very well done, but we were always soaking wet, and always lousy' (Brigadier Harry Hopthrow, reported in Kennedy 1990). However, 'The Trench Experience' is different from the Blitz in one fundamental way. In 'The Trench Experience', the visitor is not forced through in a limited time; it is possible to look at the reconstructed scenes, and listen to the recorded voices of actor/soldiers describing life in the trenches, a number of times. With a little imagination, it is possible to stop and think, and perhaps understand a little more. But this is of course reliant on the individual. Many schoolchildren seem to see the experiences as a bit of fun, a spectacle which *has* to be seen. It is unlikely that they do actually learn something about the horror of war, a horror which appeared all too absent at the time of the Gulf War.

Discussion

The heritage spectacle, including open-air museums, and the heritage centre time trips, have been described by Eco in his *Travels in Hyperreality* in the United States (Eco 1986). In part, such representations are a genuine attempt to recreate the 'real thing'. But the emphasis is on an authenticity of form, rather than an authenticity of experience. The dimensions of the trenches and the air-raid shelter, or the houses, are exact, and the accuracy of the uniforms and clothing is unquestionable, but the reality ends here. The smells can not be real, neither can the sounds, and as for the experience of day-to-day life in such contexts, thankfully this can never be a reality. Maybe such representations *should* only be seen as a marketing gimmick designed to attract visitors. This would be fine if only the rest of the representation were of educational value as well. There is a danger that the marketing gimmicks will dominate the entire museum. The Imperial War Museum also has a flight simulator which allows the visitor to go on a World War II bombing raid over Germany. This experience is somewhat ironic when during the spring of 1991, people are talking about high-tech, 'video-arcade' air attacks on Baghdad.

The attempts to re-create reality were probably best symbolized during the 1980s by the trend towards the provision of heritage smells. The company which provides most of Britain's great smells will 'visit for a survey, to advise personally on which smells may be appropriate and then provide a batch of sample oils to try' (Heritage Interpretation 1985a: 5). The system works by vaporizing some specially formulated oil in one of the company's Vortex machines. Smells produced so far include meat smells, old pub smells, coal fire and woodsmoke, fresh apples, leather, coffee, mown grass, a farmyard smell, bacon, an ironmongers and old factories. We might ask why some heritage centres don't use the real thing. There seems to be a desire to manufacture the synthetic for the sake of it, artifice for artifice's sake. Of course, the interpreters might argue that they employ these bogus smells for convenience. What we must ask is, should such a spurious form of representation be used at all if an effort can not be made to use the real when possible? Smells as signifiers might potentially possess an infinite number of meanings or signifieds. It is possible that the ambiguities initiated by smell are the most profuse and confusing: smell is an extremely acute sense, which although underdeveloped in humans, is not understood fully in terms of the ways in which it contributes to memory. There is no doubt that because it is triggered by chemical reaction, it can induce memories that are often very personal, vivid and even poignant. The decontextualizing of smells from an historical period and placement in a twentieth-century tourist attraction seems highly dubious as each person visiting the centre will have a different perception or attitude towards a smell and it is quite likely that it will be very different from those held by the people who originally produced and lived with the smells. The problem is compounded by the fact that one begins to wonder if Victorian streets, Medieval universities, Viking villages and World War II London, were all steeped in the same obviously artificial chemical-odour version of wet cats. Again, it is the homogeneity of form which contributes to the denial of difference in the past.

Smell is not the ultimate experience for the heritage sensation seeker. In June 1985, the 'Wheels' display at the National Motor Museum, Beaulieu, opened. This display has been described as 'a production typifying the "showman's" approach of many of today's commercially minded independent museums' (Heritage Interpretation 1985b). The display is concerned with the history of the motor car. The slogan of 'Wheels' is, 'Live the legend of the motor car'. Time cars take the visitor round some 20 display scenes. The displays employ sight, sound, smell, and *temperature* to 'heighten the sensations'. One display that is possibly planned for Beaulieu, would involve 'a facility representing the internal combustion engine in which visitors would be asked to imagine they are the fuel and travel around the workings of a giant engine' (Tait 1989: 41). At the other end of the heritage temperature trail is a possible trip into Scott's antarctic, which will be recreated in a deep-freeze store in Dundee.

Before long some heritage centres, and museums, may be filled with gimmicks, media of spectacle which will engulf the educational message. 'Everything looks real, and therefore it is real; in any case the fact that it seems real is real, and the thing is real even if, like Alice in Wonderland, it never existed' (Eco 1986: 16). If that which is represented is not a fake, we admire it for its antiquity and aura, while the fake or the recreation, if recognized as such, is admired as a technical achievement, a testimony to the advance of instrumental rationality and progress, and our ability to recreate that which is more real than the real thing (ibid.: 43–8). This artificial image, in my mind, is best symbolized by the use of the hologram. The holographic image of an Anglo-Saxon helmet at York is the post-modern condition at its most dire. The object is an unreal projection, a product of ultra-modern technology, fascinating to most people not because it is an Anglo-Saxon helmet, or rather the image of one, but because it is a hologram. In fact for a while some people could not even see the hologram, as the lasers were set in such a way that many small children could not distinguish the image. For some people even the gimmicky signifier didn't exist, let alone the referent itself.

All of this illustrates how interpretation centres might be seen as merely attempting to titillate the senses and develop the simulacrum. Thus the dialectic between reality and fantasy is threatened by the post-modern representation; the post-modern past is one where anything is possible, where fantasy is potentially as real as history because history as heritage dulls our ability to appreciate the development of people and places through time. Ultimately, we may be sentenced to life in fantasy space, a post-modern past, which is already articulated in the medium of 'Dungeons and Dragons', a game that cuts and mixes a science-fiction fantasy future with the characteristics of a misplaced and unknown past. Recent research in the Department of Archaeology, University of Leicester, has revealed that 15–16 per cent of UCCA candidates applying to read archaeology in this department indicated that they have an interest in Dungeons and Dragons (Lomas, pers. comm.). This is especially worrying if people who have an academic interest in archaeology are supporting and perpetuating a phenomenon which promotes the perversion of history. This is clearly the commodification of something out of nothing, the logic of the free market taken to its extreme. Reality is discarded, and the mystical Arthurian pseudo-history endorsed.

The previous chapter was concerned with the contention that heritage conservation emphasized the preservation of shallow images of the nation's 'organic' tradition, and was therefore a necessarily political or hegemonic strategy. This chapter, in contrast, has endeavoured to illustrate the development of heritage representations which have concentrated on the depiction of the past through spectacular multi-media presentations with an emphasis on image rather than historical or archaeological information, let alone historical critique.

Such representations are also an important hegemonic tool: to be bland and uncritical *is* to take a political position. An uncritical depiction of the *status quo* is undoubtedly a tacit endorsement of current political strategies. Royal Britain was, and Royalty and Empire at Windsor and The Oxford Story, are, examples of such representations.

It would appear that the imperative to shop, now recognized as the most popular leisure activity in the country, is one that has always been with us. This is hardly the case. The emphasis on reconstructed streets, especially shops, merely goes to show how perceptions of the present constitute certain groups' perceptions of the past. The representation of shopping in our past merely serves to reinforce the (post-)modern emphasis on consumption today. As Corner and Harvey observe, 'the spirit of heritage offers reassurance of continuity with a shared past' (Corner and Harvey 1991: 72). These two writers also believe that together, the spirit of heritage and enterprise during the 1980s were 'inter-connected as related elements of Thatcherite reconstruction' (ibid.: 1). The heritage served to legitimate certain ideas of organic continuity, ideas which were necessary during a period of radical economic and political restructuring. The visitor to the reconstructed shop is intended to depart feeling that they are maintaining a great historical tradition, that of going out to the shops, and contributing to the enterprise culture.

This confusion is exacerbated by the development of post-modern shopping precincts or malls. Here our actual daily consumption occurs within yet another reconstructed environment, which is also articulated through the quotation of contextless historical styles; the world is a heritage centre, and we are all shoppers within it. In Disneyland's Main Street, 'the façades are presented to us as toy houses and invite us to enter them, but the interior is always a disguised supermarket, where you buy obsessively, believing that you are still playing' (Eco 1986: 43). The heritage representation, more so than the orthodox museum display, condones the feeling that we can 'stand back' from the past and observe it. It is heritage presentations, such as Jorvik and Beamish, which attempt to promote an idea of the past as 'another country', somewhere to travel to and from, a place which is distinct and separate from the present. The *processes* of history are relegated or even forgotten. This effect is intensified in Jorvik where the archaeologist as scientist, the white-coated expert, is considered to give scientific legitimation to the recreation: it must be the 'real thing', we've measured it (Shanks and Tilley 1987: 86–90). This should be seen in the context of twelve years of Thatcherism, with its emphasis on doers rather than thinkers (see chapter three). The exact reproduction of the material surfaces of the past has become more important than the interpretation, discussion and understanding of human societies. The public's ability to differentiate between truth and falsity, or even conservative truths, must be questioned, as the role of the expert, or intellectual, is marginalized under Neo-Conservative regimes. The public are not assumed to be stupid, but they are 'being invited to relinquish the right in the verifiability of public truths per se' (Hebdige 1989: 51).

6 | *Heritage reconsidered*

The expansion of heritage during the late 1970s and 1980s was not just a response to a perceived need for the past during a period when the rigours of (post-)modern life eroded a sense of history or rootedness. It should also be considered as a product of the expansion of the wider leisure and tourism services sector, and an articulation of a service-class culture. This is not to argue for a form of economic determinism, but rather to consider that the undeniable need for some kind of relationship with the past has been satisfied in only a very limited way by those who control heritage and museums through a service-oriented commercial philosophy.

The development of heritage, indeed, any immaterial commodity, and many material commodities, are not direct responses to a need or want articulated by the society in which the commodity develops, but rather, such commodity consumption is in part an artificial desire imposed on society by capital, which must perpetuate its existence and expansion through the provision of superfluous consumables. Today such production has arrived at a position where capital can only expand through the development of commodities with ever decreasing half-lives. Fashions change with increased regularity, computer software and hardware are almost out of date the day after one buys them. This process has increased to the point where it is only images and surfaces which can be altered with an adequate expedition that satisfies capital's need to expand. It is easier to put a new label on a product or alter its colour, than it is to design an entirely new commodity. It is the most pernicious claim that the market provides what people want. The market defines the parameters of a range of commodities from which people can make choices. It should never be forgotten that it is anathema for capital to consider making a loss, unless it is potentially beneficial in the longer term. As far as the processes of capital accumulation go, it is the modernist means/ends, instrumental rationality, with the concurrent emphasis on progress, which dominates the experiences of (post-)modernity. To shop is not to make an oppositional political statement, as those who promote a kind of 'Face/ism Today' mentality might argue. Consumption of market commodities is merely the tacit endorsement of capital accumulation, an endorsement which is admittedly difficult to avoid. Whilst today, capital is, and will remain, the dominant mode of political economy, it is the ideology of progress, and unfettered accumulation which must be challenged.

The conditions of modernity and post-modernity, are modes of experience dominated by time–space compression, and an erosion of a sense of place. However, the daily experience of the majority of people has not been one constructed through a series of unambiguous ruptures or revolutions. I do not believe that anyone has ever awoken in the morning, and felt that today was the dawning of a post-modern age, and subsequently experienced a new imperative to shop. As considered in chapters two and three, the emergence of a service class, and a so-called 'post-material' world, are not radically new developments, but are in fact a part of the wider transformations of capital which have taken place since the nineteenth century. The experiences with which we are concerned do have their roots in earlier centuries, but there is no doubt that the most remarkable intensification of these experiences has occurred during the last forty to fifty years.

Leisure tourism

> One of the major trends in tourism this decade has been a move away from the traditional elements of tourism – scenery, sun, two weeks a year – towards urban, heritage-based short-break tourism. This trend has brought tourism into the forefront of regeneration and job-creation projects.
>
> (Tibbott 1987)

One sector of the service economy which has undoubtedly expanded with great intensity since World War II is the leisure/tourism sector. Thus the expansion of heritage is part of a much wider, historical expansion of all forms of leisure and tourism services. Of the tourist sites open in 1983, half had been opened in the previous fifteen years. In 1960 there were only 800 tourist sites, but by 1983 there were 2,300 (Urry 1990: 5). Between 1965 and 1985 there was a 60 per cent increase in the total of passenger mileage within Britain, but the increase in tourism activity is a global phenomenon, with world-wide tourism expanding at a rate of 5–6 per cent per annum, and tourism probably becoming the greatest source of employment by the year 2000 (ibid.: 5).

The Representation of the Past

Urry asserts that tourism is founded on the idea of a '"departure", of a limited breaking with the established routines and practices of everyday life and allowing one's senses to engage with a set of stimuli that contrast with the everyday and the mundane' (ibid.: 2). Being a tourist, argues Urry, is a part of being 'modern'. It is the notion of departure or change which is the most important. But the anticipation of such a departure is in part constructed by a multiplicity of other media, most importantly film and television. It would seem, in part, that the heritage industry is reacting to this anticipation through the construction of media which are equivalent to the televisual image, except the heritage media offer the chance to gaze upon the historical set for 'real'.

The history of mass tourism goes back about 150 years, although there were forms of tourism which pre-date this. Such a pastime was of course far more restricted than it is now. The history of tourism and leisure has been one that, in part, has been concerned with

> serving the very phenomenon it sought to denounce and escape, for the tourist industry well knows how to exploit our yearning to get off the beaten track and rediscover genuine travel, just as it well knows how to exploit our cosy, simplified view of the good old days in promoting unspoilt inns, medieval banquets, town criers, Tudorbethan teashops and all the more significant monuments now blandly classed as 'heritage'.
>
> (Ousby 1990: 7)

Tourism is an integral part of (post-)modern time–space compression and the machinations of capital. The 'shrinking' of the world, and the concomitant expansion in communication and travel networks, laid the foundations for yet another new industry, the tourism industry. Tourism was never really confined to travel in just one's own country. The Grand Tour was an early form of international tourism: 'between 1600 and 1800, treatises on travel shifted from a scholastic emphasis on touring as an opportunity for discourse, to travel as eyewitness observation' (Urry 1990: 4).

In the mid-seventeenth century, Arab bloodstock was introduced into British horse breeds. This, along with the steel coach-spring, and improving road conditions, facilitated increased access to places, which but a few decades earlier would have seemed inaccessible to many people (Ousby 1990: 10). Certain places, often those associated with the famous, emerged as tourist attractions, most notably, Stratford-upon-Avon, which by the latter half of the eighteenth century was 'more firmly established, more prominently marked on the traveller's map of England than ever before' (ibid.: 44). By the middle of the nineteenth century, Shakespeare's birthplace was receiving about 3,000 visitors a year; by 1900 this figure had risen to 30,000. In 1989 it received 571,000 visitors, and there were about another half a million visitors to the other sites in Stratford.

Country-house visiting also has its roots in the eighteenth century. In Daniel Paterson's *Roads*, a guidebook published in 1771, the strip maps contained therein noted the names and owners of country houses: 'Blenheim, Castle Howard, Chatsworth, Wilton and Burghley: all these established their reputation with visitors in the early decades of the eighteenth century' (ibid.: 69–71). The attraction of such houses was their size and cost. Then as today, the visit to the country house was founded on the auratic gaze, the appreciation and reverence of power articulated through the display of conspicuous inheritance, which in turn legitimated its foundation in tradition. By the end of the eighteenth century, country-house visiting was becoming increasingly popular.

It was Thomas Cook, a native of Leicester, who opened up travel for wider consumption during the nineteenth century. The first excursion organized by Cook was a trip to a Temperance meeting at Loughborough in 1841. During the 1840s and 1850s, he organized visits for hundreds of people to the country houses of Leicestershire. However, many country-house owners were not terribly disposed to this new development, largely as they had not come to terms with the social changes that were taking place during the nineteenth century.

It was during this period that railway travel was made more widely available. Gladstone's Railway Act ensured that railway companies made provisions for working-class travel. By 1850, over 200,000 travellers from Manchester took a trip to the coast by train during Whit week (Urry 1990: 21).

The commercialization of Stonehenge is no new thing either. By 1739, visitors to the ruins enjoyed the services of a refreshment stall of some description (Ousby 1990: 96). In 1901, 3,770 people visited Stonehenge, but by the 1920s this figure had risen to about 20,000. By the end of the 1980s about 680,000 people were visiting Stonehenge every year.

Whereas during the eighteenth and the early nineteenth centuries 'Ruins were admired as witnesses to the triumph of time and nature over man's [sic] handiwork' (ibid.: 126), today they would seem to represent a celebration of humankind's ability to preserve, and fast-freeze history, and then, put it to work in a new environment which also denies the importance of historic contexts, that of the market-place.

Early tourists were as impressed in the eighteenth century as some are today, with what might be described as a 'heritage experience'. Many visitors to the Lake District would procure the services of a servant, who would load a cannon with half a pound of gunpowder, and discharge the same. The consequent simulated thunder 'could stun the senses with nine different echoes'. A visual simulacrum could be produced by the spectator standing with their back to a scene and viewing it in a convex mirror. Desired lighting effects could complement this experience through the use of coloured background foils (ibid.: 151–5).

Leisure tourism then, was founded during the modern period. Closely tied to the processes of industrialization and urbanization, the constituency of those able to participate in such consumption continued to expand. The greatest expansion probably occurred during the decades either side of World War II.

During the inter-war period, after the railways had originally opened up some areas of the countryside to people during the nineteenth century, the advent of the affordable motor-car meant that for many, the country-side now became even more accessible. During the pre-World War I period, many rambling and cycling clubs were established. The bicycle gave freedom to many thousands of people towards the end of the nineteenth century. The Cyclists' Touring Club which had 3,356 members in 1880, had 60,449 by the turn of the century. It is estimated that by around 1900 there were 10 million bicycles in Britain (Tomlinson and Walker 1990: 231).

It is probably at this time that the idea of the rural idyll was widely popularized. Rambling clubs had their roots amongst the professional middle classes of the nineteenth century: 'These outdoor pursuits, with roots in academia, included a self-improving dimension, emphasizing an interest in the botany, geology, archaeology and history of the districts visited' (ibid.: 228). For the middle classes, self-improvement was a requirement of any leisure activity. It is apparent that visiting museums would have been an important pastime for many members of the middle classes.

'Holidays With Pay' legislation passed in 1938, along with a reduced working week and, for most people, a rise in their standard of living, meant that the potential for leisure markets had never been greater. By the eve of World War II, 4 million manual workers, and another 4 million non-manual workers, were receiving annual holiday pay. This constituted about half of the entire working population in Britain.

The expansion of leisure services has thus been a product of a number of factors, including the improvement in transport and communications, and an increase in the disposable incomes of a large sector of society. This sector, which can satisfy its needs or desires for material goods, can now make demands for 'immaterial' or luxury services. The heritage boom, from the heritage trinkets sold by companies such as Past Times, to heritage magazines, membership of organizations such as the National Trust and English Heritage, and the visiting of heritage centres, is part and parcel of a burgeoning service industry. A recent report indicates that this boom is likely to continue well into the 1990s, with spending on leisure increasing by 10.9 per cent per year until 1992, and then by 8.7 per cent until 1995 (Dane 1990: 3).

Between 1980 and 1988 there was an increase of 176 per cent in consumer spending on cultural goods and services. This does not, however, reflect just an increase in uptake. It partly reveals the increase in charges levied by the suppliers of such services (Feist and Hutchison 1990b: 2). The available data do indicate, however, that there has been an increase in consumption of leisure services. In 1980 0.87 per cent of *all* consumer expenditure was spent on such services. This steadily increased over the decade to a level of 1.14 per cent in 1988.

Heritage leisure

Most people in the First World today are more affluent and have more disposable income, and the leisure time in which to spend it, than ever before. At the same time, however, relative poverty is increasing. In Britain, actual unemployment figures are hard to obtain, as the Government has tampered with them some thirty odd times since it first came to power in 1979. The same is true of all statistics relating to poverty and deprivation in Britain during the 1980s, and into the 1990s.

This increase in disposable income has necessitated changes in patterns of consumption and production. Some have argued that there has been a shift from Fordist modes of mass consumption towards 'post-Fordist' 'individuated patterns of consumption' (Urry 1990: 13). This emphasis on individual or 'unique' consumption is part of the wider assertion of the New Right, that the individual can experience new forms of emancipation through the market.

'Post-tourism' is supposedly a move away from old-style Fordist holiday-making, symbolized by the holiday camp, which was successful through its mass repetition and standardization of production across the board. One Butlins was essentially no different from any other.

Today, the 'post-tourist' expects something tailored to their own individual needs or wants. At one level, the tourist experience is always unique to the individual as the context of reception is always potentially unique. However, what in fact has happened, most obviously in the context of heritage leisure, is a form of surface-style inflation. As with nearly all modern forms of consumption, the emphasis during the 1980s and into the 1990s was on the manipulation of image. The products themselves are not radically different, it is only their marketing surfaces which have been '(post-)modernized'.

Heritage centres and theme-parks cover the whole of the First World. Wild West themes can be experienced not only in the US and Britain, but also in Bobbejannland, Belgium, and Phantasialand in Germany. In Europa Park, Germany, a British theme, 'Victoria Square', was opened at the end of the 1980s.

The heritage 'trip' is common throughout Europe and the US. In Paris, the tourist can visit the Parc Oceanique Cousteau, where technology can create the illusion of an undersea experience. The post-modern timeless, ahistoric fantasy is represented at Parc Asterix, where the famous Gaulish cartoon hero and his friends are now part of the service sector. In the same park, the tourist can visit reconstructed streets from the Dark Ages through to the French Revolution. 'Tourism is prefiguratively post-modern because of its particular combination of the visual, the aesthetic, and the popular' (ibid.: 87).

In Britain, tourism and the heritage are officially recognized as being crucial to the country's economic success. The minister with special responsibility for tourism, in 1988, said,

> Hopefully the British public will increasingly appreciate that holiday taking in the United Kingdom is not only a stimulating and enjoyable experience but will help our balance of payments as well. Any potential visitors from overseas should realise that there can be few countries in the world offering such a range of heritage, countryside, resorts, sporting and cultural opportunities and attractions (in England 30 per cent of our existing visitor attractions have been opened since 1980, 60 per cent since 1970).
>
> (Lee quoted in Urry 1990: 51)

Part and parcel of the leisure services boom has been the expansion of museums. According to the findings of the Museums Database Project (which did not achieve a full response rate), three-quarters of museums replying to the survey had been established since World War II, and half had been established since 1971. The findings revealed that nearly half of museums in the UK are private/independent museums, and that it is this sector that has witnessed most of the recent growth.

The growth in supply was a response to a growth in demand, but it has been shown that supply by the 1990s had outstripped demand, certainly in the UK (see Middleton 1990). Between 1982 and 1988 there was an increase of 22 per cent in visits to historic properties. There were 59 million visits to museums and galleries and visiting historic buildings was, according to The General Household Survey of 1986, the most popular 'out-of-home' leisure activity apart from walking two miles or more (Hanna 1989: 5).

Visitor trends

Between 1976 and 1989 visitors to English attractions rose by 31 per cent. This percentage increase was constituted in part by a 55 per cent increase in the south-east of England, and a 40 per cent increase in the Heart of England. However, visits to London were only 4 per cent higher and this in part reveals a trend which was certainly a development of the late 1980s. As the more popular attractions were swamped by tourists, many people wanted to visit something new and smaller; less well-known sites increased in popularity. For example, Toad Hole Cottage, an eel catcher's house in Norfolk, saw an increase in visitors of over 90 per cent between 1988 and 1989. This increase was just eclipsed by Ashridge Monument in Hertfordshire, which saw an increase of 95 per cent in visitor numbers over the same period. During that same year expenditure on such services increased by 14 per cent (Leisure News 1990b).

The heritage and museums are undoubtedly a crucial part of the wider attraction of Britain for overseas visitors. But also heritage and museum visiting is an important leisure activity for a substantial proportion of the British public. The most extensive and useful survey carried out on people's attitudes towards the past, and their visiting preferences during the 1980s, was carried out by Nick Merriman for his Ph.D. He was concerned to consider British people's attitudes to museums, heritage and the past in general (Merriman 1991).

Merriman and cultural capital

Merriman's work is closely informed by the work of French sociologist, Pierre Bourdieu, whose research on French society and culture is probably some of the most useful and interesting work done by any European sociologist. Bourdieu's underlying thesis is that people, in order to appreciate or understand certain forms of cultural production, must have experienced certain forms of socialization, that is, a familial upbringing and education, that has endowed them with the 'cultural competence' necessary to recognize such productions. 'A work of art has meaning and interest only for someone who possesses the cultural competence, that is, the code, into which it is encoded' (Bourdieu 1984: 2). The argument is developed; the consumption of cultural productions is considered to be a form of conspicuous consumption, an activity which acts as a badge of distinction: 'art and cultural consumption are predisposed, consciously and deliberately or not, to fulfil a social function of legitimating social differences' (ibid.: 7). One's 'cultural capital', a form of distinguishing kudos, is articulated through the consumption of cultural products; it thus goes through a process of incrementation with each product consumed. This process of cultural capital investment, serves to distinguish the individual from one social group, whilst at the same time developing an image of association with another group, usually one perceived as being elevated from that which the individual is attempting to remove themselves. 'Taste'

> unites all those who are the product of similar conditions while distinguishing them from all others. And it distinguishes in an essential way, since taste is the basis of all that one has – people and things – and all that one is for others, whereby one classifies oneself and is classified by others.
>
> (ibid.: 56)

Merriman's survey supports Bourdieu's thesis, in that it is apparent that those who visit museums and country houses most frequently, do tend to come from the higher-status groups, and have either stayed on at school or have had a tertiary education (Merriman 1989: 152). This assessment is supported by the finding that, while only 8 per cent of frequent visitors felt that there was too much text in museum displays, 27 per cent of rare visitors, and 40 per cent of non-visitors felt the same way. This implies that it is those regular visitors who tend to come from the higher-status and 'better-educated' groups, who possess the cultural competence required to 'read' a museum display, or are better used to getting information from text.

Visiting patterns for historic buildings, castles etc. are similar to those for museums. However, structural factors, such as possessing a car, do have an effect and those of high status are therefore most likely to visit this kind of heritage attraction.

Those who visit museums, and other heritage attractions, are also more likely to attend theatre productions, concerts, ballet, and opera (English

Heritage in fact promotes a series of open-air concerts each summer in the south-east of England). Of this group 74 per cent are likely to go to the theatre at least once a year, 38 per cent are likely to go to classical concerts, and 18 per cent are likely to go to the ballet. This type of pattern is repeated in France and in Canada (ibid.: 159).

Merriman argues that museums 'divide the population into those who possess the "culture" or "competence" to perceive them as a leisure opportunity and make sense of a visit and those who do not' (Merriman 1988a: 219). Also, 'Museum visiting has in fact more to do with status affirmation in the present than it has to do with the past' (ibid.: 299).

Museum visiting may be used by people with a new-found status to legitimate their position in a new group. Merriman argues that museums are ideal places to accumulate cultural capital as they have increased in number and are relatively 'open'. 'It is possible that more and more people are taking up museum visiting as part of a lifestyle that is appropriate to their changed status' (ibid.: 222). This is commonly referred to as the 'embourgeoisement thesis'. It is the actual demonstration of visiting such places, and associating with groups of people who share a broadly common set of aspirations and attitudes, which is as important in some ways as the actual learning experience itself (ibid.: 289).

During the late twentieth century most First World nations witnessed the development of a dramatically expanded service-class culture. In Britain this development was particularly obvious. The recent expansion of heritage and museum services must be considered as an integral part of the restructured economy, and its service class.

Service-class culture

A number of researchers have identified the emergence of what can be labelled a service-class culture (for example, see Thrift 1989). This new class of people, as their label suggests, tends to be employed in the service sector. They, along with other groups which, in a post-material First World where most life-sustaining wants have been satisfied, can afford to increase their consumption of leisure services, and thus develop a new group identity through the incrementation of their cultural capital. There is no doubt that the consumption of heritage, in both its traditional conservative form and the post-modern 'experience' genre, has gone some way to satisfy the cultural demands made by this recently expanded group. For example, membership of the National Trust between 1971 and 1990 increased from 278,000 to over 2 million, an increase of nearly

720 per cent. Meanwhile, visits to National Trust properties increased by 60 per cent between 1975 and 1988.

Crucial to the success of traditional heritage, country-house visiting, and the wider consumption of images of rurality, has been the promotion by such organizations of an 'imagined community', especially that of the nation which is ideally represented by the English village and the country house. Such images have been successfully reinforced by television programmes, most notably in recent years by *All Creatures Great and Small* and *Brideshead Revisited*.

The new service class has developed its cultural capital through the 'traditionally English' method of 'integration through participation'. Here the members of a new, and potentially powerful constituency, are allowed part-way into the establishment fold. They have been given access to the *images* of traditional power, most notably, the country house.

Ousby argues that the opening of country houses to the general public was originally a part of a much wider benevolent process of democratization: 'The opening of the country house, in fact, is one aspect of that larger opening of the élite which has helped England over some of the trickiest stiles in its social and political history' (Ousby 1990: 91). The implication is here that access to the consumption of images of traditional power constitutes actual entrance into the ruling-class fold. This is of course questionable, especially as democratic access to capital and land has been continually denied to the majority of people.

Circulation of rural, or heritage, magazines, such as *The Field*, has increased dramatically (see chapter four, and Thrift 1989). There is no doubt that the most successful forms of heritage are often those which manage to combine the rural and the historic experience, symbolized today by the increasing attendance at historic gardens. In fact gardens have only recently been recognized as part of the official heritage and one of the provisions of the 1983 National Heritage Act empowered English Heritage to compile a register of gardens. By 1988 1,085 gardens and parks had been listed.

The attraction of the rural idyll is represented most clearly with the fusion of ecological and historic heritages in magazines such as *This England* and *Great Britain, The Conservation of Our Heritage*. These forms of media undeniably contribute to the construction of an idealized mythological, and historically established nation, which throughout the past, if it existed at all, existed only for a wealthy minority. There is no doubt that all societies, or nations, aim to reproduce a collective memory, which is founded on an idea of age-old *organic* traditions. This tradition demands that history is placed in a past-pluperfect, and is therefore, beyond question. In certain societies, the (re)production of such an image is achieved through force, such as in South Africa, but in most capitalist countries,

> reproduction can be accomplished through the *consent* of the
> dominated, by convincing the majority to identify and support the
> present system of rewards and power rather than opposing it, in fact
> to live their own domination as freedom. In this the media are vital
> institutions that far from providing a free marketplace of ideas work
> to legitimate the existing distribution of power by controlling the
> context within which people think and define social problems and
> their possible solutions.
>
> (Jhally 1989: 67)

There is evidence to show that the yearning for the rural idyll is mani-festing itself through the 'urban–rural push', as the service class attempts to transform its yearnings for rural stability through the buying up of property in the countryside (Thrift 1989: 34). The condition of (post-) modernity not only gave rise to a need for a rootedness in the past, but also to a need for roots in the countryside:

> The technology of the railway created the myth of a green pasture
> world of innocence. It satisfied man's desire to withdraw from society,
> symbolized by the city, to a rural setting where he could recover his
> animal and natural self. It was the pastoral ideal, a Jeffersonian world,
> an agrarian democracy which was intended to serve as a guide to
> social policy. It gave us darkest suburbia and its lasting symbol: the
> lawnmower.
>
> (McLuhan, Fiore and Agel 1967: 72)

The service-class culture which emerged during the 1980s participated in modes of consumption which enhanced their movement away from dull inconspicuous forms of consumption, towards a consumption of signs which many saw as being signs of difference and distinction. Often, these were signs of a better life-style, a life-style which usually could never be fully participated in, but one which could be mimicked through the consumption of simulacra. Despite this increase in consumption, the fundamental class boundaries still remained intact.

Mass culture, hegemony, and the commodification of pasts

The consumption of certain heritage or museum products serves to enhance the identity and cultural capital of individuals and groups. The

1980s and 1990s have witnessed an expansion in this form of consumption as the economy has been 'restructured', and new class constituencies have emerged. The provision of such cultural services has not been designed to enhance or highlight differences within societies, or to promote a critique and questioning of representations of the past. Such cultural productions have largely been bland; most cases have successfully denied difference, and have presented the history of the nation as one which is continuous, exemplary, and without discord. Such a heritage is endorsed through the promotion of a homogeneous communal identity which is in itself little different from an unquestioning corporate identity based on tradition.

Such heritage 'corporate identities' have been reinforced through a marketing strategy which provides a context of meaning for its commodities. Historic buildings and ancient monuments are situated within a unified marketing context, through the use of a corporate identity, symbolized, for example, by the English Heritage logo, or the National Trust oak leaves, which appear on signposts, advertising leaflets, and even the telephones, in English Heritage offices. Such organizations provide an identity which in many ways seems to be more important than the historical resource which they market.

'The function of Advertising is to refill the emptied commodity with meaning. Indeed the meaning of advertising would make no sense if objects already had an established meaning' (Jhally 1989: 221). This is not to say that historic buildings, for example, do not have their own meanings for people, but rather, that through an intensive marketing policy, aimed at persuading large numbers of people to travel and visit as many properties as possible, visitors may become blind to the individuality of each property and monument, and 'doing' such and such a castle, or country house, each weekend, becomes akin to going shopping, where each property visited is ticked off on the heritage shopping list. The corporate image of the organization may begin to swamp the differences or individuality of each monument. Membership of such an organization may become important, not because people have an interest in the past, but because it promotes a group identity, which in Britain, is essentially southern English, white, and middle class.

The denial of difference through the control of a large group of buildings and monuments by just two or three organizations is essentially anti-democratic. Despite the fact that organizations such as English Heritage and the National Trust call upon a number of different 'experts' to advise on the interpretation and presentation of some monuments, it is still the organization which decides who shall be consulted, and whether or not the advice should be accepted (take for example the National Trust's attitude towards the membership's concern over hunting). The myth of objectivity is necessary to such an organization's continued survival. The organization must purport to be representing the past as it was. As soon as the myth of objectivity becomes exposed, then the reputation of the organization would be irrevocably damaged in the eyes of those who believe that the 'truth' is representable *per se*.

Thus, as a corporate resource, heritage represents an ideology which is opposed to the idea of public service. For example, from 1979 to 1988 there was a total increase of 8 per cent in the number of visitors to historic buildings while (at constant prices) there was an increase of 57 per cent in revenue. We are told that this was largely due to an increase of 158 per cent in admission charges, while inflation rose by only 79 per cent during that period. The concept of public service is one that has consistently been attacked by monetarist and supply-side politicians. Even local authorities have been forced to follow this pricing trend. Admission charges to historic buildings have risen at a rate well above the rate of inflation. Taking 1984 as a starting index value of 100, the price indices in 1989 stood at the following figures: Government properties (English Heritage incl.), 210; Local Authority properties, 178; National Trust, 151; private properties, 158. The retail price index in 1989 stood at 128 (Hanna 1989: 28).

Heritage organizations have no qualms in seeing their historical resources as a product to be marketed. Their target is the members of the ABC1 socio-economic groups. Such organizations judge success, not through examinations of how the public perceives or develops an understanding of the past, but by purely financial criteria. The columns of documents detailing performance of a site are headed with the labels 'Total Retail Sales', 'Target Income Achieved', 'Average Spend Per Head' (English Heritage Spread Sheet 1990). There seem to be only restricted attempts at assessing the educational quality or academic credibility of historic representations.

Success in a market, which is perceived as the natural benign context within which all human activity occurs, is complicit with a belief that the representation of the past is a practice devoid of politics. The belief in objectivity and the denial of political content in interpretation is echoed by Rumble, the ex-Chief Executive of English Heritage: 'We ought to be seeking a passionate detachment from the past, passionate in the story it tells, and passionate in the intention to preserve objectivity in the telling of what may be an intensely subjective story' (Rumble 1989: 31).

There is in this statement again the implicit desire to see the past as that which is completed, as something which has occurred previous to the emergence of our society. It is this understanding of the past which permits its easy reification and mediation into a set of consumption choices.

For many people it is the ability to consume which permits them to develop and articulate their sense of freedom, especially in societies where the market is promoted as a benign democratic mechanism:

> The effect of such a trend upon collective consciousness and cultural relations in particular societies can not be understated. Popular culture and everyday life have always been of great concern to our political and economic masters. If popular culture can be reduced to a set of apparent choices based upon personal taste then we will see the triumph of the fragmented self, a constant lust for the new and the authentic among a population of consumer clones.
>
> (Tomlinson 1990: 6)

This book has shown that the past, most notably when it is articulated as 'our heritage', is another element within an expanding realm of flexible capital. However, it should not be assumed that there is a mass society which reads/produces and consumes heritage as a duped homogeneous collective. There is no doubt that the media, and the modes, through which the past is represented are developing as an homogeneous form, which is essentially anti-democratic. Choice is based on the market offering a limited set of surface images which all share a sense of depthlessness. Consequently, there is a danger that difference will be destroyed, as well as an awareness of place, and community identities. It should be accepted that the representation of the past has been, and always will be, political and therefore ideological. It is ideological because it is an increasingly important element in the workings of flexible accumulation in an expanding service sector. I also reject any belief that because people constitute themselves as individuals through their original readings and interpretations of the world, that the immediate corollary is the demise of the dominant ideology, or the attempt to construct a dominant ideology.

Hegemony and ideology

Merriman has contended that the results of his survey have revealed the inadequacy of the 'ideology critique' approaches to heritage and museum representations. Whilst accepting the blanket assertions which imply that all representations are a part of a wider hegemonic project, I am convinced that it is impossible for a representation not to be ideologically loaded.

Merriman's survey shows that those who hold alternative beliefs such as

'There are mysterious forces at Stonehenge' (Merriman 1988a: 262) are also keen heritage visitors, or have participated in archaeological field-work. He argues that because such visitors create their own interpret-ations, this indicates the 'redundancy of the dominant ideology thesis' (ibid.: 268). It is in fact in the interests of an hegemonic power to encourage 'alternative theses' concerning the past, as the representation and discussion of 'truths', or even controversies, in the past may not be in that power's interests.

Respondents to this survey were also asked to rank what type of history they considered to be of most importance to them. In the following summary of the results, the lower the number, the closer that opinion is to the specified group.

High Status	Middle Status	Low Status
1. British History	1. British History	1. Family History
2. World History	2. Family History/ Local History	2. British History
3. History of Homeland		3. Local History
4. Local History	4. History of Homeland	4. History of Homeland
5. Family History	5. World History	5. World History
		(ibid.: 286)

Merriman argues that the fact that the 'dominated' (low-status) class do not rank British History first reveals their non-conformity to dominant values. It could be argued that the study and discussion of British History is the last thing the ruling classes want the working classes to get involved in. Consequently, it might be seen that this lack of interest is a good thing for the existing hegemony. However, the fact that the 'dominant' classes place British History first in the table shows that the dominant ideology has been successful in controlling the classes that potentially threaten vested interest more than any other group. This is especially true when we consider the types of heritage that are presented, and the type of history that is dominant in education, that of 'chaps and maps'.

Merriman also asserts that Althusserian interpretations of museum dis-plays are 'flawed from the outset because surveys show that "the domi-nated" (those of low status, the less-well-off elderly, the unemployed) tend not to go to them' (ibid.: 293). The argument is that these theses have failed to consider the role of the reinterpreting individual, or those who reject the established didactic narrative. This is equivalent to a kind of extreme relativism, not terribly removed from the radical individualism of Thatcherism. The 'produced' interpretation does in fact have legit-imacy and validity in the eyes of the majority of visitors who read the interpretations provided. Merriman's survey actually shows that many 'high-status' regular visitors are more concerned with shallow aesthetics, and far from entering into their own reinterpretation of an object, are satisfied with the 'produced' interpretation.

A lot of Merriman's analysis regarding museums and heritage as tools of ideology and hegemony implies a belief that such displays are in fact provocative and trenchant in their analyses of the past. The fact is that many (post-)modern representations of the past are largely superficial and uncontentious, and do not really invite people to ask the questions about life and human progress that Merriman has asked them.

As far as the Right is concerned, it is perhaps this superficial non-history that is the greatest ideological strength of museums and interpretation centres. The ideological messages are not 'in the displays' as it were, but are an inherent part of a much wider socio-political construct. The presentation of the past in this context, does not need to support or criticize society explicitly, but rather, reassure tacitly with what is often perceived as an apolitical stance. The dominated, by the very definition that Merriman has employed, are economically dominated, and therefore their subjection to the ideological mechanisms designed to promote or sustain an hegemony is not necessary. However, the 'dominant' middle classes, who possess greater economic power, and potentially pose a more direct threat to ruling-class power, need to be incorporated into the dominant hegemony, through a subjection to the ideology of heritage and service consumption. This form of consumption is now so all-pervasive in many (post-)modern societies, that it is almost impossible not to be involved in some kind of continuous program of heritage consumption. Heritage now penetrates so much space in the First World, that any consideration of how the past is represented is almost pointless without an awareness of the fact that so much of the built environment is now overwhelmed by heritage quotations.

Merriman is clear that museums are contributing to a division in society, between those who possess the 'cultural capital', and therefore, visit museums, and those who do not possess such capital, and do not go to museums. He asserts that, 'This cultural division may be a phenomenon more divisive than traditional class divisions' (ibid.: 304), but this 'cultural division' is in my opinion a manifestation of what *are* in fact real class divisions. Admittedly the socio-economic goal-posts have moved in the last few decades, but there are still profound *relative* differences between the classes. Those who are employed in the leisure-service sector are among those who suffer the most: 'The new service society is not a professionalized utopia but also the site of the most unprotected, poorly paid and dehumanising of contemporary employment' (Crang 1990: 30).

Some heritage employees are even kept on *weekly* renewable contracts and fluctuations in the leisure market control the lifestyles of many leisure-sector employees.

The development of the service class, and its associated patterns of consumption, belies the fact that for some, First World societies are still societies established along lines of class. The restructuring of economies has merely redefined these class constituencies. This is reflected in the regional distribution of both classes and cultural services.

One might reasonably expect that as the service class is concentrated in certain regions, in Britain's case the south-east of England, this phenomenon might be reflected in the regional provision of heritage services.

In 1990, 66 per cent of visitors to English Heritage events went to spectacles that took place below the north/south divide, a line which runs from the Wash in the east, down to the Severn Estuary in the west. Of the attendances at special events 37 per cent were in the south-east region, whilst only 16 per cent were at events in the North. The most popular special event in 1990 was the recreation of the Battle of Hastings (on the south coast of England). This event was attended by almost 20,000 people, constituting over 9 per cent of all attendances at special events that year. These figures to an extent reflect the numbers of events organized in the regions. In 1989, 69 per cent of events were organized in the region below the north/south divide. In 1990 the balance was redressed. Attendances at National Trust properties were also biased to the south of England: 54 per cent of visits took place at properties below the north/south divide. This left 46 per cent of all visitors going to the properties in the Midlands, the north of England, Wales and Northern Ireland (National Trust for Scotland is a separate organization). The central statistical office shows us that such imbalances are to be expected. Consumer spending in the South-east in 1979 was 13 per cent above the national average, by 1986 it was 20 per cent above the national average. In the North, spending per head in 1979 was 94 per cent of the national average, by 1986 it had fallen to 89 per cent (Pond 1989: 49).

The regional biases in heritage consumption figures must contain some inaccuracies as there will be some sort of levelling out of the figures, caused by tourists who can consume anywhere in the country. The north/south imbalance will certainly continue, especially in terms of the provision of leisure services. The Channel Tunnel Link will provide leisure opportunities in both directions, with continental tourists gaining access to the South-east, and people in the South-east gaining access to the continent, which will possibly seem all the more attractive as EuroDisney developments appear outside Paris. Also, the National Sea Centre, Nausicaa, in Boulogne, expects to attract about 800,000 visitors a year from Britain, mainly from the South-east (Leisure News 1990a).

The regional imbalance is also reflected in the proportion of buildings which are officially recognized as being a part of the heritage. In England, for example, there are only five counties which possess over 15,000 listed buildings each. They are Kent, Devon, Avon, Essex and Greater London. In 1988/9, of the 6,029 Grade I listed buildings, 39 per cent were located in just five counties. The figures were as follows: Greater London (917), Avon (679), East Sussex (274), Oxfordshire (275), and North Yorkshire (220) (Hanna 1989: 10). Although the factors of preservation of pre-modern buildings which constitute the majority of those listed are probably complex, it is unlikely that the distribution of those which have been officially listed realistically reflects the pattern of actual survival. What is likely, is that these areas with a high number of listed buildings possess the type of building which the heritage bodies prefer. Even when the density of listed buildings is calculated per 100,000 people, it is the western central area of England – Gloucestershire, Wiltshire, and Hereford/Worcestershire (a solidly conservative and rural region) – which has the highest density of such buildings in the country.

In the year 1987–8 the largest share of English Heritage grants went to the south-east region (14 per cent), next was London followed by the Heart of England. The top four counties in terms of grant receipts were as follows: London, East Sussex, Gloucestershire and Wiltshire.

These regional differences are also reflected in the distribution of local amenity groups, as well as local history and archaeological societies. Of the 915 known amenity groups in England, 60 per cent of these are in the southern regions, 141 of these in the South-east, 108 in the Heart of England and 88 in the West Country (Hanna 1989: 23). In terms of history and archaeology societies, the regional breakdown is as follows: of the known national membership during the late 1980s, Scotland had 10.4 per cent, the North had 2.51 per cent, the North-west had 1.3 per cent, Yorkshire and Humberside had 5.59 per cent, Wales had 2.51 per cent, the East Midlands 1.87 per cent, East Anglia 2.83 per cent, while the South-west had 17.76 per cent and the South-east, 50.78 per cent (Spencer, pers. comm.; after Selkirk n.d.). These figures illustrate the point that the regional imbalance in Britain regarding access to knowledge about the past is one which has been established for most of the post World War II period.

There should be no doubt that to a large extent, the provision of heritage services is *not* a public service, but is one driven by economic demands. Where heritage centres and private museums do flourish in deprived regions, they flourish not out of some benevolent desire to provide a cultural service for local residents, but rather out of a desire to cash in on the tourist trade. The provision of cultural services through the market implicitly denies an idea of public service, and therefore threatens to exaggerate the class divides that already exist, as those who have will get more, while those who have not, receive less. The heritagization of space in deprived regions is not designed to provide locals with cultural services, but rather to wallpaper over the cracks of inner city decay in an attempt to attract revenue of one sort or another.

The imagineering of space

Catastrophes are transformed into lucrative opportunities for redevelopment and renewal
(Berman 1983: 95)

The dispersal of industry and the demise of organized labour are experiences which have been common to many regions of the industrialized First World. The destruction of large areas of industry has resulted in the fragmentation and weakening of certain social and cultural constituencies. Factories, mines, and docks were not just places of employment, but were places that allowed people to communicate and develop common beliefs and cultures. This destruction of the traditional centres of communication and organization, has resulted in places losing parts of their identities. This has contributed, to a certain extent, to the possibility of cultural homogenization. Such an homogenization is enhanced by the heritagization process which many places have undergone. Such heritages are comprised of certain acceptable 'national' themes: royalty, country houses, benevolent industry, and the rural idyll, all of which have already been discussed. Each area or region has its own idiosyncratic contribution to make to the heritage, but the superficiality of much heritage denies the uniqueness and importance of each of these local histories. We are left with a series of commodities, differentiated from one another only by their surfaces. Regional identities have not in fact been destroyed, indeed there is plenty of evidence to the contrary. The *potential* for the destruction of regional identities has never been greater, however, as some argue that there is no such thing as society. This doubtless implies that there can be no such thing as the regional or even community identity.

Up until the early 1980s, regional economies in Britain were identifiable, and possessed recognizable characteristics. In Wales, the North-east and Scotland, there was coal and steel production; in the North-west, textiles; in the North, shipbuilding; in the East Midlands, clothing and footwear;

in the West Midlands, motor manufacturing and engineering. Each area was to an extent symbolized by its associated industry.

Gradually during the post-war period these regional patterns of industrial production were eroded, and this process has gone some way towards a negation of regional identities. Allen believes that although there has been a *convergence* within regions, there has in fact been a *divergence* of industry. Within these old regions, there has been a process of 'fine graining'; a greater diversity of employers has moved into a region, and thus different work-force groups have proliferated. 'Class characteristics and identities within the region may have been forged by a set of industries which are now in decline, but their influence persists and informs present-day cultural and political forms' (Allen 1988: 188).

The restructuring of places has meant that new ways of attracting capital to places have had to be developed. It is this divergence which demands careful consideration. It requires a redefinition and re-articulation of class, gender and ethnic constituencies, along with what constitutes a locality or place. It is these issues and the potential role for museums which will be considered in chapters seven and eight.

Economic restructuring has led to the increasing abstraction of the characteristics of certain spaces, the emphasis on the differences that a space possesses in terms of resources and labour force. This abstraction has become more refined and intense to the point where 'The active production of places with special qualities becomes an important stake in spatial competition between localities, cities, regions and nations' (Harvey 1989: 295). Capital can occupy these spaces as access is increased through improved communications. As spaces compete with one another, they must attempt to promote an image, an attractive marketing surface, which will lure the multinational to their particular place.

The role of heritage in this process is undeniable. Beautification, through the heritagization of space, is one of the mechanisms which can be employed to attract capital. In Britain, a number of projects in de-industrialized regions, which included garden festivals and programmes of conservation and restoration of certain elements of the built environment, attempted to attract investment into these regions. Harvey believes that such projects attempt to emphasize the difference and qualities of each place, but it should be remembered, that these differences are only plaster deep. Not to put too fine a point on it, such schemes are essentially concerned with 'tarting up' space; there is in fact very little difference between one waterfront scheme and the next.

The post-modern experience of place is one defined by eclecticism. Heritage space, especially in the urban environment, is one constituted by a mixture of misquoted styles which serve to destroy the identity of a place. 'Eclecticism is the degree zero of contemporary general culture: one listens to reggae, watches a western, eats McDonald's food for lunch and local cuisine for dinner, wears Paris perfume in Tokyo and "retro" clothes in Hong Kong; knowledge is a matter for TV games' (Lyotard 1984: 76).

Often, the heritage display, with its denial of process, and its emphasis on the synchronous spectacle, removes any idea of change through time. The spectacle represents the isolated event; we are removed from history. This social distancing is reflected in the practices of 'post-Fordist' political economies. The Fordist mode of production demanded that each person only ever work on one single constituent element of the final product, but the employees were not entirely removed from that final commodity. Today, even the manufacturing industries tend to work on a trans-national basis with various parts of a product manufactured in a number of different countries, and finally assembled in yet another country. The processes of capital have always been removed from the worker who has always been just another factor in the formula for capital's ex-pansion, but today capital lives and dies in the micro-chip. Speed of light processes, devoid of human input, affect the day-to-day machinations of multinational capital. More than ever the products of capital are alien to workers. The processes which produce contemporary commodities are more and more distant from those involved in their production. All that is ever perceived is the single static constituent part which by itself is meaningless outside of the wider context of production.

As the heritage centre or the mock battle offers a representation, which at best provides a manipulated and trivialized snapshot of one element from the past, it removes that event from the wider historical process and context, and thus it serves to promote the distancing of people from places. The heritage then, gives space an identity which is different only in terms of surfaces, spaces rather than places, as it is the heritagization of space which denies the idea of historical processes across time and space. Consequently, there is the promotion, at best, of spaces which people construct as different only through the consumption of heritage pastiche, and at worst, perceive as tourist space, points on a leisure map of the mind. Both instances, I would argue, deny the potential for coming to terms with the economic, cultural, and political processes which con-stitute places.

The Representation of the Past

The heritagization of space

'What's history if you can't bend it a bit?'

(Quoted in Schadla-Hall 1990: 2)

In some cases the heritagization of space has occurred as part of a desire to improve the tourism potential of a place which is already affluent. In others, most notably the Albert Docks in Liverpool, such a project was designed to revitalize an ailing economy.

In St Albans, England, a series of events took place during the summer of 1990 with the aim of celebrating the burning to the ground of Verulamium in AD 60. The theme was therefore 'Fire'. The central feature of this season of 'Boudica Celebrations' was the staged production of a play, *Boudica*. The festival opened with a firework display, the theme of which was *Star Wars*. Other attractions included a torchlight procession, a display of vintage fire engines, folk dancing, a Bavarian evening, and a Wild West shoot-out. The most bizarre event of the programme was the PC (personal computer) users' race. This race involved competitors running around Verulamium lake, carrying personal computers. The logo for this season of bricolage-leisure was a very benign-looking dragon, whose talents included driving a Roman chariot.

Such a series of events may appear harmless, and no doubt, the ultra-relativists would argue that we should not identify the consumers of such heritage as being a part of a mass society composed of dupes. To a point this is reasonable, but at the same time we should not consider that each consumer is really a radical individual, reading, re-reading, and interpreting in a multiplicity of ways. It is in fact very difficult for someone without prior knowledge of an historical theme, to infer from such events the processes and phenomena which historians and archaeologists attempt to articulate. The consumer cannot read that which is not offered, and if the heritage promoter is not concerned with what might reasonably be considered an accurate representation, then how is access to the past meant to be facilitated?

Pembroke Castle in Wales is another example of an attempt to heritagize space, where plans to develop a marina were proposed during the late 1980s. One part of the plan included a proposal to widen the gates to the pond, thus giving access to appropriate 'heritage vessels'. A feasibility study for Pembroke was carried out by a group of heritage consultants. They picked out the following themes: 'Kings, Queens, Princes, Earls and Lords – a Royal Palace, Famous People and Families, Maritime Heritage, Commercial and Social Developments, Ecclesiastical Heritage, Battle, Siege, Peace and Tranquillity, The Life and Times of Pembroke Castle'.

The consultants went on to comment, 'The Castle not only saw wars, such as the War of the Roses where *Cromwell himself* [my italics] camped on Golden Hill, fired cannons and laid siege to the castle, but also times of peace' (L&R 1987: Appendix H). The same report claims that the first Civil War dated from 1642–9, instead of 1642–6.

The heritage consultants' contribution to the report ends with the following: 'Pembroke has an opportunity to tell its story about the everyday happenings and the life of its citizens, as well as the more important happenings, such as a baby crying – was it Henry VII?' (ibid.).

Hewison observes that 'historical *accuracy*' is a significant absence from the 'Criteria for Good Practice' listed by the heritage consultants responsible for this report (Hewison 1988). What this illustrates is that heritage is not just a problem because it commodifies, but also because it insults. It not only insults the historian or archaeologist, but also insults the consumer as well as the local community. Until local people are enfranchised *vis-à-vis* their pasts, then the heritage consultant from out of town will successfully continue to rewrite history as heritage.

It is of course arguable that the heritagization of space can help maintain an identity of place, through the emphasis on historical characteristics which stand as a metaphor for that place. The preservation of such images may be all the more important as local industries and communities are destroyed. The danger is, however, that only safe and selected images will be preserved, and the history of a place will be neglected, while the heritage, over subsequent generations, helps construct an image of place which is based on superficialities. The historical phenomena which should link places, such as modes of production and concomitant class consciousness, will be replaced by modes of heritage imagineering which unite places only through the promotion of façade and the desire to consume the spectacle.

This is well illustrated by 'Catherine Cookson Country' in South Tyneside, where imaginary characters live in a landscape that no longer exists. Here something is created out of nothing. All of the tourist attractions, including ancient monuments such as Jarrow Hall and St Paul's church, as well as areas of natural beauty, such as Marsden cliffs, are brought together in 'Catherine Cookson Country'. A brochure describes all of these places and somehow manages to link them with Cookson characters, including Rory, 'The Gambling Man', Tilly Trotter, Fanny McBride and Katie Mulholland. We are even treated to photographs of these characters in the 1988 *Catherine Cookson Country – That's South Tyneside* guide (Gillanders 1988: 2). Possibly the most extreme example of the whole image was the 'Cookson Country Carnival-Mardi Gras '88'. Here pastiche achieved a remarkable plateau when the imaginary characters of Cookson met some all-American heroes, including Mickey Mouse. The final element during 1988 was the 'Northern Lights High-Technology Illuminations'.

The Albert Dock: heritage space considered

Heritage has been a key element in many regeneration projects. At one level it has contributed, in some areas, to economic development, especially through tourism. 'The contribution that a commodified Heritage culture had made to the Thatcherite programme of the 1980s is, to a considerable extent, an economic one', but as these writers go on to note, heritage has also had a confusing ideological impact (Corner and Harvey 1991: 73).

By the beginning of the 1980s many areas in Britain were moving into a phase of what has euphemistically been termed, economic restructuring. What this 'restructuring' actually entailed was an extreme rationalization of Britain's industrial manufacturing base and a subsequent move towards service economies. On Merseyside the industrial collapse and concomitant urban decay was already well established as many of the docks had become redundant due to the loss of shipping to Northern European ports.

In order to promote the regeneration of Merseyside, the then Secretary of State for the Environment, Michael Heseltine, in March 1981 established the Merseyside Development Corporation (MDC). The MDC consisted of a core staff of only about 60 people. Of this 60 there were only three architects, four engineers and two planners (Wray 1987: 164). It should also be noted that such Urban Development Corporations were entirely separate from the responsible local authority, thus, removing local-authority control over local redevelopment.

Regeneration on Merseyside has been claimed as a 'social, commercial and physical renaissance' (BOOM 1989: 3). It has also been claimed that 'refurbishment of the South Docks has reunited Liverpudlians with their maritime heritage' (BOOM 1989: 4). Liverpool, especially since the 1960s, has developed an enigmatic image of place second to none. Despite its relatively small size, its fame and profile is probably only second to that of London, as far as English cities are concerned. The image of the city has been partially reconstructed though the media, with successful soap operas, such as *Brookside*, and films such as Frank Clarke's *Letter to Brezhnev*. The success of Liverpool's image of place was boosted during the second half of the 1980s with the reopening of the Albert Dock. Prior to this, an earlier attempt to promote Liverpool's image, and attract investment, manifested itself in the form of a garden festival. As mentioned above, the real aim of such projects has been to highlight and abstract certain characteristics of a place and exploit these differences in order to attract capital to that place.

There is no doubt that in terms of attracting numbers of visitors, the Albert Dock was probably the British tourism success of the 1980s. In 1989 it was the second most popular free tourist attraction in Britain after Blackpool Pleasure Beach. It received about 5.1 million visitors, while the British Museum, relegated to third place, received about 4.7 million visitors. It is quite apparent that the consumption of heritage or leisure spaces which offer multiple attractions, in a number of pleasant 'heritage environments' including open-air environments, is one of the most important trends in the post-tourism which developed during the 1980s.

It has been observed that the Maritime Museum in the Albert Dock 'promotes design for its own sake creating tasteful powder pink and dusty blue *Next* interiors in displays about the suffering and persecution which led to hundreds of thousands of immigrants passing through Liverpool to the hope of a new life in America' (Hall 1989: 16). Hall believes that designers are often employed to sell neat attractive saleable packages. This would certainly seem so at the Maritime Museum.

This museum's consideration of the slave trade is dispassionate to say the least. The discussion of the trade is remarkably brief, and is dealt with as if the slaves were just another commodity, like the tobacco and sugar. Certainly, during the period of slave-trading this would have been the common perception of those involved with slavery, but it might be expected that a museum in the twentieth century could afford to take a more critical stance, unless we want our children to equate slaves with cigarettes and bags of sugar.

Is the visitor meant to consider slave-traders with greater benevolence when we discover that they managed to reduce the death rate amongst slaves from 12 per cent to 4 per cent? Why was there a slave trade to start with? How were slaves caught? What sorts of work were they expected to do? What were their living conditions like? How did the slave trade come to an end? None of these questions are really broached by the museum. A whole gallery could be given over to such a display, but no, what do we have? A display on the history of Cunard, pictures of how rich people have had a good time over the decades.

The Maritime Museum is a good example of a new museum which seems intent on being uncritical. 'The Emigrants to a New World Exhibition' is a an excellent example of style mania. It supposedly vividly conveys the experience of emigrating under sail. The ship's interior is hardly any different to the most agreeable stripped-pine kitchen furniture. It is incredibly clean, well ordered, spacious, quiet, and because it is on dry-land, static. The museum could have improved its displays by linking them. For example, one such possible link could have been made with the Cunard display, which represented the history of famous cruise liners. It should have been possible to show how one class crossed the Atlantic compared with another.

Such criticism of the Maritime Museum was echoed in the *Museums Journal* by Tariq Mehmood in 1990. The response to these criticisms appeared in the issue for October 1990, and justified the trivial analysis of slavery by arguing that, 'The Maritime Museum display seeks to place the slave trade in the context of overall trading activities of the port. Reference is made to the indignities and sufferings of the slaves' (Foster 1990). This response merely compounds the original offence. The continual categorization of slavery within the context of a trading activity, rather than as a crime against humankind, consolidated by the euphemisms, 'indignities and sufferings', used to describe the horror of slavery is 'yet another injury to the descendants of those slaves who live on this island' (Mehmood 1990).

It should be pointed out that National Museums on Merseyside are aware of such criticisms and attempts to redisplay will be made.

Also in the Albert Dock is The Beatles Story, a film, sound and smell sensation. Considering the history of rock'n'roll, we are told of GIs who made the 'Blitz more bearable with chewing gum and nylons' – clearly safer than an Anderson shelter. In the reconstructed Cavern Club a single sad-looking effigy sits; in the dim light, could it be a tourist who has wised up to the great rock'n'roll heritage swindle? Again, this is the creation of artificial place. The Beatles had no obvious connection with the Albert Docks. At the time of their success, the docks were still working docks. But today The Albert Dock is the consummate heritage space. Not only do we have the refurbished dock, but there is a television studio, boutiques, bars, and pretty Victorian market-barrows selling sweets and sepia post cards, all placed within the heated shopping mall. The Heritage Shop provides the visitor with mementos of Liverpool's present past: woollen sailor-dolls and sailors' shirts, a Viking Raiders game, King Henry VIII toby jugs, and bronze busts of well-known Scouse philosophers, such as Socrates and Plato.

Style is *the* marketing watch-word. In a market where superfluousness is the key to success the only element of a product which differentiates itself from a similar product is its style. Style is about attractive surfaces, whether it be a special edition of a Metro with a sticker on the back saying 'Surf', or a pair of jeans that have that designer-worn look with holes torn into the garment before it has even left the shop. It is the image of a product that dictates its success. We are witnessing here the worryingly successful emergence of designer-history, or 'imagineering'. Each product is essentially the same, an uncritical sight, sound, smell experience, although the historical or archaeological data that each of these experiences is based on is clearly different. A combination of an emphasis on the media of representation, and a bland unquestioning approach to interpretation, has its consequence in a heritage which denies what should be the basic requirements of all history and archaeology: the investigation and questioning of the data, and its placing in its many and varied economic, political, and social contexts, including its context of production.

A locality such as the Albert Dock in Liverpool is a de-historicized place, the organization of space by the service sector for leisure consumption. In many ways it loses any real identity as a place, because its true history as an important node in the network of Imperial capital is lost. It has been remodelled by the service sector, and specifically, estate agents and tourism managers. That is not to say that the use of a locality should not or does not change. However, what is important is to understand these changes, to understand the processes that affect the context within which a locality develops, and not simply to accept any change that comes along.

In the case of the Albert Dock we should be aware of its demise as an important working dock, the consequent unemployment and the economic and political reasons for these developments. For the same reasons we should understand why, during the 1980s, Michael Heseltine decided that the docks should be redeveloped and exploited as an expensive advert for companies which he hoped would help regenerate Merseyside. Again, the socio-economic and political contexts of these developments need to be discussed, as does the recession caused by the policies of a Government of the New Right, chronic unemployment on Merseyside, and the consequent riots: is any of this remedied by a flower festival, and the development of some very expensive penthouses with a nice art gallery beneath?

What we have instead, is a contrived place; essentially it is leisure space, one of the most popular 'free' tourist attractions in the UK. Despite its obvious historical importance, the Albert Dock has become a playground where the contrived images of multiple pasts are resurrected in a pleasant environment which probably seems quite alien to many Liverpudlians. It is now an island within a city, considered as 'defensible space'; separated from the main part of Liverpool by a main road, and populated by people who can afford the inflated prices demanded for the exclusive accommodation, the Albert Dock is an imagined village within a city, and is actually promoted as such. When they visit the docks people are not visiting Liverpool as such; it is a pseudo-visit which ensures that the visitor does not have to experience the real Liverpool if they do not wish to. This is the construction of ersatz-tourism. The docks are an island suffering from amnesia, a space that can never be a place until it is returned to the people that it belongs to.

Such regeneration schemes which have taken place all over the country 'were insurance policies – inspired by the fact or fear of urban disorder. They were partly symbolic, designed to divert attention from the adverse effects of other government policies on the inner cities' (Parkinson and Evans 1988: 1).

The Merseyside Development Corporation (MDC) has been unable to follow its predefined strategy; instead it has been forced to 'respond to any marketing opportunity that has presented itself on Merseyside' (ibid.: 9). Industrial redevelopment just has not taken place. It is for this reason that the MDC decided to concentrate on leisure and tourism services. In terms of employment, the dockland regeneration programme has increased employment by 1,500 to about 2,700 (1988 figures). Of this total 550 were part-time and 770 were employed in on-site construction (House of Commons Employment Committee, figures quoted in Parkinson and Evans 1988: 13). Also, the ratio of public to private investment in the area was heavily biased towards the public sector: 'The MDC has clearly been a public sector led and financed initiative' (Parkinson and Evans 1988: 14). This was hardly what a Government of the New Right ever wanted.

There is no doubt that the dockland regeneration has been unsuccessful in its desired attempts to attract investment into the Merseyside area, but at the same time its success in attracting tourism is unquestionable. However, the economic benefits to the local community *are* questionable. Also, the perception of Liverpool represented in the various dockland attractions is unrepresentative, and the visitor from another place may undoubtedly leave Liverpool with a view of an immaculate, flourishing city, when in fact the real situation is very different, with unemployment rates as high as *c.* 20 per cent.

The danger is that history and archaeology may no longer be considered as disciplines which can help facilitate a wider appreciation and understanding of places. Instead they have become somewhat akin to a seam of coal or reservoir of water, a resource to be extracted and exploited, to be put to work in as many ways as possible in the market-place. The past has emerged as a pool of architectural styles, to be dipped into and mixed and matched in the bricolage of the new shopping arcade. Images from our pasts are exploited as inspiration for a catalogue of heritage-kitsch, to be dispatched to our not-so-loved ones at Christmas time, while on a grander scale, historical themes are manipulated in some leisure-consultant's scheme for yet another waterside development, complete with heritage centre or museum.

As Ewen argues, 'If style offers a rendition of society as defined by surfaces and commodities, the media by which the style is transmitted tend to reinforce this outlook' (Ewen 1990: 51). If we promote ourselves as a society constituted by a mere historical surface, a glossy image that appears on the front cover of *Heritage, The British Review*, or *This England*, then we are condemned to a future as a society without roots, without any real history. How can such a society, that continually insults itself, ever hope to be taken seriously by others? Such a society is one 'where image-management is a strategy of commerce, industry, and politics, style becomes the basic form of information' (ibid.: 52).

As places become increasingly constructed through the promotion of historical styles, there is a danger that each place will lose its deeper identity. As multinational capital penetrates space throughout the globe, it can only contribute to an artificial globalization of culture.

Multinational corporations are promoting an homogeneous corporate identity across the globe. Coca Cola is the most obvious example of a globally homogeneous commodity form. IBM has a presence in 130 countries. As transnational capital has eroded 'rapidly the authority of national decision making' (Schiller 1989: 318), it also erodes the culture and identity of places.

Heritage, in many of its forms, is responsible for the destruction of a sense of place. The representation of historical surfaces via a uniform set of media which tend to appear in all heritage representations, emphasize the spectacle rather than any depth of historical questioning and analysis. As similar commodities are usually only differentiated from the next by surface appearances, the same can be said of much heritage. It is this destruction of difference which many argue is common to the entire world and has led to the development of a 'global culture'. Within this global context, places are beginning to lose their distinctive identities. This is of course a slight exaggeration: 'The binary logic which seeks to comprehend culture via the mutually exclusive terms of homogeneity/heterogeneity, integration/disintegration, unity/diversity, must be discarded. At best, these conceptual pairs work on one face only of the complex prism which is culture' (Featherstone 1990: 2).

The global is the wider part of the four-dimensional web which helps constitute place and is in turn constituted by places. In the same way as the nation and the nation-state for a period had a certain level of influence on the construction of places, especially during the Industrial Revolution, the global context, through the network of multinational capital, is today influencing the construction of places more than ever before. It does not automatically follow, however, that a process of space homogenization will take place with a concomitant destruction of place.

> A global culture, so the argument runs, will be eclectic like its western or European progenitor, but will wear a uniformly streamlined packaging. Standardized, commercialized mass commodities will nevertheless draw for their contents upon revivals of traditional, folk or national motifs and styles in fashions, furnishings, music and the arts, lifted out of their original contexts and anaesthetized.
>
> (Smith 1990: 176)

Every city in every world could possess a heritage centre complete with time-cars, audio-visual displays, impressive life-size replicas, even robots and of course smells. Such heritage attractions may be consumed by people who 'do' heritage, and each one will be the same, but different. The visitor will be secure in the knowledge that what they are entering is safe and familiar – only the commodity surface will be different. These differences will play on the historical styles peculiar to that place. Places will be differentiated only by their surface appearances. As most of us are aware, and as I have already discussed (chapters two and three), multinational capital and multinational firms already dominate much of our daily lives. Before long multinational heritage could dominate, literally, all our pasts: 'a "global culture" answers to no living needs, no identity-in-the-making. It has to be painfully put together, artificially, out of many existing folk and national identities into which humanity has been so long divided' (ibid.: 180).

The global culture could be contrived in the same way as many national cultures already are: states 'are everywhere seeking to monopolize the moral resources of community, either by flatly claiming perfect coevality between nation and state, or by systematically museumising and representing all the groups within them in a variety of heritage politics that seems remarkably uniform throughout the world' (Appadurai 1990: 305).

In order to avoid the danger of a bland homogenizing culture there has to be a role for educative facilities which will permit people to come to terms with the richness of variety that can be found in different places. Crucial to such an awareness must be the appreciation of how places develop through time and how the past is always contingent upon the present.

7 | *A sense of place*

The experiences of (post-)modernity have undoubtedly resulted in the erosion of a sense of place, especially for many of us in the First World. The effects of industrialization and urbanization have transformed the lives of many millions of people over the last 200 years, and not all of these effects have been beneficial. There is no doubt that it is the working classes that have suffered most at the hands of the processes of modernization, of which time–space compression is an important element. To argue otherwise is to adopt a position of comfortable liberal impartiality, a politics of indifference, redolent of much post-modern thinking.

Throughout the (post-)modern period there has been an increasing purposive-rationalization and institutionalization of the ways in which the past has been represented to the public. Essentially the processes behind the construction and reproduction of representations of our pasts have been increasingly removed from the wider public sphere. This form of rationalization has produced neutered representations which safely mediate the subject's constructed perceptions of their historical surroundings, to the point where the past is constructed as a colourful but muted backdrop, in front of which the successes of modernization are proclaimed. Since the beginnings of modernity the past has gradually been institutionalized through museum and heritage representations, and promoted as that which modernization has overcome. Throughout modernity, historical and archaeological practitioners have often referred to a kind of 'barrier' or 'gap' which exists between the present and the past. Supposedly, the technicism of the (post-)modern world has brought us to a point where we need not want for anything. The past was a foreign country, but its identity has been subsumed in the expansion of empires of multinational capital and technical, purposive rationalization. This is not a universal experience, but it is one which potentially might be so one day.

This chapter will develop a conceptual framework which may permit the enhancement of a sense of place. The final chapter will link these ideas with developments in museums, and consider how museums might act as facilitators for developing a sense of place.

The argument is founded on a belief that the locality within which people spend the majority of their working and social lives is a place which, in the majority of cases, can be potentially knowable, and understood as a node in a network of relationships which cross both time and space. Places can therefore be perceived as localities which are at the same time both acting on, and being acted upon by, other places. It is therefore important that people realize that their places are important, and can influence institutions, including multinational capital. However, for all of this to be appreciated, it is necessary that people come to terms with the processes that have affected, and continue to affect, their place.

A future for the past?

There is still a potential for developing a sense of place, with an emphasis on the consideration of temporality in places. Much of this book has been concerned with a consideration of the impact of post-modernity, and the intensification of those experiences which have promoted the ahistoric aestheticization of space, through the exploitation of historical images.

One important characteristic of post-modern heritage has been its unnerving ability to deny historical process, or diachrony. Heritage successfully mediates all our pasts as ephemeral snapshots exploited in the present, to embellish decaying cityscapes, and to guarantee the success of capital in its attempt to develop new superfluous markets.

Meanwhile, some academics even seem to question the value of historical analyses and argue for a new emphasis on the study of space. Although the geographer, Edward Soja, does not question the validity of historical approaches to the study of society, he asserts that writers such as Foucault and Lefebvre have shown us that 'space more than time hides things from us, that the demystification of spatiality and its veiled instrumentality of power is the key to making practical, political, and theoretical sense of the contemporary era' (Soja 1989: 61). There is no doubt that the control and manipulation of space is, and always has been, a fundamental technique of maintaining political hegemony. But to deny that the exploitation of space has a temporal dimension, is to deny the existence of time itself. No phenomenon can be understood through the analysis of a single static snapshot. Soja does not appear to be asking for a denial of temporality, but rather for a re-examination of the way in which societal phenomena exist across space. However, this type of plea may result in a dangerous trend towards a form of anti- or ahistorical discourse. Places should be considered as spaces which are continually experiencing processes which occur through time, processes which are not, and never have been, static.

To move across space is to move through time. Tuan considers that 'Place is pause in movement. That is one relation between time and place. The city is time made visible' (Tuan 1978: 14). Any movement through space, therefore, is to move through time. Logically then, we can never visit the same place more than once as it is continually developing through time (see Prince 1978: 17–37). Places are continually changing, and our perceived present is always a form of pastness. It is this crucial contingency of the past on our daily experiences which must be articulated through the museum.

Cognitive mapping

The key to locating ourselves in time and space is the production of mental or 'cognitive' maps. The term map immediately implies a static, singularly spatial, representation. What I wish to consider over the next few pages is the development of an idea of maps which represent changes through time, as well as space, and show how *places* are constructed not in isolation, but by processes which originate in other times and *spaces*.

Developing a sense of place is crucial if people are to flourish and enjoy living in a world which becomes more and more complex, and subject to the whims of extensive multinational companies and corporations over which they have no control. People must be allowed to develop a sense of perspective within an area which they can manage to understand and conceptualize. Most (post-)modern representations of the past exist altogether as a synchronous shallow mass. Any attempt to develop a sense of place should be concerned with the emphasis on diachrony, an emphasis on the temporal *depth* of places.

This argument is a development of an idea mooted originally by Fredric Jameson: the idea of cognitive mapping (Jameson 1988b). Jameson argues that each stage of capital has brought with it a new experience of space. With each 'advancement' of capital there has been a kind of distancing of the social. People have become removed from the economic system of production which they serve. In the early stages of economic development people were closer to the actual markets within which they operated. During the Industrial Revolution the great migrations to urban centres removed people from the markets in which they worked. The development of imperial networks heralded the beginnings of a truly global economy, and thus markets which working people in London, Manchester and Liverpool could never really hope to understand or participate in with any power.

If placing oneself in time and space, and therefore gaining a sense of place, was difficult during the nineteenth century at the time of Imperial capital, then today, under the regime of multinational capital, or 'late-capitalism', it must be virtually impossible. Even the nation-state has a limited existence in the truly global economy. It is the multinationals such as Ford and Unilever that call the shots in the post-modern world. People are refused the opportunity to place themselves into a definable time–space location.

A new museology must concern itself with facilitating a perspective of place. Any understanding of place is going to be restricted to a certain locality, defined as

> the space within which the larger part of most citizens' daily working and consuming lives is lived. It is the base for a large measure of individual and social mobilization to activate, extend or defend those rights, not simply in the political sphere but more generally in the areas of cultural, economic and social life.
>
> (Cooke 1989: 12)

Two geographers, Gould and White, attempted to ascertain how people perceived their own localities. They were concerned with the 'mental maps' that people possessed, not just of their own areas and regions, but of the country as a whole. One phenomenon which they considered, was the degree of 'emotional involvement' that people had with an area. Basically how far, in terms of distance from their own locality, did their involvement with, or knowledge of an area extend? Although the approach has limitations, it does indicate certain trends in terms of people's conceptions of space and place. One obvious finding of such research was that 'people's emotional involvement with other places falls off very steeply with distance, and then more or less levels out beyond a certain distance' (Gould and White 1974: 42).

The maps that Gould and White developed were based on a group of participants ranking their preferences for places on maps of their countries. These data were then converted, to allow them to be used for drawing contour maps which indicated how the group of participants rated the different areas of their country. Of course, it is true that ranking likes and dislikes does not necessarily indicate how well somebody knows an area. The research showed that people tend to rank their own areas highly, what the authors refer to as a 'dome of local desirability' (ibid.: 92).

This hopefully illustrates, if it needed illustrating at all, the importance of the local and implicitly questions the legitimacy of an idea of 'nation' as promoted by modern heritage, and to an extent, the national museums. The ideal locality is of a size that people can come to terms with. The Common Ground organization, which has helped hundreds of small communities develop their own maps of *their* places, states that the parish is a useful label for a locality. This need not only mean the conventional ecclesiastical area, but any locality to which an individual or group feels some kind of attachment (Greeves 1987a: 2).

Timing space

Places are constituted through the subjective recognition of 'time marks' – elements in the environment, both humanly and naturally constructed. Such marks make time 'visible'. People gain a sense of place through a set of 'filters', a subjective engagement with these time marks. Throughout the period of (post-)modernity the power to control the timing of space, and therefore the manipulation of places, has been in the hands of a relatively small group of individuals and institutions. Such organizations have the ability to decide what will and will not be preserved, and how it will be presented and interpreted for the public.

A sense of the past is developed through an ability to locate time marks within a temporal framework and to place them in an historical perspective. The key to developing a sense of place is to allow people to develop their own understandings of place, rather than to impose institutionalized meanings onto space, thus producing artificial places.

As Kevin Lynch showed in the surveys carried out for his book *The Image of the City*, people were 'disturbed' by continual change in their environment:

> In Los Angeles there is an impression that the fluidity of the environment and the absence of physical elements which anchor the past are exciting and disturbing. Many descriptions of the scene by established residents, young or old, were accompanied by the ghosts of what used to be there. Changes, such as those wrought by the freeway system have left scars on the mental image. The interviewer remarked: 'There seems to be a bitterness or nostalgia among natives which could be resentment at the many changes, or just inability to reorientate fast enough to keep up with them'.
>
> (Lynch 1960: 45)

When Lynch wrote *What Time is this Place* at the beginning of the 1970s, he commented that 'the resistance to the loss of historical environment is today becoming more determined as affluence increases and physical change itself is more rapid. And no wonder, since the past is known, familiar, a possession in which we may feel secure' (Lynch 1972: 29). People must be offered the skills that will enable them to 'read' their environments and reconstruct a sense of place. Crucial to such projects is an appreciation of how places change through time and how each place is linked to a multiplicity of other places and influences, and thus situated within temporal and spatial contexts which are potentially infinite. Any project concerned with reconstructing a sense of place must be prepared to consider the definitions of the temporal and spatial contexts which are important to the development of different phenomena within places.

The four-dimensional web

Below is a rudimentary framework which might be considered when developing understandings of places. Museums as facilitators should first and foremost be concerned with promoting the *skills* which might enable people to read their own place, as well as other places which they may visit. One example of such skills, would be the ability to date vernacular buildings and to understand how and why they were built. The need to understand this element of the historical environment is all the more important in the light of the impact of post-modern architecture (see chapter four).

An emphasis on skills is especially important at a time when in Britain, the Government is emphasizing a facts-orientated approach to the study of history rather than a skills-based approach. Skills are portable and can be taken to any number of places, and can be used therein to develop a sense of that place. Facts are subsequently added to that framework, and may not necessarily be as portable or as useful in other contexts.

The study of particular places is preferable as the 'broad sweep' of the past is often an impossibility and more often superficial because of its potential vastness. That is not to say that broad relevant contexts are not important, in fact they are crucial. The study of places should occur within a set of four-dimensional contexts which surround that place being studied. Such contexts can extend increasingly outwards, both temporally and spatially, and will obviously decrease or expand with the nature of the study.

Any understanding of place might well be enhanced through a consideration of the 'four-dimensional web'. As may be obvious to some readers, this requires us to consider localities as nodes developing through time and space, which possess almost any number of links with other nodes, or localities, within the web or network. As far as this discussion goes, the first three dimensions are those of the physical world as perceived at any one moment in time, while the fourth dimension is time. The fourth dimension does not have to be founded on the orthodox framework of the past as linear progression through Western historical dates, but rather as a dimension or, more specifically, a characteristic of a place, or object, which implies process, change and depth.

An understanding or appreciation of place must not imply an insular aestheticization of individual places, such as the trend in the heritagization of space considered in the previous chapters. An important theme throughout this book has been that of the idea of people being consistently removed from the processes which affect their day-to-day lives, and the construction of the places within which they live. As the machinations of capital have become more and more sublime it has become increasingly difficult to make connections. In the post-modern world the 'dictatorship of the fragments' (Best 1989: 361) has contributed to the concept of individuals as entirely apart from society. Places and people are constituted through an infinite number of connections with other people and places.

In the (post-)modern world people have attempted to maintain or develop a sense of place through the development of artificial connections. A feeling of placelessness is most common in urban contexts. Certain groups of people, as discussed in the previous chapter, have attempted to create artificial roots through the consumption of representations of rurality. Many urban dwellers perceive rural localities as providing a sense of security because they are not considered to be subjected to the same extreme processes of change that occur in urban localities. The rural place is seen as more resilient and serves as a placebo for the urbanite. Things rural are more popular than ever, from cotton-waxed jackets, to four-wheel drive off-road vehicles.

In January 1991 a do-it-yourself manual, *The Country Look*, was launched. *The Country Look* instructs the reader how to arrange their best crockery on the farmhouse-style dresser, how to decorate the house in a country style, and how to prepare country fare. It would seem that many urban dwellers attempt a form of remote cognitive mapping, preferring to yearn for a lifestyle and a sense of place which is more stable and rooted.

Museums then, should be concerned with promoting a sense of place particularly for urban dwellers through a consideration of those processes which have constructed their place. An emphasis should be put on how places are nodal points in networks of production, how places are physically constructed through the exploitation of material resources, from water, clay and stone, to the manipulation of chemicals and their transformation into commodities, from bricks to nuclear power. Archaeologists have long been concerned with illustrating trading networks based on the provenancing of material. Such 'maps' can be developed to show how places have exploited different resources over time and space. The trend towards the distancing of the production of commodities away from the direct, daily experiences of those who consume them is an obvious theme. One area for consideration might be based on this idea of the distancing of people from production over time. We might consider how early farmers would have produced much of their requirements within the locality, while today, commodities manufactured on the multinational scale are consumed. Localities are even remodelled through the heritagization of their space by capital which may have come from anywhere in the world; thus, all places are a constituent part of that network.

Connections between places exist at many different levels and can be represented as such. A theme for consideration might be the development of faiths within a locality. Almost every town, city and village possesses religious buildings of some sort. Such buildings can be considered as focal points in a wider consideration of faiths in an area, region, country, continent, or even the world. These buildings are nodes in particular networks, those of religion. They can be considered in temporal and spatial contexts of various scales. For example, the development of mosques within a city over the last ten years; the development of Anglican places of worship in the British Isles between the eleventh and fourteenth centuries; or synagogues throughout the world from their beginnings to the present. Each of these areas of consideration potentially allows the development of discourses which local people might wish to become involved in, as the importance of the past is made relevant for their place today. Such discourses would need to recognize the influences of other people and other places across time and space. Such a discourse would not pretend to reveal the nature of other places – any such consideration of processes across time and space would be concerned primarily with the understanding of the development of the interested party's particular place. Of course, we should be careful to avoid the aestheticization of that place and a concomitant promotion of a debilitating patriotism. There should be an explicit awareness of the fact that shared material culture does not necessarily imply a commonality between the places and societies which share these characteristics.

When considering the construction of places, a common theme should be the idea that there is no 'gap' between the past and the present. Places are, and have been, continually constructed by processes across time and space, and of course contribute to processes which affect other places. There can be no ontological difference between the past and the present. It is unimportant whether we consider our presence as being continually constructed in the 'past', or always in the 'now'. What is crucial, is the idea that processes across time and space are continuous. It is however, necessary that considerations of such processes are contextualized, whilst realizing that such contexts are open contexts without boundaries. It is the (post-)modern consideration of the past as completed, which has allowed the isolation of our pasts and their subsequent mediation into innocuous commodities. All interpretation is constructed through the subjective reading by individuals of phenomena. The study/awareness of their own contemporary place is no different from the study of its past. If there is a 'gap', it is one that exists between subject and object. The subject is removed from all interpretation spatially. To move across space and to think, is to move through time. *All* interpretation is concerned with understanding the past.

However, the museum should always explicitly declare that cross-temporal and cross-cultural analogies are only suppositions, and care should be taken to emphasize the elements of context which are most relevant to the analogy (Hodder 1982: 26). For example, an analogy between a strimmer or hedge-cutter, and a scythe, can not be made without stressing the different contextual reasons for manipulating the environment. The beautification of the suburban lawn on a Sunday afternoon is clearly different from the necessary control of certain flora in an agrarian economy, although the achieved ends may be perceived as quite similar. Differences and similarities in practices should be highlighted.

Places are not just those localities in which people reside today, they are also areas within which exist traces of past places which are now redundant. Developing a sense of place also means understanding how previous settlement patterns in the locality have changed: how they may have expanded, contracted or have even been deserted. A place that exists today may have in its past had connections with places which no longer exist.

When considering the processes that have contributed to the construction of places we should be concerned with avoiding just mere description of the processes of power, politics, economics and exploitation. 'Archaeology is not, then, just some kind of resuscitation of the past in the present, but must involve a critique on the particular past that leads to our concrete present' (Shanks and Tilley 1987: 110).

Any interpretation will be, by its very nature, a cross-cultural interpretation before it is anything. An assumption that it is not denies the contemporary subjective construction of the person involved in the interpretive activity (see Hodder 1982: chapter one). Analogy between present and past is obviously a useful tool for museums, especially as museums expand their collections of modern material culture, and thus links between recognized modern artefacts and those from the unexperienced past can be considered. Any display based on analogy will have to consider very carefully the contexts from which both sets of artefacts are derived. An object or building can not be understood in isolation. Material culture only has 'meaning' as part of a network of relations that exist, or have existed, between many subjects and objects within a context of social relationships: 'the production of material culture is a social practice, a signifying practice situated within social, political and economic structures, structures which enable action (Shanks and Tilley 1987: 137). Therefore museums must attempt to develop displays which make 'connections', connections which must consider the economic, social, political and ritual links between peoples and places. Differences and similarities in practices should be highlighted.

Articulations of political positions and the exploitation of power through the use of material culture should also be an area of consideration. The most notable exhibition concerned with the consideration of power in a British context was the 'Symbols of Power at the Time of Stonehenge' exhibition. Held at the National Museum of Antiquities of Scotland in Edinburgh in 1985, this exhibition made explicit use of analogy between modern articulations of power through material culture and the possible articulations of power which may have been constructed during the late third and second millennia BC (see Clarke, Cowie and Foxon 1985). This type of display can illustrate the point that there are phenomena which are not peculiar to the past, but are as relevant to people today as they have always been.

Places and communities

The aim of cognitive mapping and developing a sense of place should be to allow people to develop their own sense of place. This is not an argument for a form of nihilist relativism or anarchic atomism, but rather an argument for the promotion of communication between people that allows the development of communities of discourse: 'Common meanings are the basis of community' (Taylor 1985: 39). People should be encouraged to take 'positions' vis-à-vis the past. This engagement with the construction of places demands that people be allowed to assess what they consider to be 'right' or 'wrong' about the processes which have

affected *their* place. As people make value judgements about contemporary issues in society, they should be encouraged to take positions
regarding the past, as it is processes through time which have contributed
to the construction of their societies. Some relativists might argue that
such intersubjective communities are objectionable on the grounds that
they stifle individuality. For example, one writer has asserted that

> Not only does this ideal of shared subjectivity express an impossibility,
> but it has undesirable political implications. Political theorists and
> activists should distrust this desire for reciprocal recognition and
> identification with others, I suggest, because it denies difference in
> the concrete sense of making it difficult for people to respect those
> with whom they do not identify. I suggest that the desire for mutual
> understanding and reciprocity underlying the ideal of community is
> similar to the desire for identification that underlies racial and ethnic
> chauvinism.
>
> (Young 1990: 311)

Such a simplistic decrial of the idea of community is flawed on a number
of levels. First of all, the promotion of the radical individual, supposedly
freed from the constraints of society, is, as I have detailed elsewhere, an
uncritical acceptance of Neo-Conservative ideology. More importantly it
denies the understanding that for an individual to exist with rights,
there must be a concurring society to confer those rights, 'since the free
individual can only maintain his [sic] identity within a society/culture of
a certain kind, he has to be concerned about the shape of this
society/culture as a whole' (Taylor 1985: 207). The individual can not
exist as an isolated entity removed from surrounding societal processes.
Second, Young would seem to be assuming that communities are necessarily constituted by people from the same ethnic group, the same sex, or
even, the same class. Young is possibly guilty of assuming that communities are constructed along the lines of simple binary oppositions –
black/white, male/female, or working class/landed class. As I have illustrated in chapters two and three, so-called post-material political communities transgress the traditional well-defined boundaries in the form
of single-issue groups. There is no reason why communities with positions
vis-à-vis their place should not also flourish. Such communities are of
course not restricted to understanding their place purely in terms of the
development of the material environment. Although it is a cliché, people
do make places, and an understanding of how people affect places is
crucial. Projects which aim to develop an understanding of localities
should ensure that those people who have recently moved into a place
are not disenfranchised. The history of many places is one constituted by
processes of both emigration and immigration. An overemphasis on
material culture and associated trading networks should be avoided,

whilst emphasis should be placed on the influences of groups of people on places. The myth of the 'traditional' indigenous society should be exposed, while the problems that are associated with immigration should be highlighted and discussed.

> The political consciousness of black settlers and their children draws on histories and memories of struggle beyond Britain's borders. They are combined, not only with the effects of insertion into an ailing industrial order at distinctive points but with the experience of banishment from production which has occurred with disproportionate frequency along lines marked by 'race'.
>
> (Gilroy 1987: 37)

It must be understood that communities of intersubjective understanding need not be constructed along orthodox class or ethnic lines. '*Ethnic* interests also intersect with class, gender and other dimensions in the community, the workplace, the local and national state, and – sometimes – the household' (Bagguley et al. 1990: 140). It should be clear that an understanding of place is developed through a communality which is constructed on the basis of a shared intersubjectivity, not bound by gender, race or class; positions regarding the past will necessarily be influenced by such factors, but developed through a common position regarding the processes which affect places. Such communities are not place-specific but are developed along the lines of intra- and inter-place commonality. Since the emergence of multinational capital such communities are potentially global, as many places are subjected to similar processes over time and space. The bottom line in the post-modern world must be 'making connections'.

The final chapter will consider how some of these ideas may be developed within the museum. Despite obvious criticisms of the museum as a constituent element in the institutional rationalization of society, museums may be considered as the obvious facilitators of the skills which allow people to read places. Museums should develop as providers of skills which are oriented to the specificity of their own locality. Again, care must be taken not to parochialize, an emphasis must be placed on the various contexts, both spatial and temporal, which have and do affect places.

8 | *The museum as a facilitator*

The previous chapter was concerned with sketching a relatively basic framework which might be considered when attempting to develop a sense of place. The key to a successful future for museums has to be based on an idea of *local* democracy and public service, that is, the development of the museum as a facilitator for communities who wish to learn more about the development of their place, a provision which should be available as an educational service. Essential to any such project is a transgressing of what are basically Victorian disciplinary boundaries. The 'integrated' museum is one which approaches the study of place through synthesis. This is the approach adopted by museums which consider themselves to be working within the framework of the 'new museology', the most important category of which is ecomuseums.

The concept of the ecomuseum

Nick Merriman's (1988a) research into popular attitudes towards the past and the ways in which they are represented to the public also asked the respondents to consider what they felt to be the most effective ways of developing an understanding of the past.

As only 25 per cent of respondents in his survey agreed with the statement 'Museums have nothing to do with our daily lives', it can be assumed that there is a relatively strong basis of support for a positive role for museums (ibid.: 187). However, it is clear that museums are not necessarily perceived as being the best, or most enjoyable, way of learning about the past. There is no doubt that part of the problem is the fact that museums are perceived as stuffy, temple-like institutions, which discourage interaction and questioning. Merriman believes that,

> what contemporary professional archaeology lacks is an allowance
> for the widespread participation of interested amateurs, for whom the

main attractions of archaeology are the excitement of discovery and the stimulation of the imagination caused by excavating evidence of past people. Metal-detecting and 'alternative archaeology' have at least partly arisen in response to these missing factors.

(ibid.: 248)

A new museology must concern itself with involving the public, not just during the visit to the museum through interactive displays, but also in the production of their own pasts.

When asked 'If you wanted to find out about local history or some old local place, what would be the most enjoyable way of doing it?', 20 per cent replied that they would like to visit the area by themselves, while 19 per cent said that they would prefer a guided tour of the area. Only 7 per cent indicated that they would like to go to a museum to find out about the site. What this reveals is the desire to actually be in a place, and experience it first-hand, as well as an obvious dissatisfaction with the potential of most contemporary museums to facilitate a sense of place. In fact, watching a television programme was indicated as preferable by 16 per cent (Merriman 1988b: 162). Most importantly, those people who were 'rare' visitors to museums also rated visiting the site itself well above visiting a museum (ibid.: 163).

The survey also shows that those of middle and lower status tend to rank family and local histories higher than those of high status (Merriman's term for wealthy and well-educated groups) (Merriman 1988a: 286). However, in all cases British history is ranked in either first or second place, thus possibly indicating the success of school history which tends to emphasize national histories. There is, however, an undeniable interest in local history. Such local histories then should ensure that each locality is placed within national and international contexts, illustrating the connections between different places.

Proponents of the new museology have continually emphasized the need for local museums which actually involve the community in developing an appreciation of its own places. The ecomuseum is an idea which seems to have established itself in many countries, other than Britain. The failure of the idea in Britain, to date, was highlighted by the publication of a book entitled *The New Museology* (Vergo 1989), which did not explicitly consider what the rest of the world considers to be the new museology at all.

The new museology, as defined at a meeting in Quebec in October 1984, 'is primarily concerned with community development, reflecting the driving forces in social progress and associating them in its plans for the future' (Mayrand 1985: 201). The new museology then, encompasses ecomuseology, community museology, in fact all those museologies which espouse the idea of the 'active' museum – museums which are concerned with involving people in the processes of both representation and interpretation. Some may have noticed that there is a potentially danger-ous element in the Quebec declaration referred to above, in that it declares that new museums should consider the forces in social *progress*. The architects of the new museology, no doubt, must be aware of the pitfalls associated with an idea of progress, and may not have intended the meaning that I have highlighted here.

The ecomuseum is concerned to integrate all of the disciplines which are normally involved in museology, including archaeology, social history, natural history, geology, in fact any discipline which contributes to the understanding of people and places. Ecomuseums are not, as the name suggests, purely concerned with ecological conservation issues, although many ecomuseums have developed as a result of awareness of such issues within communities. In a nutshell, the ecomuseum is 'a museum concerned with the total ecology and environment, natural and human, of a defined locality' (Boylan 1990: 32).

Just as there has been an explosion in this number of museums in Britain, there have been similar explosions elsewhere, but rather than being an explosion in the number of sites for tourism consumption, many ecomuseums have developed as a consequence of a genuine need to preserve and develop local identities. During the 1970s an ICOM survey in the USSR showed that there were about 14,000 unofficial museums. Ten years later there were no less than 20,000. As Boylan asserts, this wealth of local museums reflects the needs of local communities (ibid.: 32). These museums have doubtless been responsible for the preservation and enhancement of cultural identities once threatened by a state Com-munist machine intent on eradicating difference.

The first ecomuseum is usually recognized as that which opened in Le Creusot, central France, in 1971. The 'father' of the ecomuseum move-ment is usually considered to be Georges Henri Rivière.

It is interesting to note that the origin of the ecomuseum and decon-struction are the same. They were probably both reactions to a heavily centralized and bureaucratic French State. If deconstruction itself is con-sidered in context, then its birth too might be explicable as a phenomenon. Jameson (1981: 54, Note 31) illustrates how the desire to 'deconstruct' the 'totalization' of government in France should be seen as the context for the emergence of post-structuralism. During the post-war period French Governments were keen to centralize the government of not just

France, but the whole of the French Empire; in fact French government until recently may have been the most centralized of all Western European governments. In the light of the failure of the radical politics of the mid-to-late 1960s, the earlier war in Algiers, and the break-up of the Empire in Indonesia, the desire to develop countercultural, single-interest and local political movements in France may be seen as an obvious desire of French society during the late 1960s and early 1970s. This chapter, as was the previous, is concerned to articulate a framework which permits the possibility of communities of intersubjective meaning, and even the potential for certain 'universal' positions, as these are clearly necessary if the totalizing nature of multinational capital is to be challenged.

Rivière developed open-air museums on the Scandinavian model, but with one important difference: the buildings were to remain in their original contexts, not moved to an artificial site (Hubert 1985: 186). Essentially, the ecomuseum should be considered as a museum of place. Some may argue that many local museums already fulfil such a position. This is not so. More often than not the local museum is replete with decontextualized objects, lacking a consideration of both contexts and historical processes. More importantly, most museums fail to involve people at the level of designing and developing the museum, and at the level of exhibit interaction. The key idea must be democratization of access to the evidence for places, through the provision of a *public service*.

> An ecomuseum is an instrument conceived, fashioned and operated
> jointly by a public authority and a local population. The public
> authority's involvement is through the experts, facilities and resources
> it provides; the local population's involvement depends on its
> aspirations, knowledge and individual approach.
>
> (Rivière 1985: 182)

Rivière, considered that such a museum should be a mirror, which a local community holds up to its visitors so that the visitors may develop a respect for that locality as it is constituted by its people and their inter-action with their environment through time and space. A fundamental problem with this definition of the ecomuseum is that it has implicitly emphasized the role of this type of museum within a rural environment, partly, it would seem, because people have not tended to perceive the urban environment in the same way as the rural environment. Also, the idea of community in a rural place is apparently stronger, thus enhancing the ability of a group to define its own place; this may be more difficult in an urban locality.

'Every difficult period sees a proliferation of historical and ethnographical museums whose purpose is to smooth away worries about the future by extolling values of the past' (Hubert 1985: 187). There is a danger that many ecomuseums in France tend to extol the harvest festival and the ideal images of rurality, rather than the problems encountered by rural societies. They tend to deal only with the development of industrial techniques rather than social history (ibid.: 188). There is in fact a real danger that the ecomuseum promotes a form of micro-nationalism.

The ecomuseum is based on a locality, which can be defined as a plurality of territories 'of a family, educational, professional, associational, political and also imaginary nature' (Bellaigue-Scalbert 1985: 194). It is this plurality which should be the key to the success of the ecomuseum. The necessary democratization, or opening, of 'access to the past' should invite contradiction and debate within a community and should contribute to the demise of the stultifying, unitary, linear, didactic narrative.

It is often considered that the ecomuseum should concentrate on the character of the region, a region being defined not primarily 'by administrative or legal boundaries, unless they happen to coincide with the boundaries of a zone that forms a whole, because of the unity of its traditions, natural setting and economic life – for example a mining region, a river valley, farming country or industrial zone' (Engström, 1985: 207). Although this seems a reasonable definition of region, we should be aware that regional identities are neither environmentally nor economically determined. The successful ecomuseum should always be reconsidering how it is defined in relation to other peoples and other places; a rigid definition of boundaries or contexts is always dangerous.

The ecomuseum, or community museum, is not confined to rural localities which the term 'eco' might imply for some people. For most of the First World, it is the daily experiences of urban life which are important. One of the most successful urban community projects is the Anacostia Neighbourhood Museum. This museum was established originally by John R. Kinard in a deprived area of south-east Washington. One of the earliest displays showed how ecological ideas are of crucial importance in an urban environment. 'The Rat: Man's Invited Affliction' included an exhibit of live rats. The exhibition was concerned to increase the neighbourhood's knowledge concerning rats, which were a day-to-day problem for many people (Kinard 1985: 220).

Places and environments

The ecomuseum is therefore concerned with the facilitation of an understanding, or awareness, of how places are a construction of human interaction with environments across time and space. By environment, I do not only mean the natural resources which people often imagine as being situated in rural contexts, but the material contexts, both rural and urban, with which people interact on a daily basis, from harvesting crops to extracting stone for building, from producing synthetic chemicals to disposing of suburban household rubbish.

Places are to be understood within their landscapes, not just in terms of buildings and other monuments, but as part of a palimpsest of remains which indicates continual processes of change and stability: 'an eighteenth century hedgerow, itself now incorporating nineteenth century trees, twentieth century barbed wire and, sometimes, a Victorian bedstead, may reflect a boundary line two thousand or more years old' (Roberts 1987: 78). The number of species of flora within such a hedgerow may even give an indication of its age. Some boundaries may be based on natural features which were subsequently exploited by people, others will be the product of direct human action.

The environment should not be considered as the backdrop to human action, but rather we should be concerned with understanding 'the dialogue between peoples and their environments' (Thomas 1990: 75). All human activities have involved and always will involve some kind of interaction with the environment. The environment, whether rural or urban, should not only be seen as that which offers possibilities in terms of exploitation, manipulation and change, but also, as Bell notes, as a cultural phenomenon (1990: 70). An environment has meaning for people beyond its position as the source of food and material, as a context of social meaning. Sherwood Forest, like St Paul's Cathedral and Stonehenge, has a special meaning for people today as it probably did in the past. Built monuments have meaning not just in themselves, but because of their location as well. Bronze Age round barrows would have been eminent monuments, purposefully placed on ridges in an otherwise flat landscape.

A consideration of humankind's changing relationship with the environment is essential. The different relationships that existed between hunter-gatherers and the environment should be contrasted with that which existed between farmers and their environments, and in turn the relationship between industrial societies and their environment should also be considered.

Such themes are partly considered by the Sollerød museum in Denmark. This museum is concerned with interpretation of the Vedbæk settlements, and concentrates on the ecological contexts within which Mesolithic hunter-gatherer societies lived. The emphasis is placed on human/environment interaction, and the ways in which those peoples exploited and manipulated their localities. As the Vedbæk museum is a site museum it concentrates only on one period of prehistory. Ideally, ecomuseums should be concerned with considering the development of places through time, or at least develop a sequence of temporary projects which deal with this. A theme for consideration might be based on Butzer's assertion that, 'The subsequent prehistorical and historical records, in the wake of agricultural and pastoral origins, are marked by increasingly controlled (and simplified) ecosystems' (Butzer 1982: 319). Why has the history of the First World especially been one of increasingly labour-intensive modes of production, which have pushed the ecosystem to its limits whilst reducing the amount of free time available to most people?

An understanding of place should be based on frameworks which consider why places are located where they are. What resources do they exploit, or have they, exploited? Archaeologists have always been interested in technologies and the ways in which they may have been used to exploit the environment. There must also be a concern with the people involved in those interactions, the relations of both production and consumption of materials and goods.

In developing an understanding of why places are located where they are, there would be a need to consider what resources were available for exploitation throughout the past. Would different societies have been able to exploit those resources with the technologies available to them? What types of communication networks were available, what forms of transport did people have which would allow them to exploit available communication networks? Available resources, communications, and transport potential will then possibly have some bearing on a place's relationship with other places. Whether a place was potentially ever self-sufficient, or whether it required links with other places should also be considered. If so, how did these links develop? How did changes in other places, including environmental changes, affect the place being considered?

Another theme for consideration might be one that has importance in this and other discussions of (post-)modernity: how economic processes have gradually been distanced from individual places, and the belief that there has been a gradual trend towards places being subjected to a greater number of external influences as time has moved on. Museums should consider the processes which have contributed to this trend. One general scheme might be as follows: during the prehistoric and probably up to the Medieval period the majority of places were constituted by regional agricultural markets; local regions and nearby places had a more direct influence. Gradually, from the eighteenth century on, places were subject to greater influences from other places further and further afield, from markets of Empire and international industry, to the truly multinational global economy, with its almost instantaneous effects across space during the latter part of the twentieth century.

An appreciation of how places are linked to other places may be developed through the use of linked chronologies, illustrating what was happening contemporaneously in other places. This has been used in some conventional exhibitions, including the 'Archaeology and the Bible' exhibition at the British Museum in 1990. Here, linked chronological sequences for Egypt, Palestine and Mesopotamia were displayed. This would have been far more useful and meaningful if they had been linked with chronologies that visitors were familiar with, including those of Britain and Europe. Again, there seems to have been an assumed level of cultural competence on the part of the visitors. Also, there may be a genuine need to move away from the use of traditional chronologies, that is, the use of dates, in order to personalize the past. Perhaps an emphasis should be placed on thinking of time in terms of human generations. Dates could be referred to for example as 'when your great-great-grandparents were alive'. Such chronologies could be used in conjunction with more orthodox dates.

As discussed in the previous chapter, the best way to come to terms with places is through a form of cognitive mapping, which attempts to reveal how what we see today has developed over time. Cognitive mapping would emphasize the need to place material culture in its temporal and spatial contexts. Such projects would be greatly enhanced through the use of information technology, and more specifically, technology such as interactive video.

Interactive video

The interactive video disc (IVD) is based on an archive of images which can be still or moving. The disc is essentially a larger version of a compact disc (CD), and has a capacity of four gigabytes, which allows 26 minutes of moving images or 55,000 still frames. The image archive can be accessed randomly, which is probably the system's most important characteristic. There is also the facility for two parallel sound-tracks, and computer-generated graphics can be superimposed over an image. The image archive is controlled by software on a personal computer (PC), and it is the software which to a certain extent controls the ways in which the image archive can be accessed and manipulated (Martlew 1988 and 1990).

From the museum's point of view the introduction of IVD permits visitors to access not just images of material on display in the museum, but images of archived material, images of the places where the material was found, including maps. A catalogue approach to the image archive permits the user to access images in any order that s/he wishes, akin to a database which can be accessed at any point. The users, through the PC, can structure their own sequences of images, and can interrogate the archive to their own particular ends. The user may wish to develop an understanding of an entire region, or may wish to concentrate on a specific place, and within that place, investigate a certain period.

In terms of mapping, the interactive video disc has a number of advantages over more orthodox display methods. Most important is its ability to display images of objects that are not on display in the museum, including those in store, as well as those from other museums, including the national museums, which may have borrowed the most prestigious objects on a permanent basis. The user may decide to search for all of the objects of a similar kind, or more usefully, any material that might be associated with that object. As well as associated material from a site, the video disc can present other information, including maps and photographs of the area from whence the objects came. A map could reveal the location of similar sites in a region, or even across the country.

Trading networks could be represented, as well as other links between places. Computer manipulation and superimposition of images will become easier and more efficient as digital technology improves. Most importantly perhaps, is the development of digital video interactive, a microchip which will allow the computer to work directly on images, which it is unable to do currently (1990/1) as images are produced by analogue signals (Martlew forthcoming). Once digital images are produced, the computer will be able to alter the size and move images around the screen thus allowing the user to call up a number of different sorts of information at once, including images of objects, site plans, photographs and maps, as well as text.

In the context of the community museum, or ecomuseum, interactive video allows individuals, or groups of people, to develop their own presentations on topics of their own choice. The IVD system easily permits the development of linked sequences of images, both still and moving, along with superimposed textual information. It is possible to set up a number of different 'routes' through the presentation. A general topic might start with considering a certain period of a place's history. Routes from a general introduction might go in a number of different directions – economy, religion, leisure, conflict, and many others. Within those subtopics, a number of alternative explanations could be offered. Essentially, interactive video offers the potential for a greater democracy in access to information about the past and can allow people to develop their own cognitive maps and thus, a sense of place.

IVD might be used by a community to develop the ideas for a public map or series of maps (see Greeves 1987a & b and 1988). 'Common Ground' have been involved in hundreds of community projects in Britain that have produced maps of 'feeling' – maps which represent how people feel about their place. Such maps are far removed from orthodox maps, although such maps are an important source of information. The maps produced are ideographic representations of popular perceptions of place. They highlight the buildings and the natural features which individuals consider to be important to them. Some projects have even produced three-dimensional maps which also represent the topography of places (Greeves 1987a: 12–13). When developing such projects, care should be taken to emphasize the idea of process and change across time and space. A related project is the parish boundary project, which as the title suggests, was concerned with developing communities' awareness of how their boundaries have developed over time (Greeves 1987b).

There is, however, a danger in mapping projects that the representations produced will be static aestheticizations of place. Maps should only be considered as one element in projects which are designed to facilitate a sense of place. But they are important to any project which attempts to allow people to locate themselves temporally and spatially: 'a distinctive and legible environment not only offers security but also heightens the potential depth and intensity of human experience' (Lynch 1960: 5).

The physical forms which Lynch believed people should learn to 'read' were as follows: paths – essentially routes that a subject uses; edges – boundaries that exist in the subject's perception of an area; districts – areas with a common character, such as a city-centre shopping precinct; nodes – points at which the subject enters or leaves an area, or con- centrations of phenomena of which the subject is aware; landmarks, churches, towers etc. or possibly small elements of the environment which mean something to the subject.

For our purposes there is one major drawback in Lynch's concept of mapping. This is the fact that he is only concerned with the mapping of an area in three dimensions, whereas museums should be concerned with the fourth, that of time. This does not necessarily detract from the usefulness of some of Lynch's ideas, but we must be aware of his relegation of the temporal aspect of any built environment. Lynch has actually been quite explicit in his exclusion of the temporal dimension. He says that, 'There are other influences on imageability, such as the social meaning of an area, its function, its history, or even its name. These will be glossed over, since the objective here is to uncover the role of form itself' (ibid.: 46).

The traditional museum

In light of the above, we must ask: is there a role for the 'traditional' archaeological and historical museum? First, there should *not* be a role for the kind of exhibition which is merely concerned with promoting the fetishism of the auratic object – the emphasis on the usually prestigious object for itself, a blind aesthetics, which denies any appreciation of context. The mediation of material culture into an aesthetic object is nowhere more pervasive than in some displays of ethnic material culture. As Clifford observes, there is a tendency to destroy difference in many displays of material culture (Clifford 1988: chapter 9). Of a display at the Museum of Modern Art, New York, entitled 'Primitivism in 20th Century Art: Affinity of the Tribal and the Modern', Clifford comments that 'an ignorance of cultural context seems almost a precondition for artistic appreciation. In this object system a tribal piece is detached from one milieu in order to circulate freely in another, a world of art – of museums, markets, and connoisseurship' (ibid.: 200). Such displays impose the sense of Western rationality on the classification of the material. Not all displays deny a consideration of difference, but all displays do impose certain contexts of representation, and by their very nature, cannot really avoid this. However, museums must attempt to avoid the insulting aestheticization of the object.

The museum's possession of, or authority over the object should be criticized (Gathercole 1989: 74), as should its role in defining the contexts within which objects are placed. The key to improving an understanding of the past and the way it is represented, is to involve the public in either producing their own displays, or letting them know how exhibitions are developed.

There are many projects involved in researching how people read and interact with museum displays, and also how displays can be more efficiently designed with the visitor in mind. Also there have been some well-noted departures from the orthodox display, some of which have been the subject of this book. However, very few have been concerned with a democratization of access to the past. In fact as I have argued, post-modern heritage representations do promote an increased distancing of the producer from the consumer, as well as a denial of interaction.

Some museums have recently begun video disc projects – two exhibits opened in the summer of 1990 at the Birmingham Museum and Art

Gallery. The exhibition is commonly referred to as 'Gallery 33' and is concerned with the display of some of the museum's ethnographic collection. The IVD is designed to allow people to consider various viewpoints on certain topics, such as missionary work, cultural property and the role of museums in economic development.

A role for exhibitions?

There is no doubt that there is a positive role for certain forms of historical and archaeological museum display. Many people are still interested in just 'consuming' representations of the past, rather than being involved in the 'production' of the same. However, with the emphasis on the ecomuseum concept, museum displays might be produced not just by curators, but also by local people who wish to promote an understanding of their own place for an interested public. Some museums are already involving local people. In Glasgow, at the Springburn Museum, local people have been encouraged to become involved in the development of displays about their place. It is also important that displays are changed often, although as O'Neil points out, some people do complain if a display is removed. He also makes it clear that displays should come up to the present day in terms of chronology (O'Neil 1990: 117). A similar project at the Active Museum in Berlin has been discussed by Fred Baker (1990).

Much work has been carried out on the efficient design of exhibitions, along with a concern for how people interact with displays. The work of Chandler Screven at the International Laboratory for Visitor Studies (ILVS) is of note here. Screven has considered how museum visitors use displays: an important aim should be to encourage visitors to switch from *passive* to *active* attention. *Passive* attention is considered to be superficial, akin to window-shopping. This is very much the case with many of the heritage experiences, such as reconstructed streets, which are quite common in museums, and the heritage rides. Such passive forms of attention are 'likely to result in poor retention and information transfer' (Screven 1990: 46). *Active* learning on the other hand aims to involve the visitor with the display. Screven also asserts that displays should contain what he refers to as *intrinsic* and *extrinsic* characteristics:

> Motivation involves a group of *intrinsic* and *extrinsic* characteristics that encourage to attend, follow instructions, cooperate, and return. Intrinsic motivators include usefulness, coherence of content, timeliness, personal meaning, the opportunity to interact with (control) an exhibit, and elements of surprise and/or challenge.

Extrinsic motivators include feedback about visual content/questions, and tokens, scores, or privileges for achievement.

(Screven 1986: 113)

Where exhibitions involve feedback, which might include self-scoring mechanisms, care should be taken to avoid transforming the display into a game.

One useful strategy might be to develop methods which persuade visitors to concentrate on displays for a greater length of time. Research has shown that visitors often only spend between 15 and 30 seconds on individual display units (ibid.: 118).

There should be scope for developing Interactive displays that do not require expensive IVD set-ups. For example, it is possible to use sets of flip panels – a series of hinged flaps which can be used in a question and answer format. The visitor can be asked to respond to certain questions about a display by selecting the correct flip card. Correct answers might perhaps be on a separate panel, and the honesty of the visitor assumed. Chosen interpretive routes, similar to that outlined for the video disc, can be followed by selecting a series of colour-coded cards which are placed around an entire exhibition. There should also be the potential for the visitor to focus on key themes if they so wish. A key to all techniques is participation in the seeking of information, and hopefully, understanding.

Another important area of contemporary research is in the field of museum literacy, notably the work carried out by the museum education programme in Washington DC. Museum literacy is concerned with developing an understanding of visitor *competence* in reading museum displays (Stapp 1984: 3). The aim of this work is to enhance 'public access' to museums (ibid.: 4). The fact that entrance to many museums is free, or used to be, does not have the corollary of potential access for all. As Bourdieu observes:

> The museum gives to all, as a public legacy, the monuments of a splendid past ...: this is false generosity, because free entrance is also optional entrance, reserved for those who, endowed with the ability to appropriate the works, have the privilege of using this freedom and who find themselves consequently legitimized in their privilege.
>
> (Bourdieu 1968: 611)

The museum must be concerned with developing exhibitions which do not assume the public's ability to read displays. There should be some consideration of why museums do what they do. Each museum might develop a critical history of its own development, considering the effect of the cultural contexts within which it developed. The public should be permitted to question the interpretations offered by a museum (Potter and Leone 1986: 98).

Consumers into producers

Many of the suggestions that have been offered for consideration are based on practices which are already established in some places, some of which deserve consideration.

The first of these developments is the Archaeological Resource Centre (ARC), which opened in York in 1990. The ARC is a natural progression from the Jorvik Viking centre. There has probably been more discussion, certainly in Britain, of this latter presentation than of any other single museum or heritage representation (e.g. Hewison 1987: 83–4; Schadla-Hall 1984; Shanks and Tilley 1987: 86–90). Many of these criticisms are justified, but the popularity of Jorvik is no bad thing. In Leicester, for example, people have visited the local archaeology museum at the Jewry Wall, because a visit to Jorvik had instilled a wider interest in the past of their own place (Liddle, pers. comm.). There is no doubt that this effect has been repeated all over the country. Also, it is important to realize that Jorvik is based on an actual archaeological site, the representation is *in situ*, and it does attempt to reveal how an interpretation can be inferred from the archaeological evidence. Jorvik may actually contribute to the development of a sense of place.

In the context of a consideration of the ARC, what is most important about Jorvik is that it has allowed the development of this new project, firstly because profits from Jorvik have helped underwrite the project, and secondly, and more importantly, because it has helped create the demand for this more 'serious' venture. It is estimated that about 50 per cent of the visitors from Jorvik visit the ARC (Tweddle, pers. comm.).

The ARC is a converted church where the public can actually participate in the archaeological process. With the help of archaeologists and volunteers, the visitor is encouraged to handle archaeological finds from local excavations. For many people this is an almost magical experience. The collections in the ARC include all types of finds, from pottery, brick, bone and shell, to small finds, and microfaunal remains. The aim of the ARC is to show the visitor how archaeologists develop their interpretations. The visitor then moves on to a new set of interactive displays where they are invited to experiment with different forms of technology, including weaving and leather working. The final part of the main facility allows the visitor to use the York Archaeological Trust's database, as well as the interactive video disc, which is set up only to permit the user to take 'tours' around an archaeological site in York.

It should be stressed, however, that there are problems even with ground-breaking advances such as the ARC. For example, justified criticism has been voiced regarding what has been termed 'Scout Camp' archaeology. Nordbladh comments on the trend to promote an understanding of the past through recreations or activities 'such as house building, ship building, cooking, spinning and weaving, leather-work, flint-knapping etc.' (Nordbladh 1990: 49). Concerned specifically with prehistory, he believes that, 'It is therefore supposed that prehistory, or more precisely our version of prehistory, is reduced to what it is practical to show and to perform' (ibid.: 50). Such presentations are in fact quite superficial as they deny any consideration of the contexts within which an activity would have taken place. They are artificial, as the activities normally tend to be 'doable'. There are no real difficulties, let alone impossibilities. All the necessary materials are available, and someone is present to help you if you get stuck. This is probably not representative of the 'real' world.

Despite these problems, the ARC, and its inevitable offspring, will hopefully develop with these considerations in mind.

As well as involving people in the post-excavation process, there have been a number of projects that have involved local people in the actual retrieval of archaeological material. One example of such a project, is the Leicestershire community archaeology project.

The aim of this project is to develop and maintain community field-walking groups. There are a number of advantages with such a project. First, it obviously involves local people in 'producing' their own archaeology. Second, such community programmes are of crucial importance to any overall archaeological strategy in a region, where the various groups can contribute to an archaeological survey that would never have been carried out if they had not volunteered to carry out the work. In the Leicestershire project there are probably ten or twelve groups that cover their own areas. Over the c. 15 years that the project has existed, about 1,000 people have been actively involved. Although in terms of the county's population this is a relatively small number, this project has involved 1,000 people who would have been unlikely to have had the opportunity for involvement in archaeology without the project. Not only have these people been involved in collecting material, some of the groups are actually involved in seeing their projects through to publication (Liddle, pers. comm.).

Again the emphasis is on making 'connections'. In the context of the above discussions I have been concerned to show that many people, in museums especially, are involved in giving the public access to what belongs to them. Both the more traditional museum, and the heritage industry, have developed forms of representation that remove the past from the daily experiences of life. The representations are produced and left as static and passive objects, which often deny any potential for learning. More often than not, the representation promotes the fetishism of the object and/or peddles a single distinctively authoritarian line of interpretation. Again, there are exceptions. Some museums have started to declare that interpretations of the past are culture-specific, and that even within cultures there are important variances. At the Museum of London, the display on Iron Age hoarding has for years consisted of four pictures indicating the various possible reasons for this phenomenon; one depicts a battle scene, the next a funeral, the third an accidental deposition of the hoard, and the fourth a ritual deposition of the hoard 'invoking the help of the gods' (Museum of London display). However, in many representations of the past the authors are anonymous and the past is firmly established as something which belongs to the curator to the heritage business; at worst it is something which has to be bought.

9 | *Conclusion: the remoteness of the past*

It has been the primary contention of this book that the processes of modernization since the beginning of the Enlightenment have contributed to a distancing of people from their pasts. The most pervasive of these processes have been industrialization and 'post-industrialization', as well as the experiences of urbanization. 'Distancing' has occurred in all areas of modern experience. The experiences of time–space compression have resulted in our inability to understand or appreciate those processes which have contributed to the construction of places, and therefore our pasts. The distancing from economic process as considered in a number of chapters (especially one and two) has also contributed to the loss of a sense of place.

Throughout the Enlightenment, attempts have been made to arrest this perceived losing of the past. As the past was once a part of daily experience and consciousness, consequently it did not exact the same kind of attention or study as that which developed during the Enlightenment. As the processes of modernization developed, a need for the past became all the more urgent. Museums were therefore an important element in the maintenance and promotion of a consciousness of the past.

Museums, and the various forms of heritage derivatives, have in fact contributed to a form of institutionalized rationalization of the past. The past has been severed from the daily experiences of people, and mediated as a neutered essence which, in its institutionalized form, is often employed to legitimate the ideas of modernity and progress. Essentially, the past as occidental rationality has been situated within contexts of institutional legitimacy, which remove 'direct access' to the past from the public. This process began with the museum display and the hermetic sealing of the past within the display case, thus mediating it as something which could have no direct relevance on the daily experience of modern life. If it did, this experience was mediated by the rationalized form as legitimated by the museum. Despite this, the museum did attempt to represent an idea of process, even if this was situated in the dominant discourse of progress. The museum for much of its history was perceived as a public service, and always permitted the public to 'gaze at will', to return and look at displays when they wanted, and in what order they wanted. The heritage representation developed as the worst of both worlds.

Post-modernity then, should be seen as an intensification of those experiences of time–space compression and institutional rationalization which had originally emerged during the eighteenth and nineteenth centuries. Heritage representations should not be seen as a radical departure from those representations which developed during the previous century. The heritage and museums boom of the late twentieth century should be viewed within its various economic, political and cultural contexts. Most importantly, there probably has been a growing need for 'roots' as the experiences of (post-)modernity have intensified. The 'successes' of heritage have also to be seen in the light of increasing education and the development of so-called post-material values, along with an increase in disposable income for the majority of people in the First World. At the same time, heritage should be partly considered as an attempt to articulate an idea of 'nation' at a time when many nation-states believe their power to be under threat. This threat comes from the increasingly important role played by multinational corporations and capital, the development of supra-national organizations such as the EC, as well as the strengthening of certain regional identities, or micro-nationalisms, for example the Celtic regions of the United Kingdom, or the Basques in Spain. In Britain especially, the loss of Empire and the erosion of the power of the landed classes, certainly since World War II, should be seen as reasons for the emergence of a national heritage industry.

Heritage representations are not a profound departure from the museum display, and they rely heavily on the legitimacy of the single didactic interpretation, and the aura of the object, or rather, the aura of the hyperreal simulacrum. The past is still mediated as a single, often isolated and completed event. The emergence of the terms, *post*-industrialism and *post*-Fordism might be considered as a part of the attempt to disassociate ourselves from these pasts – a clinical operation to remove these unsightly calluses, sanitize them, and place them in a theme park. The society of the 'post' is a society without a past.

In many heritage representations, the public's gaze is controlled more so than in the museum. The ride is a once-only experience, unless you pay again! Often, there is no opportunity to return to reconsider displays; even in the walk-about representations, the visitor is told when to move, and in which direction to move. Most important, in some ways, is the denial of an idea of public service.

Some museums, and (post-)modern heritage representations especially, have been concerned with the promotion of an idea of nation. As was argued in chapter five, the idea of nation is in many ways an artificial one, and is largely a product of the late eighteenth and nineteenth centuries. The emphasis on certain forms of national heritage has also promoted the relegation of local community histories and archaeologies, which endeavour to develop a sense of place. There is no denial that monuments such as castles and country houses are important elements in the historic environment. The problem lies with the representation of an exclusive set of monuments as those which constitute a unified phenomenon representative of the nation. The preservation of an unrepresentative part of the historic environment in isolation is a crucial part of the development of a 'map' of the so-called nation's history, a history which is represented through these 'important' buildings. The monuments on this 'map' do not always relate to their immediate localities: castles and country houses are often represented as islands of historic excellence, removed from the more mundane historic environment of everyday people, whose histories are, in part, constituted by a relationship with the more ordinary elements of the vernacular historic environment. The elements of this magisterial heritage are only related to one another through their definition as being of national importance. This map of national heritage is therefore an artificial map, constructing a heritage which was never really a part of anybody's history.

All historic monuments must be considered as being places which exist as a part of localities, and therefore should be considered within those contexts, as considered in the previous two chapters. Some buildings will of course have been part of networks which did transcend the local, but they cannot be considered as apart from the local.

Public service

Something as important as the preservation and presentation of material culture should be regarded as a 'public service', the preservation and presentation of material culture as something which is important in itself, and not because of its revenue-generating potential. By public service, I mean a provision which is deemed as essential, so essential that it is crucial to the quality of life in any given society, from health and rescue services, to the provision of education. It is as a form of educating experience that the representation of the past should be considered. Crucial to any democracy is the *free* provision of such services. To put it crudely, the level of civilization in any society is related to its tax structure and specifically to the level of public provision of education services.

The total of public money spent on the arts and museums around the First World varies enormously. Public expenditure includes both central- and local-government expenditure. Arts expenditure per head in the UK in 1987 was 9.8 pounds; in the US it was 2 pounds. At the other end of the scale, in Sweden it was 27.8 pounds, in the Netherlands 20.5 per head, in France 21.4, while in what was Federal Germany 24 pounds was spent (Feist and Hutchison 1990a: 74). Although such comparisons may be misleading to a certain extent, as they do not reveal indirect funding, they do undoubtedly reveal the positions of certain governments regarding the provision of public services.

Democracy implies an unconstrained access to the decision-making bodies responsible for the perceived optimum allocation of available resources in any society. On one level it is quite clear that the governments of some nations are not adequately funding the arts and museums, and are consequently denying a democratic access to educative facilities. On another level, even if we accept the current level of funding as being that which is truly available, there is still an impeachment of the processes of democracy. In terms of a democratic access to the 'past', or rather the decisions which affect society's historic environment and material culture, the public should be given greater access to those bodies which make decisions affecting this, as well as the ways in which the past is represented. Logically, such democratic processes should take place at the local level, or at least in the region. In Britain, democracy could easily be improved at the county level.

The locality, especially in Britain, is also threatened by a national government which continuously attacks local democracy and tinkers with county boundaries. 'The reorganisation of local government has further increased the significance of local territorial politics in recent years, as some groups seek to preserve their local identities and protect local interests in the face of their absorption into larger units of administration' (Bagguley et al. 1990: 218–19). Again, the strength of each locality can be greatly enhanced through an understanding of place. There should be a developed pride in places and the history of local governments.

The possibility of devolving national conservation bodies down to regional or county level should be a serious consideration. For example, devolution to a county level would allow English Heritage employees to move into existing County Council structures and thus save most administration and operational costs. There are existing Direct Service

Organizations (DSOs) which could easily absorb many works costs. Even where the DSOs have been removed due to competitive tendering, the existing organizational structures would doubtless contribute greater efficiency. Also local context-based responses to threats to historic buildings and archaeological monuments make much more sense, especially as planning is executed in the main by local and county authorities. This removal of power away from a central unaccountable committee in London can only be a good thing. Although English Heritage is soon to move to the Midlands, it may well remain a centralized organization with limited devolution to the regions. The release of about 80 million pounds from the central government would provide about 2 million pounds per county to provide the services previously provided by the central organization. This could be topped up by a more just allocation of funds from the National Heritage Memorial Fund.

Devolution to the county level would also enhance the integration of all forms of conservation, including historical and ecological conservation. As emphasized in chapter eight, an appreciation of the past must concern itself with an understanding of human/environment interaction. As Bell and Walker note, most archaeological sites and monuments are dealt with in isolation from their landscapes; successful conservation must develop along lines of integration. The one country where an integrated approach is followed is Denmark, 'where ancient monuments, wildlife and landscape are protected by a single law: the Conservation of Nature Act' (Bell and Walker forthcoming: chapter eight).

The devolution to a county/regional level would also facilitate local interpretations of monuments as the responsibility for the presentation of these monuments would be placed in the hands of local museum services, who would integrate the interpretation of the historic environment, and show how the so-called national monuments are important elements in the history of actual places. Most importantly, an enhanced form of local democracy would bring the decision-making processes closer to the places that are affected by it. Those who fear political involvement in the 'heritage' are deluding themselves into believing that the past is not already political. The main difference at the moment (1991), is that such quangos are the products of political decisions, but the people who make many of those decisions are not elected or accountable to the public.

Part of this process of democratization would be the 'repatriation' of material culture. This is something which has long been the aim of many local museums. Thomas Sheppard, curator of Hull's municipal museum at the beginning of the twentieth century, 'felt strongly that material from the area should be provided for local people to see' (Schadla-Hall 1989: 5).

He continually endeavoured to regain material from the British Museum which had originally come from his area. Such struggles need to continue. If there is a role for national museums, it should be one which attempts to develop a more representative 'national map', a map which highlights the pasts of different regions and acts as a kind of information bureau for the country, giving visitors a 'flavour' of places they may wish to visit. Such a facility would give information on different themes in history and archaeology, and would give details of the local museums which cover these themes. As tourism in the provinces is expanding, whilst that in London contracts, this type of role for the national museum might be ideal. Of all the visits to Britain 70 per cent now take place outside of the London area (Middleton 1990: 36).

Such services, as asserted above, must remain free. Democracy must first and foremost be about unrestricted access to those processes which affect the organization of societies. Free marketeers might argue that reduced taxes permit the development of a benign free market, where the consumer directs funding in the directions that they consider to be worthy. The problem is, that until they direct funds in the direction of museums, the museums will not be able to fund a decent service. Without an attractive service, the consumer will then decide not to visit the museums, and thus fund them. A downward spiral develops and many local museums become ghettoized, or are forced to close down. As Middleton observes, the museum boom is over, and a period of rationalization will take place up to the turn of the century. Supply has outstripped demand in the private sector (ibid.: chapter 3). Public funding is therefore a necessary prerequisite if a decent service is to be provided. Museums provide what might be considered as 'minority' services which are necessary to the quality of life in a society. Take the hypothetical situation below:

> Only twelve people came to your $10,000 NEH-funded exhibit on man's [sic] inhumanity to man, but thirty years later one of the twelve wins the Noble Peace Prize for a world-wide surplus food distribution system and tells the world that your exhibit inspired her. Account for that one!
>
> (Schroeder 1980: 8)

Supposing 1,000 people turn up to a mock battle in one afternoon, and a large group of children leave believing that warfare is no different from that depicted on *The A-Team*, and no one ever gets badly hurt. Profit can not always be shown on the spread-sheet.

The free museum offers the potential of a research facility for all, a facility that can be used repeatedly on a regular basis. The idea that democratic access is improved through the market is a deception. It assumes a context of democracy in which all members of the public have equal and unrestricted access to both capital and cultural capital, access to the latter being enhanced by greater access to the former. The market is by its very nature undemocratic. This point is well illustrated if we consider those museums which have introduced charges, or 'voluntary' charges, in Britain. For example, attendance at the Victoria and Albert Museum in 1985 was 2.1 million; a voluntary charge was then introduced, and in 1986 attendance was reduced to 1.4 million and has never risen above that level (last figure, 1989). The National Maritime Museum at its most popular had well over a million visitors a year (1979). It introduced charges in 1984, and by 1989 attendance was 0.4 million. This pattern was repeated at the Natural History Museum where attendance was halved due to the introduction of charges, at the National Railway Museum, at the Royal Airforce Museum, and most dramatically of all, at the Science Museum, where attendance is about one-third of its total before charges were introduced (Feist and Hutchison 1989b: 6–7; 1990: 46–7). This pattern is not a result of a general move away from public museums to private heritage attractions, such as Beamish. Attendance at free museums has increased. In 1979 attendance at the British Museum was 4.1 million; in 1989 this figure had risen to 4.7 million. Attendance at the National Museums of Scotland was 0.7 million in 1979; in 1989 the total stood at 0.9 million.

The introduction of charges is in fact a form of disenfranchisement, a denial of access to that which should be open to all. The introduction of charges in museums is part of a much wider set of anti-democratic trends which have emerged in recent times. All of these trends have emerged from the radical individualism and supply-side theories discussed in chapters two and three.

There is today a tyranny of a commodified, synchronic past, where all our yesterdays only exist as today's commodities. The heritage industry denies historical process, and radiates only historical surfaces. The heritage consultant argues that it is s/he who knows how to communicate, and that it is the museum that reifies and obfuscates. To an extent, this may be true of some museums. It is, however, the heritage consultant who creates the sight, sound and smell experience, and the marketeers who impose the mock battles. It is they who do not communicate with the public. They never answer to the public that consumes their products. The job is done, the cheque received and they are off to the next marketing hustle. It is the museum curator who is permanently available to the public, continually caring for and studying the archive, and willing to communicate with an interested public. The expert is no longer valued in the quick-fix service society. Natural history curators are sacked as they cannot evolve to fit a profitable marketing niche, dreamed up by someone whose myopia will ensure that they do not evolve any further. The fine arts curator is made redundant, as knowledge and professionalism are going for a song.

That which is local is more important today than ever before. The story of capital has been one of an ever increasing propensity to approach the sublime, today removed from the experiences of most people's lives, and projected around the world as ethereal electronic pulses, moving at the speed of light. Nation-states are less and less able to manage their own economies, and there is no legitimate form of global, let alone, national government. It is the locality which must come to terms with the always historic processes which affect it. To understand the political and economic processes which have constructed a place is to develop the potential for manipulating those processes to that place's advantage.

Extending the temporality of place is possible through the preservation of archaeological remains *in situ*, and the development of engineering and architectural techniques that allow new buildings to be juxtaposed with the historic environment – if you like, 'peepholes to the past'. Lynch argues that we should intensify and diversify 'the sense of local time, just as we might propose intensifying and diversifying activity there' (Lynch 1972: 173).

It would be naive to expect the ecomuseum to replace the clear demand for those forms of heritage which I and others (most notably Hewison) have been concerned to criticize. Rather, perhaps a more healthy environment would be one where there is a multiplicity of choices. The heritage experience may act as a 'taster' for many people, who may subsequently develop an interest in the history and archaeology of their place, and thus require the facilities offered by the local museum. There should not be an emphasis on only one form of representation. A true democracy will offer many and varied forms of museum service. The danger is that we are in fact moving towards an homogenized monopoly of form which in itself is an attack on democracy.

Bibliography

Adorno, T. and Horkheimer, M. (1979) *Dialectic of Enlightenment*, trans. J. Cumming, London: Verso.

Alexander, E.P. (1979) *Museums in Motion*, Nashville: American Association for State and Local History.

Allen, J. (1988) 'Towards a post-industrial economy?', in J. Allen and D. Massey (eds) *The Economy in Question*, London: Sage.

Angus, I. and Jhally, S. (eds) (1989) *Cultural Politics in Contemporary America*, London and New York: Routledge.

Appadurai, A. (1990) 'Disjuncture and difference in the global cultural economy', in M. Featherstone (ed.) *Theory Culture and Society* 7 (2–3), London: Sage.

Atkinson, R.F. (1978) *Knowledge and Explanation in History*, London: Macmillan.

Bagguley, P., Mark-Lawson, J., Shapiro, D., Urry, J., Walby, S. and Warde, A. (1990) *Restructuring: Place, Class and Gender*, London: Sage.

Baker, F. (1990) 'Archaeology, Habermas and the pathologies of modernity', in F. Baker and J. Thomas (eds) *Writing the Past in the Present*, Lampeter: St David's University College.

Baudrillard, J. (1975) *The Mirror of Production*, trans. M. Poster, St Louis: Telos Press.

Baudrillard, J. (1980) 'Forgetting Foucault', *Humanities in Society*, 3:1.

Baudrillard, J. (1988a) 'Simulacra and simulations', in M. Poster (ed.) *Jean Baudrillard, Selected Writings*, Cambridge: Polity.

Baudrillard, J. (1988b) 'Fatal strategies', in M. Poster (ed.) *Jean Baudrillard, Selected Writings*, Cambridge: Polity.

Baudrillard, J. (1988c) 'The masses', in M. Poster (ed.) *Jean Baudrillard, Selected Writings*, Cambridge: Polity.

Beamish Museum (1990a) *Visitor Information*.

Beamish Museum (1990b) *Souvenir Guide Book*.

Bell, M.G. (1990) 'Cultural landscapes: some thoughts stimulated by Bill Boyd's paper', *Circaea* 7 (2): 69–70.

Bell, M.G. and Walker, M.J.C. (Forthcoming) *Late Quaternary Environmental Change: Physical and Human Perspectives*, London: Longman.

Bellaigue-Scalbert, M. (1985) 'Actors in the read world', *Museum* 148.

Bennett, T. (1988) 'Museums and "the people"', in R. Lumley (ed.) *The Museum Time Machine*, London: Comedia/Routledge.

Berman, M. (1983) *All That is Solid Melts into Air*, London: Verso.

Best, G. (1971) *Mid-Victorian Britain, 1851–70*, Glasgow: Fontana.

Best, S. (1989) 'Jameson, totality, and the poststructuralist critique', in D. Kellner (ed.) *Post-modernism, Jameson, Critique*, Washington: Maisonneuve Press.

Binney, M., Machin, F. and Powell, K. (1990) *Bright Future: The Re-use of Industrial Buildings*, London: SAVE.

Binney, M. and Martin, K. (1982) *The Country House: To Be or Not To Be*, London: SAVE.

BOOM (1989) *Business Opportunities On Merseyside*, Liverpool.

Bourdieu, P. (1968) 'Outline of a sociological theory of art perception', *International Social Science Journal* 20 (4): 589–612.

Bourdieu, P. (1984) *Distinction*, London: Routledge.

Bowler, P.J. (1989) *The Invention of Progress: The Victorians and the Past*, Oxford: Blackwell.

Boylan, P. (1990) 'Museums and cultural identity', *Museums Journal*, 90 (10): 29–33.

Brears, P. and Davies, S. (1989) *Treasures for the People*, Yorkshire and Humberside Museums Council.

Brogan, H. (1985) *The Pelican History of the United States of America*, Harmondsworth: Penguin.

Butzer, K.W. (1982) *Archaeology as Human Ecology*, Cambridge: Cambridge University Press.

Bygones (1987), *Bygones*, Torquay: Bygones.

Cannadine, D. (1983) 'The context, performance and meaning of ritual: the British monarchy and the "invention of tradition", c. 1820–1977', in E. Hobsbawm and T. Ranger (eds) *The Invention of Tradition*, Cambridge: Cambridge University Press.

Carlstein, T., Parkes, D., and Thrift, N. (eds) (1978) *Making Sense of Time*, London: Edward Arnold.

Carr. E.H. (1987) *What is History?*, 2nd edn, London: Penguin.

Checkland, S.G. (1971) *The Rise of Industrial Society in England 1815–1885*, London: Longman.

Clarke, D.V., Cowie, T.G. and Foxon, A. (1985) *Symbols of Power at the Time of Stonehenge*, Edinburgh: HMSO.

Clifford, J. (1988) *The Predicament of Culture*, Cambridge, Massachusetts: Harvard University Press.

Cooke, P. (1989) 'Locality, economic restructuring and world development', in P. Cooke (ed.) *Localities*, London: Hyman.

Cormack, P. (1978) *Heritage in Danger*, London: Quartet.

Corner, J. and Harvey, S. (1991) 'Mediating tradition and modernity', in J. Corner and S. Harvey (eds) *Enterprise and Heritage*, London: Routledge.

Crang, P. (1990) 'Contrasting images of the new service society', *Area* 22 (1): 29–36.

Dane, J. (1990) 'Leisure spend shines in economic slump', *Leisure News* 47: 3.

Degler, C.N. (1984) *Out of our Past*, New York: Harper & Row.

Dellheim, C. (1982) *The Face of the Past: The Preservation of the Medieval Inheritance in Victorian England*, Cambridge: Cambridge University Press.

Denning, Lord (1990) 'Fanfare on being British', *The Field* 272 (7028): 80–1.

Eco, U. (1986) *Travels in Hyperreality*, London: Picador.

Engström, K. (1985) 'The ecomuseum concept is taking root in Sweden', *Museum* 148: 206–10.

Ewen, S. (1990) 'Marketing dreams: the political elements of style', in A. Tomlinson (ed.) *Consumption Identity and Style*, London: Routledge.

Faiers, R. (1990) 'Don't let Europe rule Britannia', *The Field* 23 (1): 12–15.

Featherstone, M. (1988) 'In Pursuit of the postmodern: an introduction', in M. Featherstone (ed.) *Theory Culture and Society* 5 (2–3), London: Sage.

Featherstone, M. (ed.) (1990) *Global Culture*, London: Sage.

Feist A. and Hutchison, R. (eds) (1989) *Cultural Trends 1989: 4*, London: Policy Studies Institute.

Feist, A. and Hutchison, R. (eds) (1990a) *Cultural Trends 1990: 5*, London: Policy Studies Institute.

Feist, A. and Hutchison, R. (eds) (1990b)

Bibliography

Cultural Trends in the Eighties, London: Policy Studies Institute.

Fekete, J. (1988). *Life After Post-modernism*, London: Macmillan.

Foster, H. (1984) '(Post)modern polemics', *New German Critique* 33 (Fall): 67–78.

Foster, H. (ed.) (1985) *Postmodern Culture*, London: Pluto.

Foster, R. (1990) 'Not a black and white issue', *The Museums Journal* 90 (10): 20–1.

Foucault, M. (1970) *The Order of Things: An Archaeology of the Human Sciences*, London: Tavistock, Routledge.

Gamble, A. (1988) *The Free Economy and the Strong State*, London: Macmillan.

Gathercole, P. (1989) 'The fetishism of artefacts', in S. Pearce (ed.) *Museum Studies in Material Culture*, Leicester: Leicester University Press.

Gibbins, J.R. (1989) *Contemporary Political Culture: Politics in a Postmodern Age*, London: Sage.

Giddens, A. (1984) *The Constitution of Society*, Cambridge: Polity.

Giddens, A. (1990) *The Consequences of Modernity*, Cambridge: Polity.

Gillanders, P. (1988) *Catherine Cookson Country – That's South Tyneside*, South Tyneside Council.

Gilroy, P. (1987) *There Ain't No Black In The Union Jack*, London: Hutchinson.

Glyn, A. (1989) 'The macro-anatomy of the Thatcher years', in F. Green (ed.) *The Restructuring of the UK Economy*, London: Harvester Wheatsheaf.

Gould, P. and White, R. (1974) *Mental Maps*, Harmondsworth: Penguin.

Green, F. (ed.) (1989) *The Restructuring of the UK Economy*, London: Harvester Wheatsheaf.

Greeves, T. (1987a) *Parish Maps: Celebrating and Looking After Your Place*, London: Common Ground.

Greeves, T. (1987b) *The Parish Boundary*, London: Common Ground.

Greeves, T. (1988) 'Placing ourselves – conservation in a changing world', *Royal Society of Arts Journal* April.

Habermas, J. (1981) 'New social movements', *Telos* 49 (Fall): 33–7.

Habermas, J. (1984) *The Theory of Communicative Action Vol. 1*, trans. T. McCarthy, London: Heinemann.

Habermas, J. (1987a) *The Theory of Communicative Action Vol. 2*, trans. T. McCarthy, London: Heinemann.

Habermas, J. (1987b) *The Philosophical Discourse of Modernity*, trans. F.G. Lawrence, Cambridge: Polity.

Habermas, J. (1989) *The New Conservatism*, Cambridge: Polity.

Hale, J. (1989) 'Gentlemen versus players', *The Weekend Guardian* 11 Nov.: 111–12.

Hall, J. (1989) 'Gilding the lily', in S. Mossman (ed.) *Tourism: Museum Dream or Nightmare*, 23rd Transactions of the Museums Professionals Group.

Hamnett, C., McDowell, L. and Sarre, P. (eds) (1989) *The Changing Social Structure*, London: Sage.

Hanna, M. (1989) *English Heritage Monitor 1989*, London: British Tourist Authority and English Tourist Board.

Hanna, M. and Binney, M. (1983) *Preserve and Prosper*, London: SAVE.

Harland, R. (1987) *Superstructuralism*, London: Methuen.

Harris, L. (1988) 'The UK economy at a crossroads', in J. Allen and D. Massey (eds) *The Economy in Question*, London: Sage.

Harvey, D. (1985) *Consciousness and the Urban Experience*, Oxford: Basil Blackwell.

Harvey, D. (1989) *The Condition of Post-modernity*, Oxford: Basil Blackwell.

Hebdige, D. (1988) *Hiding in the Light*, London: Routledge.

Hebdige, D. (1989) 'After the masses', *Marxism Today* 33 (1): 48–53.

Heller, A. and Fehér, F. (1989) *The Post-modern Political Condition*, New York: Columbia University Press.

Heritage Interpretation (1985a) 'Not to be sniffed at', *Heritage Interpretation*, 29 (Spring): 5.

Heritage Interpretation (1985b) 'Driving ahead with wheels', *Heritage Interpretation*, 31 (Winter): 8–9.

Heseltine, M. (1990) 'Fanfare on being British', *The Field* 272 (7028): 78–9.

Hewison, R. (1981) *In Anger: Culture in the Cold War 1945–60*, London: Weidenfeld and Nicolson.

Hewison, R. (1987) *The Heritage Industry*, London: Methuen.

Hewison, R. (1988) 'Making history: manufacturing heritage', unpublished paper.

Historic Buildings and Monuments Commission (1987) *Report and Accounts 1986–87*, London: HBMC.

Historic Buildings and Monuments Commission (1988) *Report and Accounts 1987–88*, London: HBMC.

Historic Buildings and Monuments Commission (1989) *Report and Accounts 1988–89*, London: HBMC.

Historic Buildings and Monuments Commission (1991) *Diary of Events 1991*, London: HBMC.

HMSO (1980) *National Heritage Act 1980*.

HMSO (1983) *National Heritage Act 1983*.

Hobsbawm, E. (1983a) 'Mass-producing traditions: Europe, 1870–1914', in E. Hobsbawm and T. Ranger (eds) *The Invention of Tradition*, Cambridge: Cambridge University Press.

Hobsbawm, E. (1983b) 'Inventing traditions', in E. Hobsbawm and T. Ranger (eds) *The Invention of Tradition*, Cambridge: Cambridge University Press.

Hobsbawm, E. and Ranger, T. (eds) (1983) *The Invention of Tradition*, Cambridge: Cambridge University Press.

Hodder, I. (1982) *The Present Past*, London: Batsford.

Hooper-Greenhill, E. (1988) 'The museum: the socio-historical articulations of knowledge and things', unpublished Ph.D. thesis, University of London.

Hooper-Greenhill, E. (1991) *Museums and the Shaping of Knowledge*, London: Routledge.

Hoover, K. and Plant, R. (1989) *Conservative Capitalism in Britain and the United States*, London: Routledge.

Horne, D. (1984), *The Great Museum*. London: Pluto.

Hubert, F. (1985) 'Ecomuseums in France: contradictions and distortions', *Museum* 148: 186–90.

Hudson, K. (1975) *A Social History of Museums*, London: Macmillan.

Hudson, K. (1987) *Museums of Influence*, Cambridge: Cambridge University Press.

Hunter, M. (1985) 'The cabinet institutionalized: the Royal Society's "Repository" and its background', in O. Impey and A. MacGregor (eds) *The Origins of Museums*, Oxford: Clarendon Press.

Huyssen, A. (1984) 'Mapping the post-modern', *New German Critique* 33 (Fall).

Impey, O. and MacGregor, A. (eds) (1985) *The Origins of Museums*, Oxford: Clarendon Press.

Jameson, F. (1981) *The Political Unconscious*, London: Methuen.

Jameson, F. (1983) 'Postmodernism and consumer society', in H. Foster (ed.) *Post-modern Culture*, London: Pluto.

Jameson, F. (1984a) 'Postmodernism, or the cultural logic of late capitalism', *New Left Review* 146: 52–92.

Jameson, F. (1984b) 'The politics of theory', *New German Critique* 33 (Fall): 53–65.

Jameson, F. (1988a). 'Beyond the cave, demystifying the ideology of modernism', in *The Ideologies of Theory, Essays, 1971–1986, Vol. 2, Syntax of History*, London: Routledge.

Jameson, F. (1988b) 'Cognitive mapping', in C. Nelson and L. Grossberg (eds) *Marxism and the Interpretation of Culture*, London: Macmillan.

Jameson, F. (1989) 'Introduction' to D. Kellner, *Critical Theory, Marxism and Modernity*, Oxford: Polity.

Bibliography

Jhally, S. (1989) 'The political economy of culture', in I. Angus and S. Jhally (eds) *Cultural Politics in Contemporary America*, London and New York: Routledge.

Kellner, D. (1988) 'Post-modernism as social theory: some challenges and problems', in M. Featherstone (ed.) *Theory Culture and Society* 5 (2–3), London: Sage.

Kellner, D. (1989a) *Critical Theory, Marxism and Modernity*, Oxford: Polity.

Kellner, D. (ed.) (1989b) *Postmodernism, Jameson, Critique*, Washington: Maisonneuve Press.

Kemp, M. (1988) 'Museums and scholarship', in T. Ambrose (ed.) *Working with Museums*, Scottish Museums Council, Edinburgh: HMSO.

Kennedy, M. (1990) 'Soldiers find a better hole', *The Guardian* 30 June.

Kern, S. (1983) *The Culture of Time and Space, 1880–1918*, London: Weidenfeld & Nicolson.

Kinard, J.R. (1985) 'The neighbourhood museum as a catalyst for social change', *Museum* 148: 217–23.

Kroker, A. and Cook, D. (1988) *The Post-modern Scene, Excremental Culture and Hyper Aesthetics*, London: Macmillan.

Kulik, G. (1989) 'Designing the past: history-museum exhibitions from Peale to the Present', in W. Leon and R. Rosenzweig (eds) *History Museums in the United States*, University of Illinois Press.

L & R (1987) *Report on the Development of Pembroke Waterway*.

Lash, S. (1990) *Sociology of Postmodernism*, London: Routledge.

Lawson, D. (1990) 'Interview with Nicholas Ridley; saying the unsayable about the Germans', *The Spectator* 265 (8453): 8–10.

Leisure News (1990a) 'SE tourism faces new French rival', *Leisure News* 61: 1.

Leisure News (1990b) 'Tourists turn to regions', *Leisure News* 61: 5.

Leon, W. and Piatt, M. (1989) 'Living-history museums', in W. Leon and R. Rosenzweig (eds) *History Museums in the United States*, University of Illinois Press.

Leon, W. and Rosenzweig, R. (eds) (1989) *History Museums in the United States*, University of Illinois Press.

Levitas, R. (1985) 'New Right utopias', *Radical Philosophy* 39 (Spring): 2–9.

Lowenthal, D. (1985) *The Past is a Foreign Country*, Cambridge: Cambridge University Press.

Lumley, R. (1988) *The Museum Time Machine*, London: Comedia/Routledge.

Lynch, K. (1960) *The Image of the City*, Massachusetts Institute of Technology.

Lynch, K. (1972) *What Time is this Place?*, Massachusetts Institute of Technology.

Lyotard, F. (1984) *The Postmodern Condition*, trans. G Bennington and B. Massumi, Manchester: Manchester University Press.

McCarthy, T. (1984) 'Introduction' to J. Habermas, *The Theory of Communicative Action Vol. 1*, London: Heinemann.

MacGregor, A. (1985) 'The cabinet of curiosities in seventeenth-century Britain', in O. Impey and A. MacGregor (eds) *The Origins of Museums*, Oxford: Clarendon Press.

McLuhan, M., Fiore, Q. and Agel, J. (1967) *The Medium is the Massage*, London: Allen Lane, The Penguin Press.

Marquand, D. (1990) 'Smashing times', *New Statesman and Society* 3 (111), 27 July.

Martlew, R. (1988) 'Optical disc storage: another can of worms?' in C.L.N. Ruggle and S.P.Q. Rahtz (eds) *Computer and Quantitative Methods in Archaeology, 1987*, Oxford BAR Int. S393.

Martlew, R. (1990) 'Videodiscs and the politics of knowledge' in D. Miall (ed.) *Humanities and the Computer*, Oxford: Clarendon Press.

Martlew, R. (forthcoming) 'Multi-media in museums: potential applications of interactive technology', *Society of Museum Archaeologists Journal*, Proceedings of the 1990 conference in Hull, England.

Marwick, A. (1989) *The Nature of History*, 3rd edn, London: Macmillan.

Marwick, A. (1990) *British Society Since 1945*, 2nd edn, London: Penguin.

Marx, K. (1954) *Capital: A Critique of the Political Economy, Vol.1, Book 1*, trans. S. Moore and E. Aveling, F. Engels (ed.), Moscow: Progress Publishers.

Massey, D. (1988) 'What's happening to UK manufacturing?' in J. Allen and D. Massey (eds) *The Economy in Question*, London: Sage.

Mayrand, P. (1985) 'The new museology proclaimed', *Museum* 148: 200–1.

Mehmood, T. (1990) 'Trophies of plunder', *The Museums Journal* 90 (9): 27–30.

Merriman, N. (1988a) 'The role of the past in contemporary Britain', unpublished Ph.D. thesis, University of Cambridge.

Merriman, N. (1988b) 'The social basis of museum and heritage visiting', in S.M. Pearce (ed.) *Museum Studies in Material Culture*, Leicester: Leicester University Press.

Merriman, N. (1989) 'Museum visiting as a cultural phenomenon', in P. Vergo (ed.) *The New Museology*, London: Reaktion.

Merriman, N. (1991) *Beyond the Glass Case: The Past the Heritage and the Public in Britain*, Leicester: Leicester University Press.

Middleton, V.T.C. (1990) *New Visions for Independent Museums In the UK*, Chichester: Association of Independent Museums.

Murray, T. (1989) 'The history, philosophy and sociology of archaeology: the case of the Ancient Monuments Protection Act (1882)', in V. Pinsky and A. Wylie (eds) *Critical Traditions in Contemporary Archaeology*, Cambridge: Cambridge University Press.

Museum of London (1985) *The Museum of London*, London: Thames & Hudson.

Museums Journal (1990) 'One a fortnight', *Museums Journal* 90/9: 21.

National Heritage Memorial Fund (1988) *Treasures for the Nation: Conserving our Heritage*, London: British Museum Publications.

Nordbladh, J. (1990) 'Prehistory as a scout camp: where did the archaeology go?' in F. Baker and J. Thomas (eds) *Writing the Past in the Present*, Lampeter: St David's University College.

Norman, G. (1989) 'From stately homes to horseshoe bats (an interview with Lord Charteris of Amisfield)', in Office of Arts and Libraries, *The Arts in Britain*, London: Central Office of Information.

Olmi, G. (1985) 'Italian cabinets of the sixteenth and seventeenth centuries', in O. Impey and A. MacGregor (eds) *The Origins of Museums*, Oxford: Clarendon Press.

O'Neil, M. (1990) 'Springburn: a community and its museum', in F. Baker and J. Thomas (eds) *Writing the Past in the Present*, Lampeter: St David's University College.

Ousby, I. (1990) *The Englishman's England*, Cambridge: Cambridge University Press.

Parkinson, M. and Evans, R. (1988) 'Urban regeneration and development corporations: Liverpool style', University of Liverpool Centre for Urban studies.

Pearce, D. (1989) *Conservation Today*, London: Routledge.

Pearce, S.M. (ed.) (1989) *Museum Studies in Material Culture*, Leicester: Leicester University Press.

Perkin, H. (1989) *The Rise of Professional Society: England Since 1880*, London: Routledge.

Phillips, P. (1984) 'One man's view of teaching Tudor domestic life', *Heritage Interpretation* 26 (Spring): 10–11.

Pinsky, V. and Wylie, A. (eds) (1989) *Critical Traditions In Contemporary Archaeology*, Cambridge: Cambridge University Press.

Plouviez, J. (1988) 'Rescue survey on the funding of British archaeology', Unpublished paper.

Pond, C. (1989) 'The changing distribution of income, wealth and poverty' in C. Hamnett, L. McDowell and P. Sarre (eds) *The Changing Social Structure*, London: Sage.

Poster, M. (ed.) (1988) *Jean Baudrillard, Selected Writings*, Cambridge: Polity.

Potter, P.B. and Leone, M.P. (1986) 'Liberation not replication: archaeology in Annapolis

Bibliography

analyzed', *Journal of the Washington Academy of Sciences* 76 (2): 97–105.

Prince, H. (1978) 'Time and historical geography', in T. Carlstein, D. Parkes and N. Thrift (eds) *Making Sense of Time*, London: Edward Arnold.

Raban, J. (1989) *God, Man and Mrs Thatcher*, London: Chatto & Windus.

Relph, E. (1987) *The Modern Urban Landscape*, London: Croom Helm.

Rifkind, M. (1989) 'Introduction' to Scottish Office, *Scotland's Heritage*, Scottish Office.

Rivière, G.H. (1985) 'The ecomuseum – an evolutive definition', *Museum* 148: 182–3.

Roberts, B.K. (1987) 'Landscape archaeology', in J.M. Wagstaff (ed.) *Landscape and Culture*, Oxford: Basil Blackwell.

Rowse, A.L. (1990) 'Fanfare on being British', *The Field* 272 (7028): 79–80.

Royal Britain (1989) *Royal Britain*, London: Unicorn Heritage plc.

Royal Commission on the Historical Monuments of England (1990) 'National hospital survey', *Newsletter* 3 (Summer): 2.

Rumble, P. (1989) 'Interpreting the built and historic environment', in D. Uzzell (ed.) *Heritage Interpretation, Vol. 1*, London: Belhaven.

Sahlins, M. (1974) *Stone Age Economics*, London: Tavistock.

Samuel, R. (1989a) 'Introduction: the figures of national myth', in R. Samuel (ed.) *Patriotism: The Making and Unmaking of British National Identity, Vol. 3: National Fictions*, London: Routledge.

Samuel, R. (1989b) 'Continuous national history' in R. Samuel (ed.) *Patriotism: The Making and Unmaking of British National Identity, Vol. 1: History and Politics*, London: Routledge.

Schadla-Hall, R.T. (1984) 'Slightly looted: a review of the Jorvik Viking centre', *Museums Journal* 84 (2): 62–4.

Schadla-Hall, R.T. (1989) *Tom Sheppard, Hull's Great Collector*, Beverley: Highgate Publications.

Schadla-Hall, R.T. (1990) 'What's history if you can't bend it a bit?', *NADFAS News* Spring/Summer.

Schiller, H.I. (1989) 'The privatization and transnationalization of culture' in I. Angus and S. Jhally (eds) *Cultural Politics in Contemporary America*, London & New York: Routledge.

Schroeder, F.E.H. (1980) 'Accountability: a covenant with the people', *Midwest Museums Quarterly*, 40 (3–4): 4–11.

Scottish Office (1989) *Scotland's Heritage*, Scottish Office.

Screven, C.G. (1986) 'Exhibitions and information centers: some areas for controlled research', *Curator* 29 (2): 109–137.

Screven, C.G. (1990) 'Uses of evaluation before, during and after exhibit design', *International Laboratory for Visitor Studies Review*, 1 (2): 36–66.

Selkirk, A. (n.d.) 'Survey of British archaeological societies', unpublished paper.

Shanks, M. and Tilley, C. (1987) *Reconstructing Archaeology*, Cambridge: Cambridge University Press.

Shoard, M. (1980) *The Theft of the Countryside*, London: Temple Smith.

Shoard, M. (1987) *This Land is Our Land*, London: Paladin.

Smith, A.D. (1990) 'Towards a global culture', in M. Featherstone (ed.) *Theory Culture and Society* 7 (2–3), London: Sage.

Soja, E.W. (1989) *Postmodern Geographies: The Reassertion of space in Critical Social Theory*, London: Verso.

Spadafora, D. (1990) *The Idea of Progress*, Yale University Press.

Stapp, C.B. (1984) 'Defining museum literacy', *Journal of Museum Education* 9 (1): 3–4.

Stapp, C.B. (1990) 'The "public" museum: a review of the literature', *Journal of Museum Education* 15 (3): 4–10.

Tait, S. (1989) *Palaces of Discovery: The Changing World of Britain's Museums*, London: Quiller.

Taylor, C. (1985) *Philosophy and the Human*

Sciences: Philosophical Papers 2, Cambridge: Cambridge University Press.

Tebbit, N. (1990) 'Fanfare on being British', *The Field* 272 (7028): 76–8.

Thomas, K.D. (1990) 'What's in a name? Anyone can be an environmental archaeologist', *Circaea* 7 (2): 72–76.

Thrift, N. (1989) 'Images of social change', in C. Hamnett, L. McDowell and P. Sarre (eds) *The Changing Social Structure*, London: Sage.

Tibbott, R. (1987) 'The tourism vision', *The Estates Gazette* 2 May.

Tomlinson, A. (ed.) (1990) *Consumption, Identity, and Style*, London: Routledge.

Tomlinson, A. and Walker, H. (1990) 'Popular movements, collective leisure and the pleasure industry', in A. Tomlinson (ed.) *Consumption, Identity, and Style*, London: Routledge.

Trigger, B. (1989) *A History of Archaeological Thought*, Cambridge: Cambridge University Press.

Tuan, Y. (1978) 'Space, time, place: a humanistic frame', in T. Carlstein, D. Parkes and N. Thrift (eds) *Making Sense of Time*, London: Edward Arnold.

Urry, J. (1990) *The Tourist Gaze*, London: Sage.

Uzzell, D.L. (1988) *The Hot Interpretaion of War and Conflict*, London: Belhaven Press.

Vergo, P. (ed.) (1989) *The New Museology*, London: Reaktion.

Wallace, M. (1989) 'Mickey mouse history: portraying the past at Disney World', in W. Leon and R. Rosenzweig (eds) *History Museums in the United States*, University of Illinois Press.

Wells, J. (1989) 'Uneven development and deindustrialisation in the UK since 1979', in F. Green (ed.) *The Restructuring of the UK Economy*, London: Harvester Wheatsheaf.

Whitrow, G.J. (1988) *Time in History*, Oxford: Oxford University Press.

Wray, I. (1987) 'The Merseyside development corporation: progress versus objectives', *Regional Studies* 21: 163–7.

Xenos, N. (1989) *Scarcity and Modernity*, London: Routledge.

Young, I. M. (1990) 'The ideal of community and the politics of difference' in L. J. Nicholson (ed.) *Feminism, Postmodernism*, New York: Routledge.

Index

Index

Index

Index

Index

Index

Index

Robin Hood, The Tales of, heritage centre, Nottingham 108–9
Rockefeller, John D. 96
Roman philosophy, and concept of time 10
Rowse, A.L. 88
Royal Airforce Museum, admission charges 182
Royal Britain heritage experience, London 106–7, 114
Royal Commission on the Historical Monuments of England 80, 84
Royal Family 91–2; and heritage industry 73–4; representation of in heritage centres 106–7
Royal Society museum, London 20
Royalty and Empire, heritage experience, Windsor 114
Rudolph II, Emperor 20
Rumble, P. 129
rural environment, and ecomuseums 163–4; popularity with urban dwellers 154
rural idyll, concept of 120; and move of service-class to countryside 127
Rutherford 11

Sahlins, M. 9
St Albans, England, Verulamium events (1990) 138
St Andrew's Village, Toronto 85
St Paul's Cathedral, London 165
St Pauls's Church, Jarrow, South Tyneside 82, 139
Saltram Hall 76
Samuel, R. 91, 93
SAVE Britain's Heritage 82–3
Scandinavia, development of folk-life museums 95–6
Scandinavian Folklore, Museum of 95
scarcity, invention of 29
Schadla-Hall, R.T. 138, 173, 180
Schiller, H.I. 145
schizophrenia, and perception of time 60
Schliemann, Heinrich 15; Mycenae 15
Schroeder, F.E.H. 181
Science Museum, London, admission charges 182
scientific discovery 23–4; and concept of time 11; and origins of modernity 7
Scotland, National Museum of Antiquities 157; new Museum of 89; preservation of ancient monuments 71; Society of Antiquaries of 16
Scottish Office, Scotland's Heritage 89
Scottish Photographic Survey 71
Screven, Chandler 171–2
Scruton, Roger, The Meaning of Conservatism 47
sense of place 148–59; and community 157–9; constructed by human interaction with environments 164–7; destruction of in re-creation of historical period 102; distorted by concept of nation 93; effects of wartime bombing and demolition 75; and four-dimensional web 153–7; global homogenization of 145–7; and immigration 158–9; importance of 150; loss of 23, 28, 65, 176; and mock battles 104–5; museums as facilitators 149, 160–75; and need to make value judgements 158–9; and preservation of industrial buildings 83; reconstruction of 153; and religious centres 155; and settlement patterns 156; and unity of past and present 155–6; ways of enhancing 149–59
service sector, development of 47–9
service-class culture 4, 84, 125–7; and expansion of heritage 116
sexual stereotyping 101–2
Shanks, M. and Tilley, C. 35–6, 104, 115, 156, 157, 173
Sheffield Society for the Promotion of Useful Knowledge 20
Sheppard, Thomas 180
Sherwood Forest, Nottingham 165
shopping, as most popular leisure activity 114–15; precincts 115, 145
signifiers, in Lacan's concept of language 60; smells as 112
simulacra, and mock battles 103
single-issue groups 74; see also pressure groups
slave-trade 24; museums' depiction of 141–2
smells, heritage 112–13, 146
Smith, A.D. 146
Smith, Adam, Wealth of Nations 13
Smith, T. Dan 75
social control, post-modern view of 57–8; through culture of post-modernity 63
socialism 73, 76
society, existence of denied by New Right 61, 135
Society of Antiquaries of Scotland 71
Society for the Interpretation of Britain's Heritage (1977) 75
Society for the Preservation of Ancient Buildings 71
Soddy 11
Soja, Edward 149–50
Sollerød museum, Denmark 165–6
Solutrean Epoch 17
Sons and Daughters of America 24
Sorbonne, Paris, Ecole Pratique des Hautes Etudes 15
space, heritagization of 4, 135, 136, 137–40, 154; timing of 152–3
Spadafora, D. 8, 9
sponsorship, of open-air museums 96; see also funding

Index

Index